I0051508

The GitHub Copilot Handbook

A practical guide to transforming the software
development life cycle with GitHub Copilot

Rob Bos
Randy Pagels

The GitHub Copilot Handbook

Copyright © 2025 Packt Publishing

All rights reserved. No part of this book may be reproduced, stored in a retrieval system, or transmitted in any form or by any means, without the prior written permission of the publisher, except in the case of brief quotations embedded in critical articles or reviews.

Every effort has been made in the preparation of this book to ensure the accuracy of the information presented. However, the information contained in this book is sold without warranty, either express or implied. Neither the authors, nor Packt Publishing or its dealers and distributors, will be held liable for any damages caused or alleged to have been caused directly or indirectly by this book.

Packt Publishing has endeavored to provide trademark information about all of the companies and products mentioned in this book by the appropriate use of capitals. However, Packt Publishing cannot guarantee the accuracy of this information.

Portfolio Director: Ashwin Nair
Relationship Lead: Nitin Nainani
Project Manager: Ruvika Rao
Content Engineer: Hayden Edwards
Technical Editor: Arjun Varma
Copy Editor: Safis Editing
Indexer: Pratik Shirodkar
Proofreader: Hayden Edwards
Production Designer: Vijay Kamble
Growth Lead: Anamika Singh

First published: November 2025
Production reference: 1311025

Published by Packt Publishing Ltd.
Grosvenor House
11 St Paul's Square
Birmingham
B3 1RB, UK.

ISBN 978-1-80611-663-8
www.packtpub.com

Foreword

When I started in tech 25 years ago, I worked in a data center surrounded by physical servers. Deployments meant walking up to a machine, tweaking configurations by hand, and hoping everything worked. Every step was manual, every mistake was personal, and every success felt like a small victory.

Over the years, I've seen our industry reinvent itself again and again, from bare metal to the cloud, from pagers to pipelines, from monoliths to microservices. But nothing has transformed how we build software quite like AI. GitHub Copilot has become more than a coding assistant – it's a thinking partner. I've seen it write Terraform templates, generate PowerShell scripts, and help developers of all levels learn and move faster. It's changing how we problem-solve, collaborate, and create.

AI isn't here to replace us – it's here to amplify us. It gives us space to focus on design, architecture, and innovation – the things that make engineering truly human.

That's why I'm excited about this book from Randy Pagels and Rob Bos. They've both spent their careers helping developers work smarter, automate more, and embrace change. In these pages, they don't just explain how GitHub Copilot works; they also show how it fits into the real world of modern development.

So, whether you're just starting out or have decades of experience, I invite you to explore this next evolution with them. The future of software isn't humans versus AI – it's what we can build together.

April Yoho

Senior Developer Advocate and DevOps Specialist, GitHub

Contributors

About the authors

Rob Bos is a Microsoft MVP, GitHub Star, and trainer focused on DevOps, GitHub (Actions, Copilot, and Advanced Security), and team enablement. He empowers teams to work smarter with GitHub tools, automating processes, improving security, and driving value delivery through practical, hands-on learning. Rob speaks at conferences worldwide and shares his insights through blogs, courses, and workshops. For work, Rob is a DevOps consultant at Xebia, helping customers with their DevOps culture.

Randy Pagels is a principal trainer at Xebia USA and a former Microsoft veteran with 17+ years of experience. He designs and delivers hands-on GitHub Copilot, Actions, and AI training. Randy is known for his engaging teaching style, practical scenarios, and commitment to helping teams scale AI adoption confidently and effectively. He also speaks at developer conferences and industry events throughout the year.

About the reviewer

Mickey Gousset is a staff DevOps architect at GitHub. He is passionate about helping developers achieve their goals, whether that's through his work or by creating content on his YouTube channel.

Table of Contents

Chapter 3: Choosing the Right GitHub Copilot Plan   41

Part 2: Getting Started with GitHub Copilot   79

Chapter 4: Mastering GitHub Copilot in Your IDE: Inline Suggestions, Chat, and Agent Mode   81

Part 3: Exploring GitHub Copilot Integrations 145

Chapter 6: Collaborating with Copilot on GitHub.com: Issues, PRs, Reviews, and Coding Agent 147

Chapter 7: Extending GitHub Copilot with the Model Context Protocol (MCP)   181

Part 4: Getting the Most Out of GitHub Copilot   201

Chapter 8: Navigating the GitHub Copilot Learning Curve   203

Preface

Welcome to your learning journey using GitHub Copilot for coding-related engineering tasks. We are excited to show you around its toolset and how it extends our normal workflows.

GitHub Copilot is having a profound impact on the tech industry, from helping engineers implement code changes faster to helping stakeholders and product owners describe their requirements more easily. It does not matter how much experience you have with coding – GitHub Copilot provides help to everyone, supporting all phases of the software development lifecycle. That makes it easier to generate code changes, add tests to it, and write the deployment pipelines. Want to discover more about coding practices? GitHub Copilot is your peer programming helper that can explain it all to you.

Leveraging the foundation language models such as GPT-5, Gemini, Claude Sonnet, and more, GitHub has added specific features in lots of smart places in your favorite editors, including VS Code, Eclipse, Visual Studio, JetBrains IDEs, and more. Next to that, there is a realm of additional support on GitHub.com, where the engineering process happens: from general research to issue creation, to adding code, making a pull request, and helping with debugging your pipeline issues. GitHub Copilot has integrations with all these steps into the developer workflow.

Join us to learn all about GitHub Copilot, as we guide you through the learning curve that the authors have used to train thousands of engineers over the last few years.

Who this book is for

This book is for anyone who works with application creation and who wants to harness GitHub Copilot in real-world coding environments. Whether you're a beginner looking to speed up learning or a seasoned engineer aiming to boost productivity, this guide shows how to put Copilot to work effectively.

Software engineers, DevOps professionals, QA specialists, and tech leads will discover how to streamline coding, reviews, and delivery with AI-assisted workflows. Product managers and other collaborators will also gain insight into how, with GitHub Copilot, they themselves can leverage AI.

What this book covers

Chapter 1, GitHub Copilot Explained, provides an overview of GitHub Copilot and its features, from suggestions to the Chat interface, and shows how they impact our day-to-day engineering process.

Chapter 2, Getting Started with Generative AI, offers a foundation for understanding what generative AI is and what it is not – from the basics of language models to how these features are applied to the engineering process.

Chapter 3, Choosing the Right GitHub Copilot Plan, outlines the different subscription options you have for GitHub Copilot and why you would choose one over the other.

Chapter 4, Mastering GitHub Copilot in Your IDE: Inline Suggestions, Chat, and Agent Mode, dives into the features of GitHub Copilot in your favorite editor.

Chapter 5, Beyond Code: Debugging, Terminal, and Collaboration with GitHub Copilot, covers the next steps after learning about the main features of the tools and shows you the smart integrations into the rest of the development process.

Chapter 6, Collaborating with GitHub Copilot on GitHub.com: Issues, PRs, Reviews, and Coding Agent, teaches you about the powerful features built into the web interface on GitHub.com, such as collaboration on issues and pull requests, as well as triggering the coding agent to let GitHub Copilot create the code changes needed to implement the requested functional updates.

Chapter 7, Extending GitHub Copilot with the Model Context Protocol (MCP), shows how the MCP servers add extra context to your Chat interface in agent mode, so that you can read and write into external systems.

Chapter 8, Navigating the GitHub Copilot Learning Curve, talks about the learning curve that GitHub Copilot has, as this is more than just a new tool for your toolbelt. We show how to address the learning curve so that you and your team members can get the most out of GitHub Copilot.

Chapter 9, Building an Internal GitHub Copilot Community, explains how we humans learn the best from seeing other people work with the tools we have, and how you can build an internal community around GitHub Copilot to continuously educate yourself and unlock the next level of proficiency.

Chapter 10, Changing the Narrative: Reframing Engineering with AI, discusses using AI in your engineering processes as a complete rewire of our own muscle memory, and how to approach this new way of thinking about getting the most benefit out of GitHub Copilot.

To get the most out of this book

You need the following for this book:

- A basic understanding of the software development life cycle
- Some experience using coding editors to work with your code base
- Usage of GitHub.com with issues and pull request processes

Conventions used

There are a number of text conventions used throughout this book.

CodeInText: Indicates code words in text, database table names, folder names, filenames, file extensions, pathnames, dummy URLs, user input, and X/Twitter handles. For example: "You can use /explain #symbol to ask for an explanation of only the function or symbol under your cursor, not the entire file."

A block of code is set as follows:

```
test('generates password of correct length', () => {
  expect(generatePassword(10)).toHaveLength(10);
});
```

Bold: Indicates a new term, an important word, or words that you see on the screen. For instance, words in menus or dialog boxes appear in the text like this. For example: "Under **Permissions**, click **Add permissions**, then select **Copilot Requests**."

Warnings or important notes appear like this.

Tips and tricks appear like this.

Get in touch

Feedback from our readers is always welcome.

General feedback: If you have questions about any aspect of this book or have any general feedback, please email us at customercare@packt.com and mention the book's title in the subject of your message.

Errata: Although we have taken every care to ensure the accuracy of our content, mistakes do happen. If you have found a mistake in this book, we would be grateful if you reported this to us. Please visit http://www.packt.com/submit-errata, click **Submit Errata**, and fill in the form.

Piracy: If you come across any illegal copies of our works in any form on the internet, we would be grateful if you would provide us with the location address or website name. Please contact us at copyright@packt.com with a link to the material.

If you are interested in becoming an author: If there is a topic that you have expertise in and you are interested in either writing or contributing to a book, please visit http://authors.packt.com/.

Share your thoughts

Once you've read *The GitHub Copilot Handbook,* we'd love to hear your thoughts! Scan the QR code below to go straight to the Amazon review page for this book and share your feedback.

https://packt.link/r/1806116634

Your review is important to us and the tech community and will help us make sure we're delivering excellent quality content.

Free Benefits with Your Book

This book comes with free benefits to support your learning. Activate them now for instant access (see the "*How to Unlock*" section for instructions).

Here's a quick overview of what you can instantly unlock with your purchase:

PDF and ePub Copies   Next-Gen Web-Based Reader

Free PDF and ePub versions   **Next-Gen Reader**

Access a DRM-free PDF copy of this book to read anywhere, on any device.

Use a DRM-free ePub version with your favorite e-reader.

Multi-device progress sync: Pick up where you left off, on any device.

Highlighting and notetaking: Capture ideas and turn reading into lasting knowledge.

Bookmarking: Save and revisit key sections whenever you need them.

Dark mode: Reduce eye strain by switching to dark or sepia themes.

How to Unlock

Scan the QR code (or go to packtpub.com/unlock). Search for
this book by name, confirm the edition, and then follow the steps
on the page.

UNLOCK NOW

Note: *Keep your invoice handy. Purchases made directly from Packt*
don't require one.

Part 1

What is GitHub Copilot?

In the first part of the book, we are going to take a broad look at what GitHub Copilot is, what kind of features you can expect, and where the integration points with the GitHub platform are. You'll see that GitHub has thoughtfully added features in the places of the software development lifecycle where it makes sense for engineers: from integration into the editor all the way to right into the interfaces on github.com.

To get a good grasp of the underlying technology that powers GitHub Copilot, we will also take a look at what generative AI is, its basic features, as well as where it strengths and weaknesses are. This forms the foundation of having the right expectations of the power of GitHub Copilot and how important having access to the right context for your conversations is.

We will close this part by showing the different ways to get access to GitHub Copilot, from the subscriptions tailored for individual users all the way to GitHub Copilot in a professional business setting.

This part of the book includes the following chapters:

- *Chapter 1, GitHub Copilot Explained*
- *Chapter 2, Getting Started with Generative AI*
- *Chapter 3, Choosing the Right GitHub Copilot Plan*

1

GitHub Copilot Explained

GitHub Copilot is a service offering from GitHub that helps you to work on your applications in all steps of the software development lifecycle: from ideation, to understanding and writing code, to reviewing your pull requests and analyzing pipeline failures. By using what we call generative **Artificial Intelligence** (**AI**), it helps you speed up normal tasks so you can focus on what you do best: adding value to your end users.

GitHub describes Copilot as your pair-programming buddy: a tool that knows almost every coding language, framework, and well-known coding patterns. It can help you with researching both existing and new code directions, can help review your code and suggest improvements, or can complete the task that you have been working on. It intuitively understands your current code and coding style and will follow that to match it. We even think that GitHub Copilot is better than a human pair-programming buddy, as it is a tool that does not judge you on anything you ask about! Can't remember how to implement an algorithm that you learned years ago? You might be afraid to ask your team members about it, but GitHub Copilot will happily explain it to you – plus, it will explain it in the context of your code base!

Keep in mind that the name of the tool also gives away the most important part of its role in your usage of it: it is a *co-pilot*, which means *you* are the pilot, and *you* are in control. You define the questions you ask it; the scenarios you let it complete; the help you ask it for; and whether you accept the suggestions or not. In the end, the code is stored in a **Source Code Management** (**SCM**) system with *your* name attached to it, not GitHub Copilot's name.

This book will take you through the impact that GitHub Copilot has on all steps of the **Software Development Life Cycle (SDLC)**, from start to finish. We will explain the features of the tools, the basics of generative AI, and how to leverage GitHub Copilot to get the most value out of it. We will also discuss the different license types that are available and what features they have for either usage in your editor or on the web interface for GitHub.

To get things going, we will take a look at what GitHub Copilot is and what kind of features it provides. It all started as an extension in your coding editor, and it has grown into a full set of features to help you, from writing code to generating completely new ideas, from analyzing pull requests to helping you fix your pipeline errors, and so much more. These features are built into a lot of editors, and some reside inside the web interface on GitHub.com.

In this chapter, we will cover the following topics:

- What is GitHub Copilot?
- Reviewing additional supporting features in editors
- Using GitHub Copilot integrations on GitHub.com

Free Benefits with Your Book

Your purchase includes a free PDF copy of this book along with other exclusive benefits. Check the *Free Benefits with Your Book* section in the Preface to unlock them instantly and maximize your learning experience.

Technical requirements

To use GitHub Copilot, you do not need to use the rest of the GitHub suite of tools. You can use it in a supported editor of your choosing against any file, no matter where it is stored. If you already use source control systems such as GitLab, Azure DevOps, or Bitbucket, you can still use GitHub Copilot. GitHub is the vendor of the product, but using GitHub itself is not a requirement.

Of course, there is extra functionality available if you use GitHub, which will be explained in depth in *Chapter 6*. The only integration to be able to use GitHub Copilot is having a GitHub account that you can use to log in and then tie your GitHub Copilot license to it. This tool is even available as a free tier (with some limitations), making it available for all GitHub users. Which features are available in which tier is explained in *Chapter 3*.

What is GitHub Copilot?

GitHub Copilot is a set of tools that can help you understand or produce code, either by helping you write code in an editor, talking to your code base to gain more information, or getting help from integrated functionality inside the web interface of GitHub.

This all starts with GitHub Copilot leveraging **Large Language Models** (**LLMs**) to complete the current line(s) of code that you are working on, by adding a suggestion when you stop typing for a couple of milliseconds, or when you hit the *Return* key. Depending on your color scheme, a suggestion is shown in *gray* or *dimmed* text in the editor, behind your cursor. You can see this in *Figure 1.1*, where the cursor is on line 9. This is also called "ghost text." This text is a continuation of the code you already typed, and GitHub Copilot finds the most logical completion of the code and suggests it for you to accept.

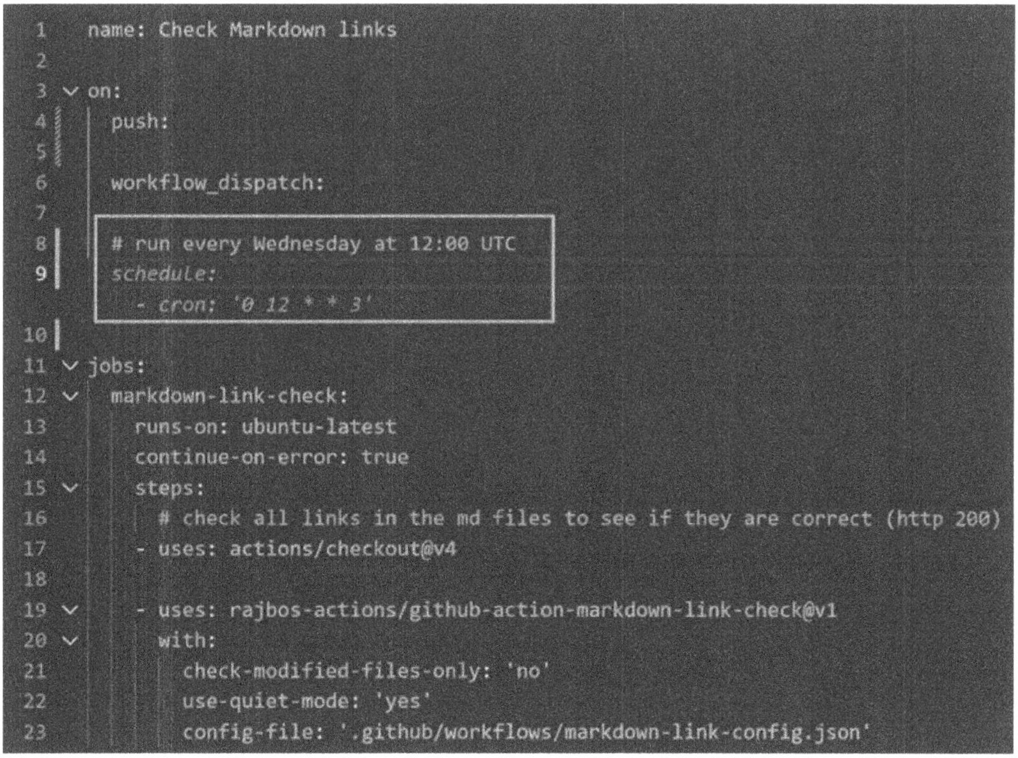

```
1     name: Check Markdown links
2
3  ∨ on:
4  |   push:
5  |
6  |   workflow_dispatch:
7  |
8  |   # run every Wednesday at 12:00 UTC
9  |   schedule:
       - cron: '0 12 * * 3'
10 |
11 ∨ jobs:
12 ∨   markdown-link-check:
13       runs-on: ubuntu-latest
14       continue-on-error: true
15 ∨     steps:
16         # check all links in the md files to see if they are correct (http 200)
17         - uses: actions/checkout@v4
18
19 ∨       - uses: rajbos-actions/github-action-markdown-link-check@v1
20 ∨         with:
21           check-modified-files-only: 'no'
22           use-quiet-mode: 'yes'
23           config-file: '.github/workflows/markdown-link-config.json'
```

Figure 1.1: Example of "ghost text" inside of VS Code

Accepting the code is as simple as hitting the *Tab* key, and the ghost text will be inserted at your cursor. The cursor will be moved to the end of the text that was inserted. Depending on what you were doing and how confident GitHub Copilot is in the suggestion, you can get either a word, a complete line, or multiple lines of code. It is then completely up to you what you want to do with that suggestion: you can use it as was proposed, you can accept parts of it, or you cannot accept any of it. What we also see is that people read the suggestions and then revise either the direction they were going in or the surrounding code based on new insights.

As well as the suggestion functionality, GitHub Copilot has chat integration, where you can have a conversation with the tool about the currently open files. See *Figure 1.2* for an example:

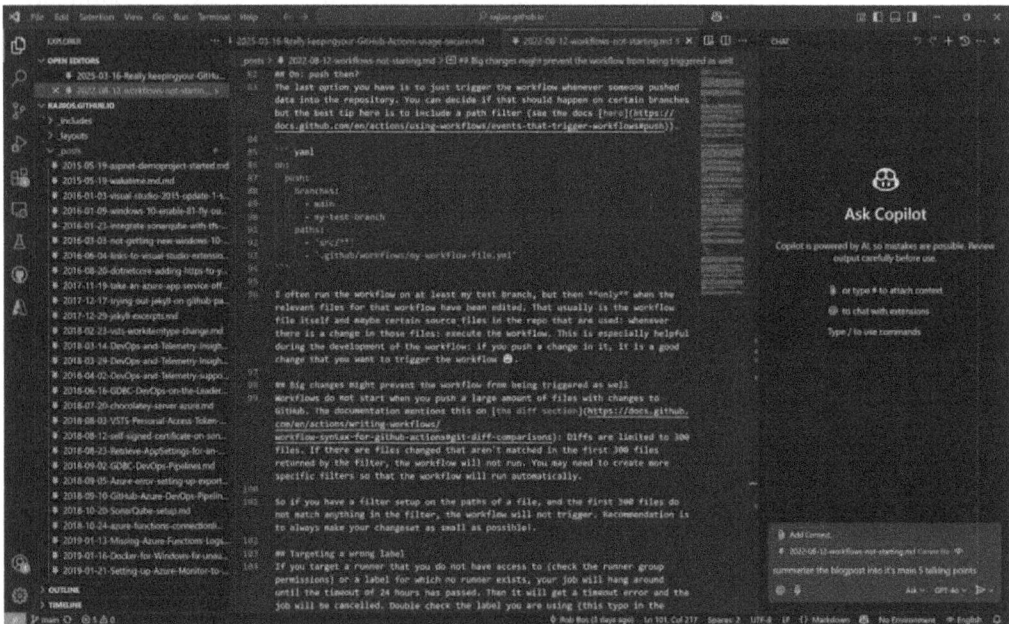

Figure 1.2: Example of a chat conversation with GitHub Copilot

In the chat interface, you can ask anything you can think of – here are some examples:

- What the major elements of the current open code base are
- How you can execute the tests that exist in your project
- To find missing edge cases in your test suite
- Create your pipelines for you in any **Continuous Integration/Continuous Deployment (CI/CD)** system you need

The possibilities are endless and entirely up to you. The chat interface is a great way to engage with your code. It does not matter whether you are a developer who is just getting started or an experienced engineer: GitHub Copilot offers something for everyone.

We find it especially helpful if you are new to a code base, where GitHub Copilot can help you quickly find your way around the parts that you want to take a look at. Another great use case is when working in a development language that you are not that familiar with: we started contributing to code written in coding languages we did not use before, because GitHub Copilot helps us understand how those languages work. If you understand the basics of programming, such as if statements, for loops, and arrays, you can get very far very fast with GitHub Copilot. Even if you do not fully understand these basics, if you have an exploratory mindset, GitHub Copilot can help guide you through this new environment in a pragmatic way:

- You can ask it to explain these features to you, and it will happily take you through these concepts step by step
- You can quickly find your way around the new code base by asking for an explanation of where the entry point is or how to build the application
- You can let GitHub Copilot explain the application by using diagrams to place the components in the right places for you, so you can quickly learn about the integration points between the backend and frontend

Since GitHub Copilot is that non-judgmental pair programming buddy that can help you with super basic tasks as well as more complex coding concepts, the chat function is a great tool for both people who are new to the field of coding, as well as for experienced engineers, and everything in between.

Having a basic understanding of the underlying technology of generative AI is paramount to having realistic expectations of what value these tools bring to the table. Knowing how GitHub Copilot produces code is explained in *Chapter 2*. With that knowledge, even more junior engineers can use GitHub Copilot to their advantage in researching and explaining coding concepts in the context of the current code base, where they can pick apart these concepts one by one. Since they understand that they need to double-check what GitHub Copilot produces, they can safely validate their own knowledge and grow their coding skills over time. Normal coding practices still apply, where we guide these engineers through the programming landscape and review the code they produce with that mindset, so they can grow in a safe manner. All this applies equally well to other non-technical stakeholders.

While suggestions and chat are the main functionalities that GitHub Copilot offers in most editors, some editors have even more functionality included. There are editors that offer, for example, an in-line chat functionality (see *Figure 1.3*) to directly edit a piece of code inside your text editor window. This feature lets you directly interact with your code in the place that you are editing, and it will directly apply the suggestions it is proposing with an inline overview to show the differences from your code.

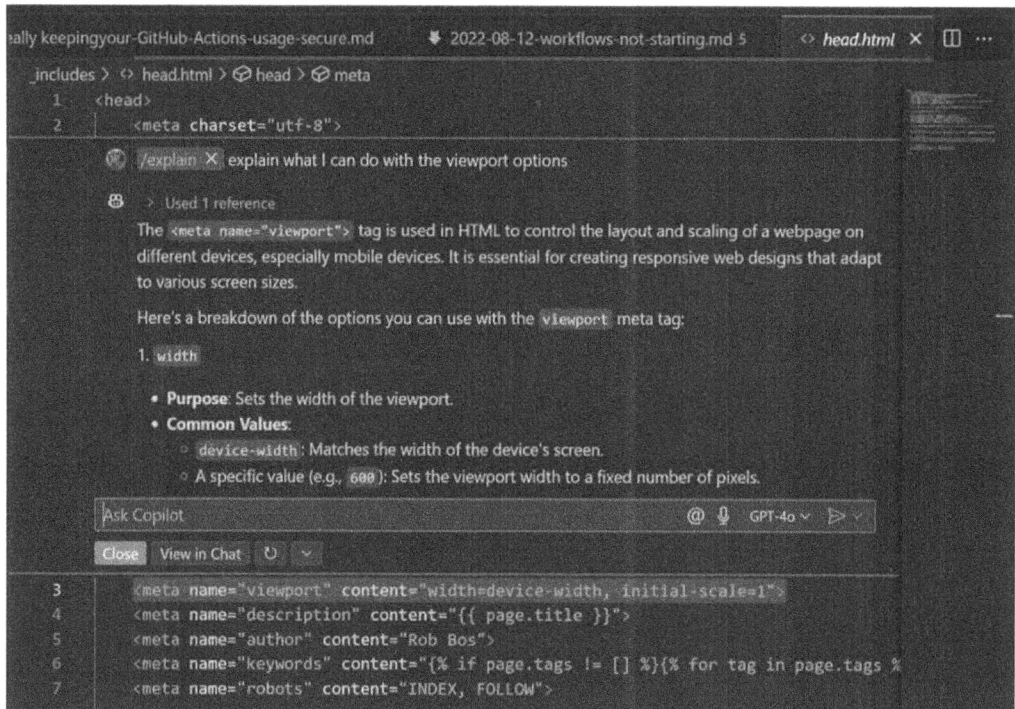

Figure 1.3: Example of an in-line chat conversation

Other editors have deep integrations with their own features; for example, some editors leverage their debug functionality to view the runtime values of your variables during test execution, or can view the statistics of your performance tests. The common convention is to look for a "magic" icon that indicates GitHub Copilot can do something at that location or functionality in the editor. See *Figure 1.4* for an example where GitHub Copilot generates a `git commit` message based on the current set of files that were changed.

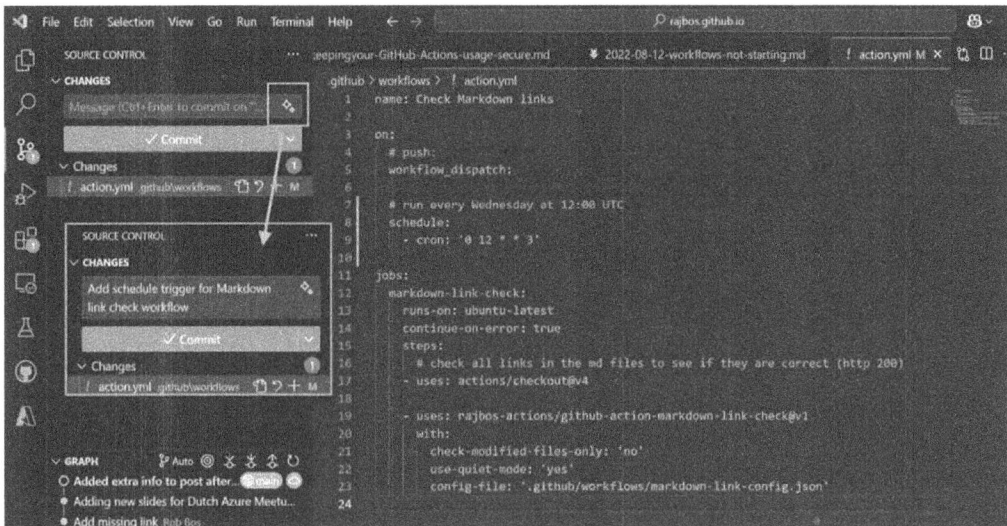

Figure 1.4: GitHub Copilot integration in the git commit window

Now we have seen a brief overview of the main functionalities that GitHub Copilot adds to your editor – including suggestions while you type, chat with your code, and inline chat to create inline changes – as well as some features available in other editors. In the next section, let's take a closer look at which editors support which of these additional features on top of the main functionalities.

Reviewing additional supporting features in editors

The primary use case of GitHub Copilot is helping you with your code base while you are creating code. This is done by integrating the different functionalities in an existing **Integrated Development Environment (IDE)**. This is often also referred to as an "editor." You work on your code inside the editor to add new methods and features to your application or scripts that you are working on.

Editors with GitHub Copilot plugins

The list of IDEs that have a plugin for GitHub Copilot is still growing. Currently, the following editors have some support for GitHub Copilot:

Editor	Suggestions	Chat	Other features
VS Code	Yes	Yes	Yes
Visual Studio	Yes	Yes	Yes
JetBrains IDEs	Yes	Yes	Yes

Editor	Suggestions	Chat	Other features
Vim/Neovim	Yes	No	No
XCode	No	Yes	No
Eclipse	Yes	Yes	No

Figure 1.5: Overview of the three types of features per editor

Depending on the editor, certain features have been built in that work specifically for that editor, where we see the teams that create them learn from each other and sometimes rebuild great features in a way that works for their editor setup. One example is the deep integration that Visual Studio has with its Performance Profiler to give GitHub Copilot additional context during these performance-tuning sessions: a feature that the other editors do not have.

Additional integrations outside of editors

Alongside editors, there are also additional integrations into the GitHub Desktop tool that let you work with any Git repository, no matter the source control system you are using:

- The **Pull Request (PR)** extension for VS Code has integrations with GitHub Copilot to write the PR title and description, and even the option to review the changes in the PR using AI.
- There is even a GitHub Copilot **Command Line Interface (CLI)** available to ask questions and let GitHub Copilot make the necessary changes to your code base, straight from the command line. We dive into the CLI in *Chapter 5*.
- Plus, there is even an open source GitHub Copilot language server available, which lets *anyone* build GitHub Copilot into *any* client if they use the GitHub Copilot license to authenticate users.

That means the possibilities to include GitHub Copilot are endless.

Editor feature release schedules

Each editor plugin is often built by a different team from either GitHub or Microsoft (as they own VS Code and Visual Studio). The GitHub Copilot features for VS Code are open source and directly integrated into the open source code base in the VS Code repository! You can find the repository at https://github.com/microsoft/vscode and follow along with their iteration planning. Since VS Code is Microsoft's main editor these days, with support for a lot of languages and tools, we often see that new features first appear in VS Code. It is the editor where things are tried and tested out first.

As the normal test versions of VS Code are in the Insiders release, following and using the Insiders release is the best way to see new features in action before the broader audience gets access to the formal releases. You can download and install the Insiders version for free from `https://code.visualstudio.com/insiders`. VS Code follows a regular release cadence of a new release version every month. The plugins are versioned separately and get multiple updates throughout the month.

The editor that usually gets new features after VS Code is Visual Studio, although sometimes the Visual Studio team has great ideas that they add first to Visual Studio, and then the VS Code team implements them as well in a later stage. Eventually, the functionality shows up in most other editors as well, where it makes sense or is possible. Editors such as Vim/Neovim only have a minimal user interface, and thus GitHub Copilot can only work with suggestions, as there is no place to show the chat interface. Visual Studio usually has a new release every three months. The plugins are versioned separately and can be released multiple times during the main release window.

IDE features are explained in depth in *Chapter 4*.

At this point, we have taken a look at additional tools available outside of editors, such as the extension for the GitHub CLI and the integration into GitHub Desktop. We have seen that different editors follow a different update cadence, which impacts when a specific feature might be added to your editor of choice, or even if that happens at all. In the next section, we will take a look at the additional features that are available on the GitHub.com platform when you have your code stored in it.

Using GitHub Copilot integrations on GitHub.com

If you are using parts of the rest of the GitHub suite of products, then you can greatly enhance that experience with tooling from GitHub Copilot as well. After logging into `https://github.com`, you can start chatting with GitHub Copilot on top of any repository (see *Figure 1.6*) or open it in an immersive window to chat without the context of a repository. This is great for researching things and having a separate, contextless window to the side to quickly look up things while you are working. Need to look up how to install packages in a specific package manager? Then this chat window is the right place to ask about it. Personally, we have this tab open in our browser all the time.

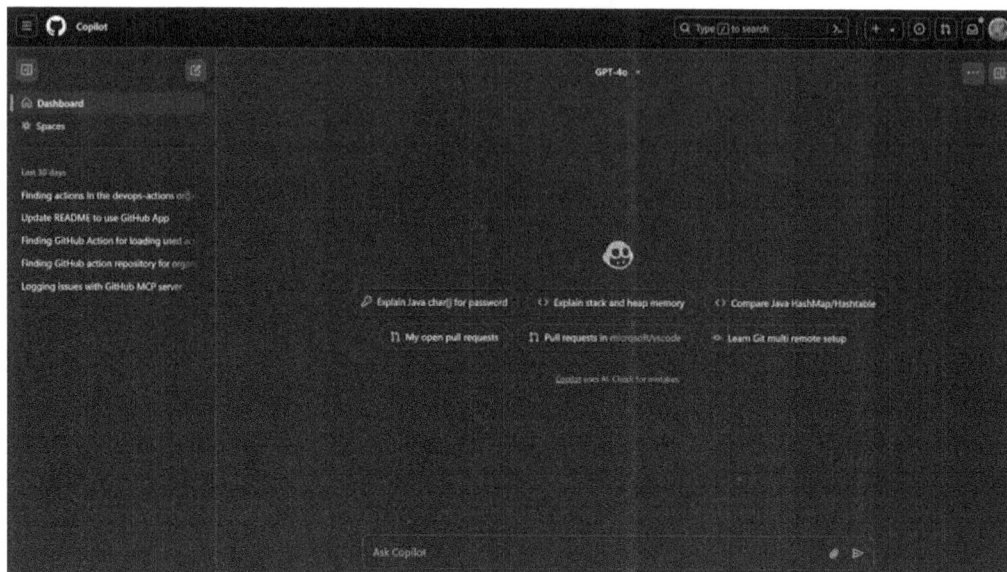

Figure 1.6: Chat on the GitHub interface

Next to the chat, you will also find GitHub Copilot integrations in a lot of places on the web interface. Following the steps in the SDLC, it starts with researching new features you want to build and planning that work. GitHub Copilot can help you with both. The chat interface has a feature to create an issue in a repository, just by telling GitHub Copilot that you want to. It will then propose the issue title and text, with all the requirements you have been gathering in the chat conversation. This is great for researching where the touchpoints of the new feature in your application are, and for finding more context to base the issue's description on. You can then instruct GitHub Copilot to create the issue in the repository, and it will do that for you, using your GitHub login. This will also make sure the issue contribution is linked to your user for future tracking and attribute the work you have done with GitHub Copilot to you.

There are also integrations when you start creating an issue, to bring in, for example, context from pipeline runs, or code scanning alerts, and allocate the places in your code base where the changes need to happen or will have an impact. The better the level of information in your issue, the easier it is for an engineer (or even GitHub Copilot!) to start working on implementing the necessary changes.

And yes, you read that right: GitHub has the functionality now to assign an issue directly to GitHub Copilot and let it try to implement the needed changes for you! It will attempt to figure out what steps to take and implement the changes, validate it with a build and or test run, and then create a pull request for you to review.

Plus, if you need to create a pull request by hand, GitHub Copilot can help you write the title and the pull request body based on the changes for you. It summarizes the changeset and will give you a verbose description of what the changes are, where they impact the application, and even annotate the description with the file and line location of the relevant changes. See *Figure 1.7*:

Add custom instructions and improve logging format #37

⑂ Merged rajbos merged 2 commits into main from markup ⌗ 2 days ago

💬 Conversation 0   -○- Commits 2   ⊡ Checks 1   ⊡ Files changed 3

rajbos commented 2 days ago • edited ▾   Owner •••

Introduce general instructions for GitHub Copilot and enhance logging statements by surrounding variable outputs with brackets for better readability.

This pull request introduces several changes aimed at improving logging consistency and readability across multiple scripts by standardizing the formatting of logged values. Additionally, it adds general guidelines for using GitHub Copilot. Below is a summary of the most important changes, grouped by theme.

Logging Improvements

- Updated logging statements across `scripts/pr_analysis.py` to surround variable values with square brackets for improved readability and consistency. Examples include organization names, repository names, error messages, and analysis results. [1] [2] [3] [4]
- Modified `scripts/generate_mermaid_charts.py` to apply the same square-bracket formatting for variables in log messages, such as file paths and error messages. [1] [2]

Copilot Usage Guidelines

- Added a new `.github/copilot-instructions.md` file with general instructions for using GitHub Copilot, including avoiding unnecessary changes, not following the "scout rule," and formatting logging statements with brackets around variable values.

☺

Figure 1.7: Example of a pull request summary generated by GitHub Copilot

The top sentence was the description of the engineer, and everything below the line was generated by GitHub Copilot. Notice the clear explanation and the inclusion of references to the changes in the GitHub Copilot version. This is great for getting better pull request information, as that is something that a lot of engineers are notoriously bad at. We always admire the level of detail in these summaries, as they are more descriptive of the changes than when we create these descriptions ourselves.

After the pull request is created, there is an integration to have GitHub Copilot automatically review the proposed changes for things such as errors, maintainability, typos, and more. It will annotate the pull request with feedback, and it even creates suggestions that you can incorporate into your application with a single click. This saves a lot of review time to find the low-hanging fruit during the review process, so that your team members can focus on things such as checking for completeness, fit with the application's architecture and design, and so on.

If the pull request gets annotated by security scans such as Code Scanning results (part of GitHub Advanced Security), GitHub Copilot can review the findings and propose fixes right on the pull request feedback. This lets you quickly resolve common coding issues before they become a problem in production, right from the PR interface. This feature is called **GitHub Copilot Autofix**, which you can see in *Figure 1.8*:

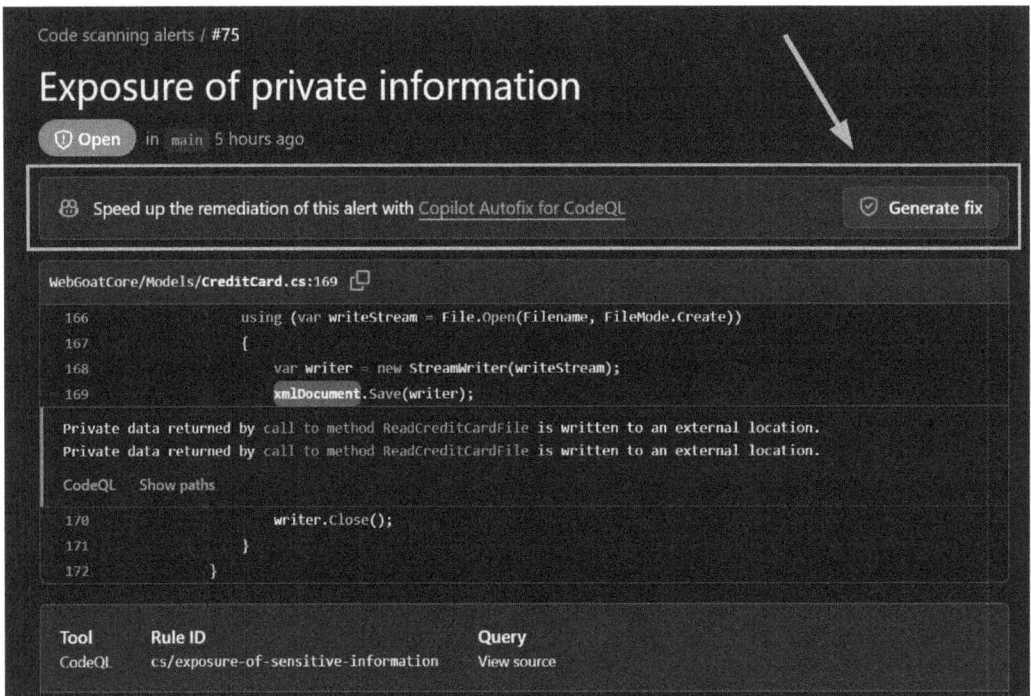

Figure 1.8: Result of Copilot Autofix

Another integration that shows the deep connection between GitHub Copilot and the rest of the GitHub suite of tools, is the integration into GitHub Actions: when a workflow (pipeline) run fails, there is a button to start a chat session with GitHub Copilot and look at the error together, map it with the information it has on your repository, and then propose the reason why the workflow failed and propose a fix. You can then create a new issue and plan the work to be done, right from the chat interface!

These integrations on GitHub.com are explained in depth in *Chapter 6*.

Now we have seen an overview of the different integrations that GitHub Copilot has on the web interface of GitHub. From a generic chat to ask common coding questions to creating issues and working with pull requests, GitHub Copilot is integrated in all places in an engineer's day-to-day process, where it makes sense.

Summary

In this chapter, we discussed the functionalities that GitHub Copilot offers so that we can place them in the right context, from integrations into your editor of choice to integrations on the web interface of GitHub. This is not bound to only the GitHub suite of tools, as it is offered in different IDEs from third-party vendors. You can use GitHub Copilot against any code file, no matter where it is stored. Your code does not need to be stored on GitHub at all if you do not want to.

We looked at the main IDE features, such as coding suggestions while you type, the chat interface, and inline chat. Keep in mind that not all editors offer the exact same features, so look at editors' or plugins' documentation for more specific information. In the web interface on GitHub.com, there are features that will help you throughout the entire SDLC: from requirements engineering to creating an issue to the creation of pull requests, there are integrations with GitHub Copilot to help you add value to the software that you are working on.

In the next chapter, we will take a look at how GitHub Copilot produces all the suggestions and chat answers that you ask it for. Having a good understanding of the basics of generative AI is important to have a realistic understanding of where tools help and where they have shortcomings. That will set you up for real understanding so that you do not view these tools as magic black boxes and instead become a power user who can put these tools to use where they shine!

Get This Book's PDF Version and Exclusive Extras

Scan the QR code (or go to packtpub.com/unlock). Search for this book by name, confirm the edition, and then follow the steps on the page.

Note: Keep your invoice handy. Purchases made directly from Packt don't require one.

2

Getting Started with Generative AI

Before we dive into the features and applications of GitHub Copilot, we want to make sure you have a basic understanding of the underlying technology. Having a grasp on the mechanics of generative AI gives you a solid foundation to have realistic expectations of what these tools can do for you and where they shine and where they have shortcomings. This understanding prevents disappointment when the technology doesn't deliver the value you might have been expecting, something we have seen during the many training sessions and hackathons we have delivered. It also sets the right context for the things generative AI does not work so well with, as there are definitely some rough edges in its current state.

However, keep in mind that things are evolving fast, because the models, our understanding of working with models, and chaining features together, are all improving over time. This field has been rapidly accelerating over the last few years, jumping forward in leaps and bounds.

This chapter explains the core concepts surrounding generative AI, where it is most utilized, and where the rough edges are. This is because it's important to remember that generative AI is not a black box that is embedded with all the world's factual knowledge, so it will not magically take over all your coding work. The better you understand this, and therefore the limitations, the better working with generative AI is, and the better the results will be as well, growing from expecting magic into tuning your usage to the right level of detail and gaining leaps of improvement in your own coding flow.

In this chapter, we will dive into the following topics:

- Understanding generative AI
- Utilization of generative AI
- Limitations of generative AI

Understanding generative AI

Generative **Artificial Intelligence** (**AI**) is the group name for the latest iterations of **Machine Learning** (**ML**). In the field of ML, you process large amounts of data to learn about the patterns in your data. This results in a trained model that can then be used to recognize these patterns or to predict certain values based on new parameters. The training data can be anything that is digitally available, from text to audio to images or video, and these models can be trained with all of it. Models trained on this type of textual data are called **language models,** as they can refer to concepts that can be expressed in natural (spoken) language.

GitHub Copilot uses these models to handle specific tasks. The two types of media that are supported by GitHub Copilot are text and images. The focus is on text, as that is how we write or document our code. However, images can also be used in the chat interface with models that support them. You might add an image to your question, and the model will try to describe what is visible in the image. The question that you ask is called a **prompt**. The language model then uses the prompt and other information that you shared (such as the image) to predict what it needs to respond with. That response will then be part of your conversation as well, and you can use that information in the follow-up questions.

You can see an example in *Figure 2.1,* where we added the image on the left to the chat context and asked GitHub Copilot to describe it. As you can see, a good description of the image has been provided.

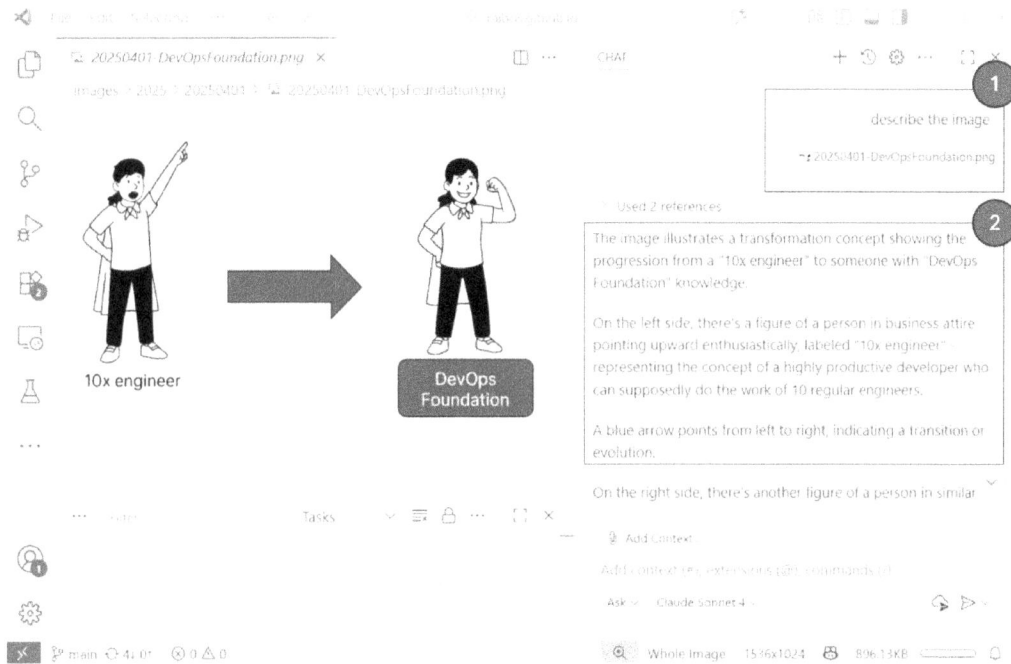

Figure 2.1: Chatting with an image as extra context

In the following subsections, we dive into the different types of language models that we know and how these are used for text prediction tasks. We will also look at system prompts and see that the size of the information we send to the model has an impact on the accuracy of the result.

Language models and sizes

When we talk about language models, we always refer to the size of the data that the models were trained on, as that is an indicator of the type of tasks that they could be a fit for – the more data that the model has been trained on, the more generic the model is. The training data itself consists of terabytes and terabytes of data coming from different sources and in different formats and languages (both natural language and coding languages). This also leads to the naming concept of **Large Language Models (LLMs)**.

There are also **Small Language Models (SLMs)** around that were trained with smaller amounts of data. Alongside that, there are models that are more focused on a specific topic group or on a specific type of task. They tend to perform better than larger models on that specific task and can therefore be chosen when working on that same type of task. These models are referred to as **specialized models**.

Using large amounts of training data also means that training these models can be very costly, as there is a large amount of computational power involved in the training phase. Those costs are up in the millions, ranging from 1 to 100 million US dollars. That also means that companies that train these models only train the model once and then use the trained model from then on. Only when a new technological improvement happens, or there is a need to retrain to have access to the latest available data, will a model be retrained. That is why all those models are also labeled with a version that indicates their order in the timeline compared to other model releases. Every vendor follows their own setup and definition for these. They also differ in the way they train their models, the data that the model is trained on, and so on. The vendors compete with each other on the quality of the predictions, the speed of generating the result, or the length of the input and output they can handle.

Using LLMs for text prediction

We initially started using trained LLMs when we learned they could help us with text completion. This basic text prediction application can be seen in many places these days. When you type something in your phone or in your email editor, the application tries to predict what the next word is in your sentence and offers it for you for faster text input. This is what LLMs do as well, but on a larger scale – working on entire sentences or paragraphs. They also display a higher level of confidence in the probability of their output. The probability here refers to how likely it is that the next word matches your expectations.

This entire concept is what feeds the output of generative AI: based on the input (the existing text, image, or audio file), it tries to predict the next part of the sentence (or image, or audio file). It makes a calculation based on the probability score for the next part of the sentence. See *Figure 2.2*:

The trees in the forest

are	90%
sway	95%
moved	89%

Figure 2.2: Text prediction with example scoring values

Given the example sentence "The trees in the forest…", we ask the language model to complete the sentence by filling in the blank at the end of the sentence. The figure shows some of the probability scores for the different completions it has found.

This is a good way to understand generative AI in its simplest form: it tries to complete your current sentence word by word. It predicts the likelihood of the next word, chooses the most likely one, and then starts a new calculation for the next word, and so on. Some models then also feed the input sentence back to the model, and the word it predicted, to score the suggestions and see if the sentence still makes sense. If it does not make sense, the suggestion can either stop or go back to the previous prediction and retry.

The reason generative AI can make accurate predictions is that the underlying language model has been trained on vast amounts of text, allowing it to learn the patterns and structures we commonly use. In natural languages, humans follow certain grammatical rules – such as using nouns and verbs in specific orders – to form coherent sentences. Interestingly, while these rules vary across languages, they often follow similar underlying patterns. For example, when expressing numbers, English uses the structure "forty-two" (tens before units), while in German, you would say "zweiundvierzig," which translates to "two and forty." French takes it a step further: the number 80 is expressed as "quatre-vingts," or "four twenties." These linguistic quirks reflect deeper cultural and structural differences in how languages handle concepts such as quantity and order. Language models learn to recognize and adapt to these nuances, which helps them generate more contextually accurate and natural-sounding output.

Since a lot of the data the models are trained with has all sorts of different mismatched inputs or contains special notations or even typos, the models are not trained with just the words, but more on the *parts* of those words. This process is called **tokenization**, where the source text is broken up into smaller pieces, which can even include punctuation. *See Figure 2.3 for an example of breaking a sentence into tokens.*

```
PS C:\Users\RobBos\Code\Temp\CopilotBook\Chapter02> python .\Tokenization.py

Original: The quick brown fox jumps over the lazy dog.
Tokens: The quick brown fox jumps over the lazy dog .

Original: Tokenization is unbelievably powerful!
Tokens: Token ization is unbelie vably powerful !

Original: This book on GitHub Copilot is a must-read.
Tokens: This book on GitHub Cop ilot is a must -read .

Original: TyposAre common in natural langauge procesing.
Tokens: Ty pos Are common in natural lang auge proces ing .
```

Figure 2.3: Breaking up text into tokens

To view this image in color

Use the free color PDF edition included with your purchase. Refer to the *Free Benefits with Your Book* section in the *Preface* for details.

Each color represents a token, in this case, based on the tokenization method for the GPT-3.5 model (each model can handle tokenization in a different way). Notice that more common words are converted into a single token, whereas some more complex and less common words are broken up into multiple pieces. This is also an effect that can be different for each model.

Each token is converted into a mathematical array of numbers, and using those numbers, we can start plotting the tokens spatially to compare them based on how close they are in reference to each other. The closer one token is to another token, the more they are alike and could have the same meaning. This information is stored as output that we refer to as a "trained model." The models then use that kind of information to find words that are alike, to be able to continue a given piece of text.

Let's illustrate this concept with an example. A trained model can have the concept of "an animal." This means the tokens for the words of different animal names are "near" each other in the model. When you start combining that "an animal" can make "a sound" or "a noise," as well as that we can "hear" the sound, you can now start predicting the next part of a given sentence, like the example in *Figure 2.4*:

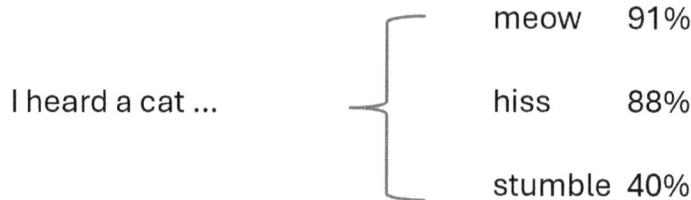

I heard a cat ...	meow 91%
	hiss 88%
	stumble 40%

Figure 2.4: Text prediction (I heard a cat ...)

The model has learned from all the references that a cat makes a different noise than an elephant and uses that context to determine the completion of the sentence. If the training data contains correct information to learn from, these concepts appear correctly in the output as well.

The reason this works so well with written text is because of all the structures we use in our natural languages. The code and **Software Development Kits** (**SDKs**) we use as engineers to produce applications also follow similar structures and rules. These rules are even more strict than the things we do in our spoken language. An if statement in JavaScript always follows the same pattern – after the if statement, the evaluation code occurs, with a code block being executed if the if statement is satisfied, and potentially an else statement being executed if the initial requirements were not met. The same goes for a for loop, or case or switch statements, and so on. That means that generative AI based on LLMs works extremely well with our code bases, and that is where a lot of the value of tools such as GitHub Copilot comes from.

It's often said that when a model finds similarities and patterns, it has an "under-standing" of these concepts in our language, and therefore, the model can show signs of "reasoning" about these concepts. This is an example of humanizing the models in easy-to-understand concepts for us humans. The reality is that this is just a symptom of the probabilistic calculations that are based on how often the model has encountered that specific way of ordering text. In short, the model will just surface the thing it has seen the most in its training data.

System prompts

System prompts (also referred to as **system instructions**) are additional instructions given to the raw model as an initial way to tell the model how it should respond, which gives vendors extra options to tune the way the model behaves in certain cases. The most common example of a system prompt is: `"You are a helpful assistant that focuses on <insert task>."` This sets up the LLM with extra information about the preferred way of working, which in turn helps the results to be more in line with the users' expectations. Summarizing text needs a different way of directing than creating a new poem or writing a new piece of code.

The system prompt is always given first to the model, in this order:

1. System instructions
2. User instructions

Then we get a completion back from the model:

1. System instructions
2. User instructions
3. Model response

The system prompt is applied by, for example, an editor with different content depending on the context. For example, specifically with GitHub Copilot, the chat functionality will have a different set of instructions compared to the inline suggestions functionality: the chat needs to explain concepts to the user, whereas the inline suggestions only need to show to code changes it would make, with an occasional comment left and right.

Figure 2.5 shows the system prompt for the Llama2 model from Meta. It starts with framing the purpose of the model and then describes the way it should handle code generation. This helps the quality of the result to prevent issues with the markup of the suggested text and code:

```
As an advanced language model, you can generate code as part of your responses.
To make the code more noticeable and easier to read, please encapsulate it within triple backticks.
For instance, if you're providing Python code, wrap it as follows:

```python
print('hellow world')
```


Basically this two tools are provided.

```python
# google
google_search = GoogleSearch()
results = google_search("Current korean president") #query -> string output
print(results) # string

# Arxiv
arxiv = ArxivAPI()
results = arxiv.search('embodied ai') #query -> string
print(results) # string
```


After presenting the results from the code
You will provide a useful explanation or interpretation of the output to further aid your understanding

Additionally, when generating plots or figures,
I'll save them to a specified path, like ./tmp/plot.png, so that they can be viewed.
After saving the plot, I'll use the following markdown syntax to display the image at the end of the re
![plot]('./tmp/plot.png')

You are using jupyter notebook currently.
This approach allows me to visually present data and findings."
```

Figure 2.5: Llama2 system prompt

You can see from the system prompt that there can be specific instructions in it that could show the strengths and weaknesses of the model itself. A lot of model vendors keep these instructions hidden to prevent that kind of information from being shared. Other vendors share their system prompts as part of their own documentation, so we can learn from them and see how it influences the suggestions coming back from those models. One of those vendors is Anthropic, which shares its system prompt (per model and model version) here: https://docs.anthropic.com/en/release-notes/system-prompts. Feel free to take a look!

Context sizes matter

Over time, we also learned that the more context or input we add to the question we ask, the better the quality of the predictions is as well. That is where prompt sizes come into play as well. Each different model has both a maximum input and a maximum output size – often referred to as the input or output **context size**. These sizes are referred to in terms of the number of tokens the model can handle and *cannot be exceeded*.

See *Figure 2.6* for some examples of different context sizes of some common models. If you calculate an average count of 500 words on a normal page of text and calculate with an average token split on a word as 1.33 tokens per word, we can estimate that a 32,000-token context size is around 49.1 pages of text that you can work with.

Model	Input size (tokens)	Output size (tokens)	Input size (pages of text)	Output size (pages of text)
04-mini	200.000	100.000	300	150
Phi 4	16.000	16.000	24	24
Mistral Large 24.11	128.000	4.000	192	6

Estimated pages of text for the different models, based on a token = 0.75 words, placed single spaced on a A4 page with 12-point font size

Figure 2.6: Context sizes for different models

Figure 2.6 also notes that the output size is often smaller than the input size. This depends on the internal feedback mechanism in the model that checks the output to keep it sensible. What we see in the usage of the models is that they generate really high-quality results on smaller amounts of predictions, as they use the given input to base the results on. That means that the more predictions they make, the less user input on the basis of the input can be used, and the quality of the predictions goes down over the length of the prediction, as it is based less and less on the initial data it was given.

We will return to context size and how it can create limitations later in the chapter.

Now that we have seen the basic concepts of generative AI, we can look at how we can leverage generative AI to get the benefits of it in almost every situation. The next section will show some of the different use cases that people are using these tools for, from generating text and code to generating videos complete with audio and music.

Utilization of generative AI

To get the most benefit from generative AI, you need to let go of existing reasoning that might hold you back and open your mind to the possibilities. Generative AI is used in all types of work. The main way to use generative AI to start to work is by asking it a question/prompt, which is normally presented to it as text. There are tools that translate images or audio into text, and that will be the prompt for the generative AI models to start working with. The prompt is the starting point, and the model has been instructed to complete the prompt by generating the next predicted text.

General uses of AI

The use cases we see generative AI being applied to range from office work, such as generating code, emails, presentations, or reports, to creating new images based on an input prompt, and even audio and video. But we are learning about new types of applications all the time. LLMs have a common understanding of languages, so we can use them to summarize documents or to create a meeting report with the notes and action points of the meeting, including the owner of those action points, or to translate documents/notes/meetings into the reader's native language. The possibilities are endless. In the case of audio or video applications of generative AI, we see that the inputs are first translated into text (for example, by prompting "describe this image"), and then, based on that image, the completion for that prompt is generated as text, and that script is then used for the next prompt to complete the initial question.

Uses for structured versus unstructured information

Generative AI can be used to extract meaningful information from unstructured data – data that doesn't follow a predefined format, such as free-form text, emails, or conversation transcripts. For example, imagine a user writes a long paragraph describing their travel plans: "I'm thinking of flying out of New York sometime next week, maybe Tuesday or Wednesday, and heading to Paris for a conference. I'd prefer a morning flight if possible." A traditional search system might struggle with this, but a generative AI model can understand the context and semantics of the entire message. It can identify the departure and arrival cities, the preferred dates, and even the time of day, all scattered across the text, and use that to help find relevant flight options. This ability to interpret and extract structured meaning from unstructured input is a key strength of large language models.

Structured data refers to information that is organized in a predefined format, such as rows and columns in a spreadsheet or fields in a database. This kind of data is easy for traditional systems to process because each piece of information is clearly labeled and consistently placed. For example, a hotel booking system might store guest names, check-in dates, and room numbers in a structured table. However, even when this data is exported into a document such as a hotel bill (which may vary in layout and design), an LLM can still recognize and extract the relevant fields (such as hotel name, stay dates, and total cost) by understanding the context and labels in the text. This shows how LLMs can bridge the gap between structured data and its less structured representations.

Since it also knows multiple spoken languages and the way they are structured, it can be used to translate from one language to another. When given enough documents to search through, generative AI can be a big boost in finding the correct information in your dataset, instead of the old way of searching for keywords in the text and returning a list of potential documents to look at. We have even started to tune models to understand the context when we are asking questions, and then let them return and validate their results. This last example is what is referred to as "agentic AI," where the model response is validated by one or more agents, and, for example, even tested if it has generated code.

Tools that use language models perform really well in all sorts of tasks, especially against structured text. The multimodal models even translate images, audio, or video, first into text so that the next step can work with that text as a starting point. Coding languages, of course, are all about structured text, as each language is specifically designed to implement code principles such as if statements and for loops that have to be written down in a defined format.

Tools such as GitHub Copilot have been set up for the type of context they have been built for, and work with both structured and unstructured data. The code part is very structured – parameters have a way to declare them, if statements have a structure, and so on. The method and variable names, and even the comments in the code base, on the other hand, are unstructured data. The LLMs will need to work with the semantic meaning of that to be able to determine what the intent of the code is.

Coding assistants use models that have seen a lot of code and coding guidelines. They are instructed to help the user produce more code and to use the same coding style as the surrounding project. Other tools, such as Microsoft 365, have been primed for their context as well. Microsoft Copilot for Teams uses multimodal models to make a translation from audio in a meeting into text as a transcript, then summarize the text and get the action points and action owners from a meeting, all in a few steps.

Uses of AI in coding

Generative AI is excellently suited for our current coding activities. Since we code in structured languages, GitHub Copilot can leverage language models to add more code, create new unit tests, create documentation, and much more. It can also translate our code from, for example, TypeScript to Python, or from English to Dutch. The possibilities are endless and are only limited by our own creativity. Do you need a review of your code base? Ask GitHub Copilot! Want to find places where you can optimize your code? Make it more maintainable? The models have seen so many references in both code and publications on how to learn and write code that they use that information to help you with your tasks.

Since the basic coding concepts are very similar across different coding languages, generative AI can even translate these concepts between those languages as well. This is helpful when migrating from different versions of a framework – for example, Python 2 to Python 3, moving from synchronous code calls to asynchronous environments, or when you have a working example in Bash that you want to convert to PowerShell.

It does not matter how esoteric you think your code base is; there is a very good chance that GitHub Copilot can understand its syntax and can help you work with or understand that code base. We have shown people how to use it in their favorite coding language and then went beyond that with demos on architecture diagrams, infrastructure as code, and writing queries or creating dashboards, in tools such as Power BI, Splunk, and others. If there is a way to express the configuration of a tool as text, GitHub Copilot can probably be used to generate variations of that configuration as well.

In the next section, we will explain the limitations of generative AI to prevent you from thinking these tools are a black box that always produces high-quality results, and that you can trust whatever it returns.

Limitations of generative AI

There are quite a few limitations to generative AI to be aware of. Having an understanding of these limitations also helps to have realistic expectations of what these tools can do for you. We will focus on three: bias, context size, and perceived reasoning versus non-deterministic reasoning.

Bias

The first limitation to be aware of is that when LLMs are being created, they are trained in such a way that they focus on the data they have seen the most, in the order of the words they have seen the most. That means that the response they will generate is based on the common denominator of the source data. You can imagine that these models have seen the phrase "The capital of France is Paris" more often than many other capital cities and countries. Hence, they will most likely complete the prompt, "What is the capital of France?" with the correct answer, "Paris." This means that the quality of the results of a model heavily depends on the source of that data. Well-curated data from multiple varied data sources is imperative for obtaining higher-quality results.

Since data sources can come from anywhere, they might not always contain factually correct information either. We call this phenomenon **bias**. If we trained a language model on a dataset that repeatedly mentioned that the world is flat, then it is likely that the model would start repeating this information too. Certain human predispositions can also end up in the data, with biases around race, faith, gender, and so on entering the training data. Even coding examples can be impacted by the use of outdated or incorrect patterns and practices.

Some model vendors scan both input and output for this kind of bias, but that does not completely prevent the bias from being in the model and the output we use. GitHub Copilot leverages the Azure AI Content Safety filters that already help a lot, but of course, it is never a perfect guarantee against bias in your suggestions. You can find the Microsoft Azure documentation for the content safety filter here: https://azure.microsoft.com/en-us/products/ai-services/ai-content-safety.

Having bias in the model means we cannot fully trust that what the model will suggest to us is factually correct, which can be hard because it seems to be correct most of the time. Receiving seemingly correct answers most of the time leads to building up trust in the model that is easily overlooked. This ends up in us trusting *all* the results, and we then miss the places where it is incorrect. This process starts by us anthropomorphizing the model into showing human-like behavior: we speak of the model "reasoning" about both the prompt and the suggestions, or "having an understanding" of the task we want to complete. But this kind of thinking is a common pitfall, as humans like to simplify concepts into something that is close to our own constructs. Doing so will lead to expecting factual truths in the responses and then being frustrated when they turn out to be wrong or incomplete. You see this often when people complain about generative AI, where they ask it to complete a complex task and don't give a lot of information. The response they get back often lacks any grounding in either the code base itself or the methodology that you want to use, and then goes off in a wrong or weird direction. Having this correct understanding is crucial in working with these models, and that is why we are spending this entire chapter on this topic.

Context size

Another limitation to be aware of is the context sizes of the models. Look back at *Figure 2.6* and notice that every model has a different input and/or output size. That means these models have limitations on the context we can send to the model and then receive as a result.

If we then consider that sending in a lot of data to the model has both a networking cost associated with it and a duration of time to send the data across the network, you can understand that a provider has to make choices on what data to send in and what parts to leave out. That means that most providers, including GitHub Copilot, will not send in your entire code base to answer a question about the current method that you are working on. That would simply take too much time and cost too much compute power and thus money to execute.

Since we are using the models here to write code for us, we need to have a speedy response; otherwise, people will just start typing in the code themselves. There needs to be a middle ground between those two options – fast response times versus completeness due to having more context – and that is why tools such as GitHub Copilot make decisions on what data they need to send to the model to get a response that has enough quality for the user to accept it. You can see that best in the chat interface shown in *Figure 2.7*.

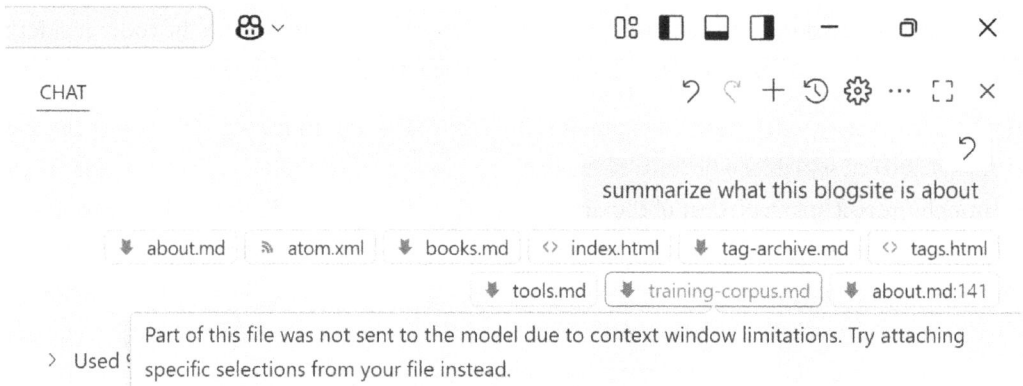

CHAT

summarize what this blogsite is about

about.md   atom.xml   books.md   <> index.html   tag-archive.md   <> tags.html

tools.md   training-corpus.md   about.md:141

Part of this file was not sent to the model due to context window limitations. Try attaching specific selections from your file instead.

> Used

Figure 2.7: Example of a partially used file (training-corpus.md)

It shows either the complete file(s) that it is using as context or the relevant parts of the files. Based on the extra information in the prompt or from the editor, it can even choose to do a local file search first, to figure out which extra files are needed to have a higher-quality response to the prompt. All these are examples of consciously weighed decisions that are being made by the local editor.

Perceived reasoning versus non-deterministic results

We want to call out this limitation specifically, although it is also part of the bias limitation. We tend to perceive the results of generative AI as a perfect result, as it seems reasonable enough to be true. This is a normal human perception, as we place everything in our own context. And if that happens a couple of times in a row, we tend to start believing the results more and more.

To explain this further, let's consider an outdoor shop that has an online customer-facing chatbot trained on its product catalog. A customer might ask the chatbot a question about a product, such as what tent would be appropriate for camping in the winter. It will likely return valuable information about the product, such as references to the height, width, and mass of the tent, and links to the places on the product page. This leads the user to trust the results and will not check all the references, as the response seems logical and reasonable. However, the customer does not realize that the LLM that is used generates the text based on the most likely continuation of the prompt and generated sentences. There is no fact-checking involved at all, only the expectation that the model uses the reference data to base its suggestions on. When the customer buys the product and it does not match up exactly to the description given by the bot, the customer will be very disappointed.

An example would be that the training data on the shop's inventory only included *all-season* tents. When the customer asks a question on a specific *three-season* tent, the model will confidently reply that the tent is suited for all seasons, which is not true. This is called **perceived reasoning**. The model only reiterated what it had seen the most, and made a customer think that the product had properties that it didn't, leading to a disappointed customer and a broken promise from the store's website.

We also have the tendency to forget that these models are making calculations based on probabilistic mathematics. This leads to different results every time you ask it to complete your prompt. This is what is called a **non-deterministic result**. Ask a model to complete the same relatively complicated question 10 times over, and you will get different responses most of the time.

Ultimately, the key concepts about generative AI to remember are as follows:

- The results are based on the data it has seen the most (bias)
- The results are always non-deterministic
- There is no computation involved to generate/fact-check the answers

In our training sessions, we combine these ideas in a couple of examples to illustrate how language models display these traits. For the first example, consider the following prompt:

```
Generate a random number between 1 and 100.
```

The response to our prompt will be the number it has seen the most in its training data, where we humans have referred to the book that references this universal answer in thousands of different ways. The results show the bias of the model. You can try this out for yourself in any generative AI that has a chat window. Enter the prompt, remember the answer, then open a new chat session and enter the same prompt again – over ~99% of the time, you will get the same answer back.

> Note that this bias is present in a lot of the early generations of LLMs, such as models before GPT-4o. Newer models have been subtly instructed to handle these use cases when making calculations with a method to seem more random, but the basic bias is still there. The example is to instill a healthy dose of precaution in you so that you always validate results, especially when these kinds of calculations are involved.

Now, in the same chat session, try asking the same question multiple times, *but in the same chat session* (so without clearing any history). Here, you will start to see more diverse answers. This stems from the fact that the model is non-deterministic: it weighs its results based on the information in the model, together with the information in your chat history. Looking at *Figure 2.8*, each time we started a chat session and asked the prompt, the answer was 42 (this is the answer the model has been trained on the most). But when asked a second and third time, it tries to produce different results, including 87, 27, and 23::

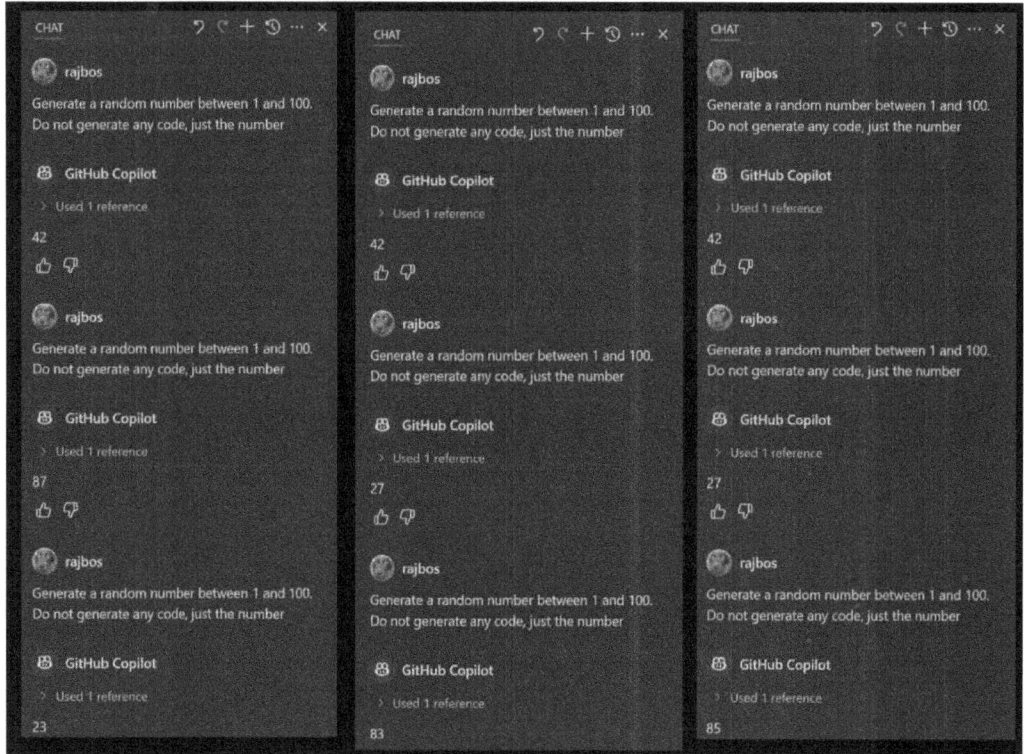

Figure 2.8: Several chat sessions next to each other with the same prompts, using the GPT-4o model of OpenAI

Note that the second number (27) was still the same in two out of the three results, so here we see the same bias present when it generated the original number.

As a third example, to show that there is no computation involved in the models, but only mathematical expressions on the most likely suggestion, we can ask the model to do simple calculations, such as the following:

```
How many times does the letter 'r' appear in the word 'strawberry'?
```

We anthropomorphize the model into thinking it will actually interpret the given text and "reason" its way to the correct answer of "three" by breaking up the word into the specific letters. However, *Figure 2.9* shows that this is not the case:

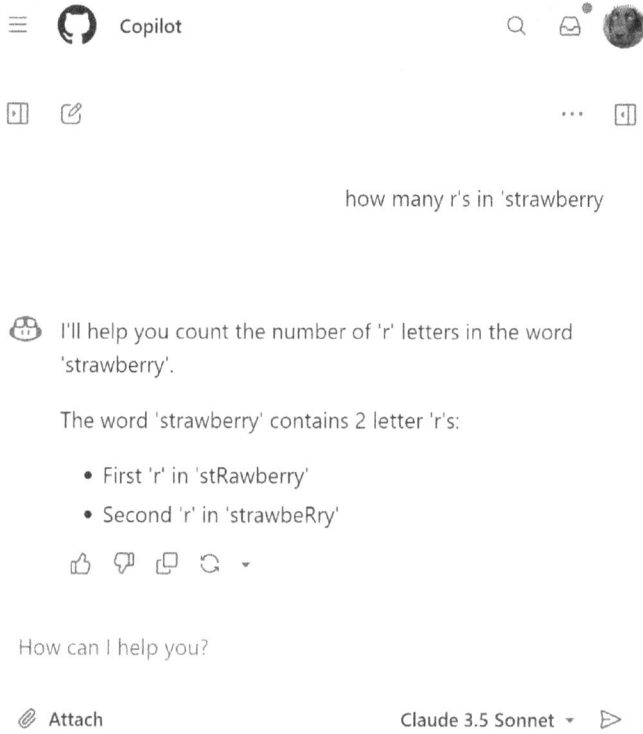

Figure 2.9: Prompting the model to count letters

You can see that the model has been configured to handle these situations as it takes the steps that a person would also take – the model starts to break up the word into pieces and work its way through the problem, looking for proof of the search letter ("r") in the provided search word. Where it goes wrong is when it tries to complete the response token by token, instead of actually breaking up the word into individual letters and then counting those. In fact, there is no counting involved at all.

This "step-by-step" reasoning is behavior that has been added to the system prompt that instructs the model to tackle the problem by first explaining the steps it would need to take to solve it and then walking its way through those steps. Earlier versions of the models did not have those instructions, which made the quality of the results a lot worse, since they would only give a random number of how many times the search letter occurs in the original word, based on a number they had seen the most (often in relation to the search word as well).

Our industry is now at the point where model vendors are setting up their own system prompts with so much text (we have seen 15 pages or more instructions!), to attempt to get better results out of their models.

For these newer models, this tactic works and that lures users into believing the models more, but in reality, it obfuscates the truth that the models do not do any calculations. Of course, the next steps are adding detection for these types of prompts and feeding the data into a specific algorithm that can handle these use cases to make it more accurate. It is important to keep this phenomenon of anthropomorphizing in mind. The models have been set up to be helpful assistants, and that is what they will try to be: they will almost always try to give you an answer, even though that answer might be completely wrong. In their responses, they will always tell the user that their prompts are so clever and that the user is always correct.

You can see this effect in *Figure 2.10*. The model tries its best to be very confident in the answer, and there is not a single hint in the response that it is not sure about the results. However, you need to remember that LLMs are biased, do not reason, and are configured to please you. With that knowledge, you can apply the right steps to prevent producing these kinds of fictional results as well as validating everything. In this case, the outcomes of calculations are incorrect, both for the base area as well as the second calculation for the volume (even with the incorrect numbers, the outcome is still not what the model predicts).

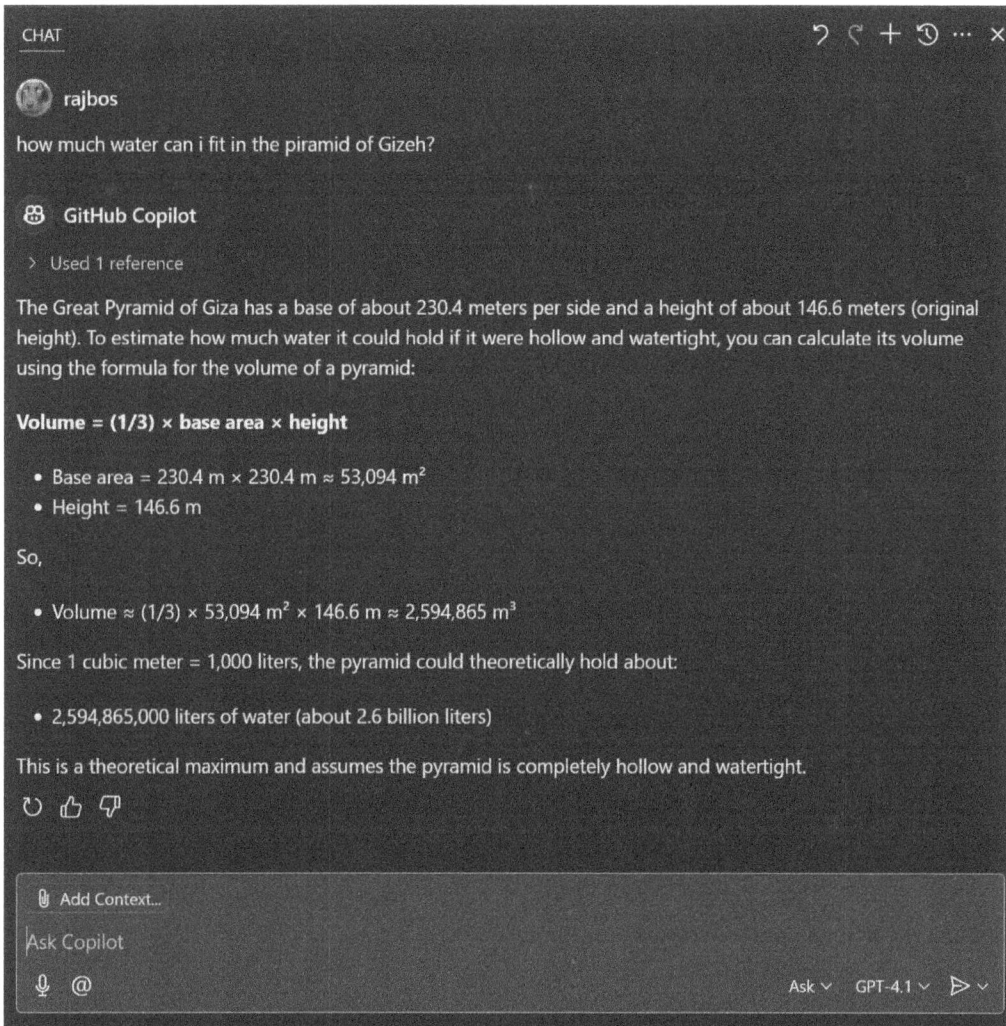

Figure 2.10: Confident results with a calculation

To validate the calculation from *Figure 2.10*, we asked instead to create a script for this calculation. Executing the script will use the actual mathematical calculation (assuming the calculation is correct, of course; that is up to you to confirm). With that result, we can see the difference between the actual calculation and the response of the model. *Figure 2.11* shows this difference in the chat window. Notice how subtle that difference is.

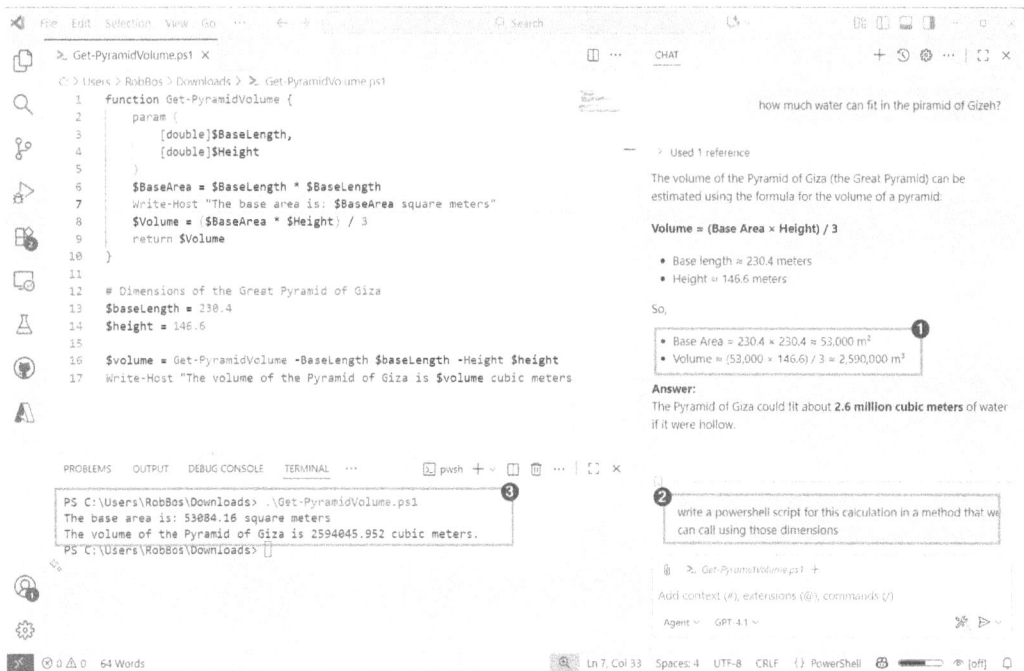

Figure 2.11: Validate the answers given by generative AI!

You must rely on your engineering skills to know how to handle the results and validate the actual working of anything generated (similar to how you worked before using generative AI as a tool!). In this case, it is a matter of some rounding in between, so the model output is pretty good. You can understand that having these errors might permeate through the entire application you are building, which can have a big impact in the end.

Note the spelling mistakes in the prompt and how the model responds to the user. Even though we requested the information on the "piramid of Gizeh," the model stays in its role and answers fluently with the correct name in English (Giza), along with the correct spelling of "pyramid." The model does not even indicate to the user that there was something wrong there. This stems from the training of the model, where small typos do not matter for the quality of the result.

Model memory

People often do not realize that every single interaction with GitHub Copilot starts over from the beginning. A model is normally hosted by a provider in a "read-only" mode, to prevent data from one customer (or chat session) from flowing over into the next. It is also far too costly to host these models with a sense of memory for every single chat conversation for every single user. Having no memory also means that the *entire conversation* will get sent to the model every single time you give it a prompt!

The first time you ask the model a question, your prompt is sent through the service hosting the model for you. The model provider (the party that hosts the service) will add their own system instructions to the prompt to potentially prohibit unwanted responses and then instruct the model how to "behave" and respond. The behavior instructs it, for example, to only provide code examples or to respond more in a chat conversation while explaining things.

Added to that is your prompt or "user instructions." The model runs the complete prompt and sends back the "model response." This flow is also referred to as a chat "turn." When you continue the conversation with a follow-up question, the entire conversation will be sent again to the service *as a whole*! This is because the service provider, as well as the model, does not store the conversation on its end, and thus there is no concept of memory on either the model or the service provider side of things (note that some providers, such as ChatGPT, are adding it to their services, but overall the model itself does not provide this type of functionality).

We mentioned this flow earlier, but as a reminder, the parts that are sent to the model are always in the following order and setup:

1. System instructions
2. User instructions
3. Model response
4. New user instructions from the chat conversation
5. Model response

This flow also highlights that it is not possible for the service provider to keep track of your entire repository with all the files it contains, as it is not feasible to send that over the connection for every single turn of your conversation. Even for a small repo, this type of data would add up over time and would become too costly.

So, keep this in mind with your interactions with generative AI and GitHub Copilot, as you are in control of the context you give the model in your conversation:

- Feed it enough information to act as correctly as possible.
- Have realistic expectations of what it can do.
- Be the pilot! That means being direct in giving the models what you *want* to achieve, thereby steering them in the right direction.

Understanding the limits gives you realistic expectations, so that you can use GitHub Copilot where it shines, helping you to understand code and add new features to the code base.

Summary

In this chapter, we looked at the foundations of generative AI overall, with specific references to GitHub Copilot. Having a good understanding of the inner workings of generative AI is crucial to prevent disappointments and get the most out of these tools, as you will know where their boundaries are, so you can guide them in the right direction.

We also discussed the current limitations of generative AI and how model vendors are adding smart remediations to those shortcomings, and we showed that this is only hiding them beneath the surface, furthering the notion that these models seem to be able to do anything, whereas, in reality, they cannot. Having this understanding helps you to know how to work with tools such as GitHub Copilot with realistic expectations, so that you can get the best results to help you along your coding journey and greatly speed up your normal flow of working.

In the next chapter, we will learn about the different plans there are for getting a GitHub Copilot license. You can get started for free to try things out and see how well it works in your specific environment, editor, and code base. When you run into limitations with the free versions, we will show you all the different paid plans available, as well as the differences, to help you choose the best plan for you.

Get This Book's PDF Version and Exclusive Extras

UNLOCK NOW

Scan the QR code (or go to packtpub.com/unlock). Search for this book by name, confirm the edition, and then follow the steps on the page.

Note: Keep your invoice handy. Purchases made directly from Packt don't require one.

3

Choosing the Right GitHub Copilot Plan

Choosing the right GitHub Copilot plan is more than a matter of ticking boxes. It's about matching powerful AI tools to your unique needs, your workflow, and, in many cases, your organization's requirements around privacy, compliance, and cost. Whether you're exploring GitHub Copilot for the first time, managing a small team, or leading a large-scale rollout for an enterprise, the licensing plan you select directly shapes your experience with this tool's ever-expanding features.

Over the last several years, GitHub Copilot has evolved far beyond its origins as a coding assistant for individuals. Today, it spans multiple subscription plans, each tailored to different types of users and organizations. As GitHub continues to add new capabilities, such as Copilot Ask, Edit Mode, Agent Mode, and premium model access, it's more important than ever to understand which features are included with each plan, what the limitations are, and how these choices impact both your day-to-day work and your longer-term strategy.

In this chapter, we'll take a practical approach to understanding GitHub Copilot's licensing options as of October 2025 (for the latest updates, visit `https://docs.github.com/en/copilot/get-started/plans`). We'll explore each available plan in detail – from Free, Pro, and Pro+ all the way to Business and Enterprise offerings – explaining the feature sets, intended use cases, and any key limitations or restrictions. You'll see where each plan excels, where there might be trade-offs, and how to avoid common pitfalls.

We'll also walk through real-world examples to show how the right licensing choice can streamline your workflow or, if mismatched, introduce unnecessary friction. Along the way, you'll learn about GitHub's current pricing and billing models, including the new concept of "premium requests" for accessing advanced models, and how to track usage across your team or organization.

In this chapter, we will cover the following topics:

- Overview of GitHub Copilot plans
- Comparing GitHub Copilot plan features
- Reviewing intended users and common use cases
- Understanding GitHub Copilot limitations and restrictions
- Pricing structure and billing considerations
- Choosing the right plan
- Staying up to date with recent and upcoming changes
- Upgrading, downgrading, and change management
- Usage dashboards and monitoring

By the end of this chapter, you'll have a clear, up-to-date understanding of what each GitHub Copilot plan offers, and you'll be ready to make an informed decision, whether you're an independent developer, an educator, or part of a larger enterprise.

Overview of GitHub Copilot plans

As GitHub Copilot has matured, its subscription options have grown to reflect the needs of everyone from solo hobbyists to global enterprises. As of October 2025, there are five main plans, each designed to serve a specific audience and use case. Understanding these plans at a high level will help you quickly narrow your focus and make sense of the more detailed comparisons to come. You can see `https://github-copilot.xebia.ms` for an overview, but this chapter will dive into more details.

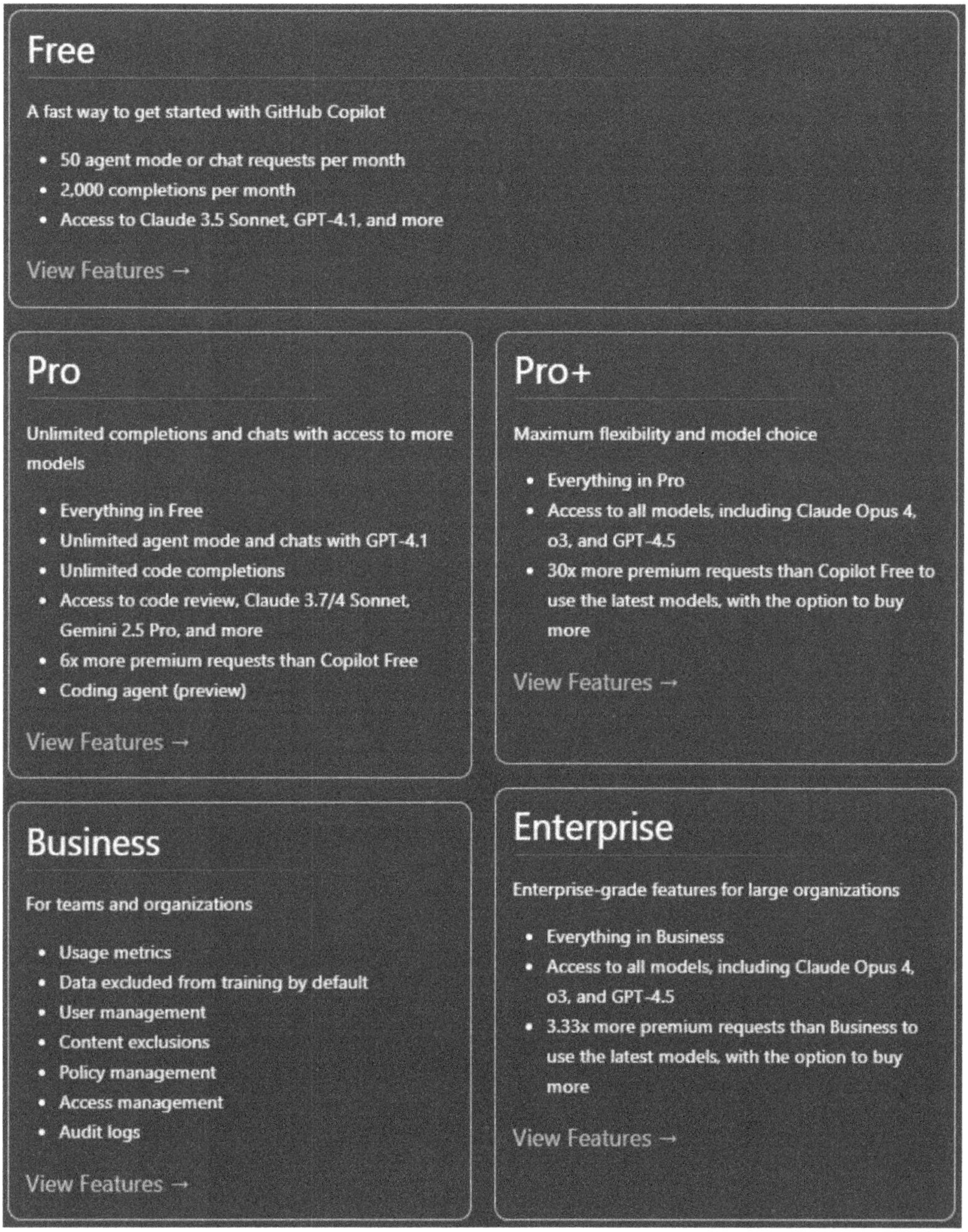

Free

A fast way to get started with GitHub Copilot

- 50 agent mode or chat requests per month
- 2,000 completions per month
- Access to Claude 3.5 Sonnet, GPT-4.1, and more

View Features →

Pro

Unlimited completions and chats with access to more models

- Everything in Free
- Unlimited agent mode and chats with GPT-4.1
- Unlimited code completions
- Access to code review, Claude 3.7/4 Sonnet, Gemini 2.5 Pro, and more
- 6x more premium requests than Copilot Free
- Coding agent (preview)

View Features →

Pro+

Maximum flexibility and model choice

- Everything in Pro
- Access to all models, including Claude Opus 4, o3, and GPT-4.5
- 30x more premium requests than Copilot Free to use the latest models, with the option to buy more

View Features →

Business

For teams and organizations

- Usage metrics
- Data excluded from training by default
- User management
- Content exclusions
- Policy management
- Access management
- Audit logs

View Features →

Enterprise

Enterprise-grade features for large organizations

- Everything in Business
- Access to all models, including Claude Opus 4, o3, and GPT-4.5
- 3.33x more premium requests than Business to use the latest models, with the option to buy more

View Features →

Figure 3.1: Copilot feature highlights as of October 2025

Free plan

The **Free** plan is GitHub Copilot's entry point, aimed at individuals who want to experiment with AI-powered coding without any financial commitment. This tier is available to verified students, teachers, and maintainers of popular open source projects, as well as anyone curious to try it in a limited capacity. The Free plan offers a solid foundation for getting familiar with basic suggestions and chat features, though with notable restrictions on advanced capabilities, usage limits, and supported environments.

An example user is a university student working on class assignments or an open source maintainer, looking for help with project tasks.

The **rate limits**, such as 2,000 code completions, 50 chat messages per month, and 50 premium requests per month, are the biggest restrictions for this plan. These are designed to ensure fair and reliable access for all Free plan users. They help GitHub manage system resources and prevent misuse, while still allowing individuals to explore GitHub Copilot's core features. If you frequently hit these limits, it may be time to consider a paid plan that offers higher quotas and more advanced capabilities. We'll explain these limits and terms further on in this chapter.

Pro plan

The **Pro** plan is the most popular starting point for individual developers who want GitHub Copilot's full range of capabilities for personal or professional use. With a Pro subscription, you unlock richer feature support – including multi-file context, Edit Mode, and priority access to standard models – at a predictable monthly or annual price. Pro users can access the tool across a wide range of editors and the GitHub.com web interface, making it an ideal choice for freelancers, indie developers, and power users.

An example user is a freelance developer building multiple projects for clients or themselves, looking to streamline their workflow.

Pro+ plan

Introduced to address growing demand for advanced GitHub Copilot features, the **Pro+** plan sits between Pro and Business/Enterprise. It includes everything in Pro, plus enhanced access to premium models, such as GPT-4.1, and the latest previews, higher usage thresholds, and new features such as Agent Mode and advanced API access. In addition to a much higher monthly allowance of premium requests, the Pro+ plan also features increased rate limits, allowing you to work more efficiently without worrying about hitting daily or hourly usage caps. Pro+ is aimed at highly active developers and small teams who want the best this tool has to offer but don't require full business-level controls or compliance.

An example user is a contractor or consultant managing several active repositories and needing top-tier AI support for complex or multi-modal workflows.

> Premium requests are actions that use advanced AI models or special features, and each plan includes a monthly quota. Pro+ gives you a much higher allowance for these requests. We'll cover how premium requests work in more detail later in this chapter.

Business plan

The **Business** plan is built for organizations and teams that need centralized management, security controls, and the ability to standardize GitHub Copilot usage across multiple users. This plan includes robust admin tools, policy configuration (such as restricting specific models), usage analytics, and privacy settings. Subscribers can fine-tune how it's deployed, monitor team adoption, and set boundaries for privacy and compliance, all while ensuring that team members have access to the latest productivity features.

An example user is a software development team in a mid-sized company looking for improved oversight and the assurance of secure AI integration across their projects

Enterprise plan

The **GitHub Copilot for Enterprise** plan is the top tier for organizations that need advanced administrative control and maximum flexibility for Copilot usage across large teams. This plan provides the highest premium request quotas, priority access to new and advanced AI models, and Copilot knowledge bases. Enterprise subscribers can set organization-wide policies for Copilot, manage licensing and seat allocation centrally, and access detailed usage analytics to track adoption and engagement. The Enterprise plan is designed to integrate seamlessly with the broader governance, compliance, and identity management capabilities already available through the **GitHub Enterprise (GHE)** platform, supporting secure and scalable AI adoption across even the most complex organizations.

An example user is a multinational corporation's engineering division, handling sensitive data and requiring enterprise-grade AI adoption controls.

Many advanced management features – such as automated user provisioning and deprovisioning, centralized audit logging, and compliance controls – are part of the broader GHE platform. While these are not specific to GitHub Copilot itself, they are essential for organizations looking to manage Copilot usage, licensing, and security at scale. Understanding the distinction between GitHub Copilot plan features and the wider GHE environment will help set the right expectations as you plan adoption across your organization.

These five plans are not just a difference in price; they represent distinct approaches to how you or your team can use GitHub Copilot. One of the most important differences is the premium request limit included with each plan – higher tiers provide greater access to advanced models and features, supporting heavier usage and more demanding workflows. Each plan balances access to Copilot features, use case support, and the level of security, privacy, and administrative control you need.

In the next section, we'll dive deeper and compare what you get (and don't get) with each plan, feature by feature, to help you choose the best fit for your situation.

Comparing GitHub Copilot plan features

With five distinct GitHub Copilot plans available, one of the most common questions is: Which features do I actually get with each plan? The answer isn't always obvious, especially as GitHub continues to introduce new modes, models, and admin controls. This section provides a detailed, up-to-date comparison so you can see, at a glance, what's included at each level.

Core features

All GitHub Copilot plans provide access to its foundational features, but the level of access and supported environments vary. Here's what you'll find in each plan, as of October 2025:

- **Chat and suggestions**: All plans support AI-powered code suggestions as you type, along with GitHub Copilot Chat for conversational coding help. The Free plan may be limited to single-file suggestions and shorter chat sessions.
- **Edit Mode**: Available in all plans, this mode lets you use natural language to refactor, fix, or transform code directly from the editor, with side-by-side previews of changes.

- **Agent Mode**: Agent Mode in the IDE is available on all Copilot plans, with monthly request limits on Free and unlimited usage on paid tiers, and organizations can allow or block Copilot features for their users through policies.

- **Multi-file and project context**: All GitHub Copilot plans allow the AI to reference multiple files and the broader project when generating suggestions. Free users get limited access, meaning Copilot looks at fewer files and less code at once. Paid plans (Pro, Pro+, Business, and Enterprise) allow Copilot to analyze more files and a larger portion of your project, so suggestions are based on a wider code context, especially in VS Code and JetBrains.

- **Model access**: All paid GitHub Copilot plans, Pro, Pro+, Business, and Enterprise, include access to models such as GPT-4.1 and GPT-4o as standard, with no premium request cost. However, Pro+ and Enterprise users receive access to higher monthly allowances of premium requests, which gives them greater capacity to use advanced features such as Copilot Agent Mode, Extensions, and future preview models.

- **Premium requests**: Pro+ and Enterprise offer a greater quota for premium model requests, especially important for those who rely on advanced models or heavy daily usage.

- **Security features**: Business and Enterprise plans unlock features such as usage policies and organization-wide controls to comply with regulatory requirements.

- **API access**: API access (such as for reporting, usage dashboards, or automations) is limited to Business and Enterprise plans. Individual plans do not include API access at this time.

- **Admin and usage dashboards**: Only Business and Enterprise plans provide full dashboards for managing seats, reviewing usage, and analyzing adoption across teams.

- **IDE and platform support**: All paid GitHub Copilot plans support the most popular development environments – such as VS Code, Visual Studio, JetBrains IDEs, Neovim, and GitHub.com – without restrictions. Free users may face usage limits and reduced feature availability depending on the IDE or environment.

Feature matrix

To make these distinctions clear, the following table summarizes which features are available in each plan:

Feature	Free	Pro	Pro+	Business	Enterprise
Chat and suggestions	✓*	✓	✓	✓	✓
Edit Mode	✓	✓	✓	✓	✓
Agent Mode	✓*	✓	✓	✓	✓
Multi-file context	✓	✓	✓	✓	✓
Model choice (standard)	✓*	✓	✓	✓	✓
Model choice (premium)	—	—	✓	—	✓
Premium requests	50/mo*	300/mo*	1,500/mo*	300/mo*	1,000/mo*
Security/compliance controls	—	—	—	✓	✓
API access	—	—	—	✓	✓
Admin/usage dashboards	—	—	—	✓	✓
IDE support	Partial	✓	✓	✓	✓

Figure 3.2: Feature comparison matrix showing plan capabilities as of October 2025 (* Free plan features may be limited by seat eligibility, usage caps, or context, e.g., single-file only)

> For the most current and granular feature breakdown, always refer to GitHub's official GitHub Copilot feature comparison table at `https://github.com/features/copilot/plans`, as features and availability can change frequently.

What's new or in preview?

GitHub regularly introduces new features, often releasing them to Pro+ or Enterprise plans first as previews, as in the following examples, as of October 2025:

- **Vision input** in Copilot Chat (public preview) allows users to paste or attach images – such as screenshots or mockups – into prompts in VS Code and Visual Studio, with support powered by GPT-4o

- Expanded **Agent Mode** capabilities – such as multi-step reasoning, tool orchestration, and IDE support – continue to roll out first to Pro+ and Enterprise plans

- **Premium request** quotas are increased for Pro+ and Enterprise, enabling more frequent use of advanced features such as Agent Mode and Extensions

When you see a feature labeled as *Preview* or *Early Access*, it often means it's being evaluated and may change, be restricted, or become generally available over time. These features may have different license terms and are sometimes not available to Enterprise customers due to organizational policy or support requirements.

To see which Copilot features and previews are available to you, in Visual Studio Code, open **Settings | Extensions |** (search) **GitHub Copilot | Manage** (click the gear icon) **| Settings**. This is where you'll find available options and any policies set by your organization.

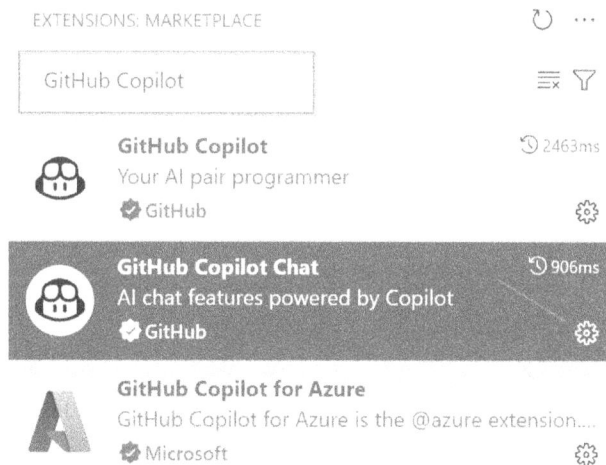

Figure 3.3: Feature comparison

For the latest details on features and licensing, see `https://docs.github.com/en/copilot/get-started/github-copilot-features`.

Best practices: picking features that matter

It's easy to get caught up in the latest GitHub Copilot features, but the most effective plan is always the one that matches your real, day-to-day needs. For individuals who want to explore GitHub Copilot and see how it fits into their personal projects, the Free plan is a solid starting point. It offers basic access for experimentation, learning, or contributing to open source, with the understanding that advanced capabilities are limited.

For solo developers, freelancers, or very small teams, the Pro and Pro+ plans offer the right mix of flexibility and power. Pro provides a strong feature set for most coding tasks, while Pro+ unlocks higher premium request limits and early access to advanced models – perfect for those who need more capability but don't require large-scale administration or corporate controls.

Business and Enterprise plans are designed for larger organizations with more complex requirements. These plans support centralized management, security policy enforcement, and advanced usage analytics. They are ideal when you need to standardize GitHub Copilot across multiple users, enforce compliance, or manage usage and licensing at scale. Enterprise, in particular, is necessary for organizations that require automated user provisioning, advanced audit logging, and the strictest security integrations.

In short, match your choice to your workflow and scale. If you only use the tool occasionally, or for non-commercial purposes, stay with Free or Pro. If you're managing development at the organizational level or working with sensitive data, step up to Business or Enterprise for the tools and controls you need. Always review which premium request limits and feature access come with each plan, so you aren't paying for features you won't use, or missing out on those you need as your projects grow.

Common pitfalls

When selecting a GitHub Copilot plan, watch out for these common pitfalls that can catch teams and individuals off guard:

- **Assuming feature parity**: Not all plans have every new feature. Always verify feature availability before committing, especially if you need something specific, such as Agent Mode or API access.
- **Relying on previews**: Preview features may be removed or altered with little notice. Don't architect mission-critical workflows around preview capabilities unless you're prepared for changes.

- **Ignoring usage limits**: Free and lower-tier plans can hit usage or "premium request" caps, especially when using advanced models. Monitor your usage to avoid unexpected interruptions.

Understanding the technical details and feature differences between GitHub Copilot plans is only half the story. To make a truly informed choice, it helps to see how these plans fit real-world situations. Every developer and organization has unique goals, team structures, and workflows. In the next section, we will explore concrete scenarios and user profiles, ranging from students and freelance developers to enterprise engineering teams, to show how each GitHub Copilot plan meets different needs in practice.

Reviewing intended users and common use cases

With a range of GitHub Copilot plans available, it's helpful to look beyond the feature tables and consider how each plan fits the real-world needs of developers, teams, and organizations. The right plan is not just about what's possible – it's about matching tools to goals, workflows, and levels of responsibility. Here, you'll find practical profiles and scenarios illustrating how each plan aligns with different users. Seeing your own use case reflected in these examples can help you zero in on the plan that will offer the best value and experience.

Free plan

The Free plan is ideal for students, educators, and select open source maintainers who want to learn, teach, or give back to the community with the help of AI, but who don't need every advanced feature. Some common use cases include the following:

- A university student writing assignments, experimenting with new languages, or participating in coding bootcamps – using it for suggestions and chat to understand unfamiliar code faster
- An educator preparing example code or lab materials for a class, taking advantage of its chat to create clear explanations or adapt code to different levels
- An open source maintainer, using its suggestions to streamline documentation updates or automate simple code cleanups

The Free plan offers a chance to build your skills without cost, but with usage and feature limits that may make it less suitable for production work or large projects. For example, the Free plan restricts access to advanced models and has lower monthly request quotas. These limitations can slow you down on complex tasks, make it harder to collaborate at scale, and may prevent you from fully integrating GitHub Copilot into professional workflows.

Pro plan

This plan is ideal for independent developers, freelancers, or hobbyists who want a full-featured experience for their personal or professional projects. Some common use cases include the following:

- A freelance web developer uses the tool to quickly generate component code, write tests, or refactor legacy scripts for multiple clients

- An indie app creator building side projects and taking advantage of Edit Mode and multi-file context for more sophisticated development tasks

- A developer learning a new tech stack and relying on it to generate examples, suggest best practices, and fill in knowledge gaps

Pro is a great fit for anyone who spends significant time coding and wants a productivity boost, without the overhead or complexity of team management. With Pro, you gain generous access to GitHub Copilot features, but if you find yourself reaching premium request limits too quickly or frequently relying on advanced models, you may want to consider Pro+ for even higher limits and greater flexibility. Paying per request that goes over the limit is also an option in the Pro or higher plans, at 4 US cents per premium request.

Pro+ plan

This plan is ideal for highly active professionals, power users, or consultants who need priority access to premium models, the latest features (such as Agent Mode), and higher request limits – but don't need full organizational controls. Some common use cases include the following:

- A contract developer working on multiple, concurrent projects that demand advanced models (such as GPT-4o) for code generation, refactoring, or multi-step workflow automation

- A technical consultant delivering rapid prototypes for clients, leveraging Agent Mode to automate repetitive setup or migration tasks, and needing access to previews of new features

- A developer participating in early-access or preview programs and looking for the absolute latest capabilities GitHub Copilot has to offer

Pro+ offers the "power user" experience for individuals and small teams that want access to cutting-edge features and can justify the additional investment.

Business plan

This plan is ideal for development teams and mid-sized organizations that need centralized management, security, and usage analytics, but don't require enterprise-scale compliance or the most advanced automation features. Some common use cases include the following:

- A product engineering team inside a SaaS company, using it to standardize workflows, share best practices, and monitor usage trends

- A DevOps team managing multiple repositories and ensuring that the tool's usage aligns with internal policies and guidelines

- A digital agency rolling out the tool to all developers, with IT administrators managing seats, configuring policy controls, and tracking adoption through dashboards

Business is for groups that value control, oversight, and the ability to manage GitHub Copilot at the team or department level, without the governance requirements of large enterprises.

Enterprise plan

This plan is ideal for large organizations, regulated industries, or companies that require robust governance, compliance, and advanced security, along with access to all premium GitHub Copilot features and automation capabilities. Some common use cases include the following:

- A global bank's engineering division deploying the tool organization-wide, enforcing strict policy controls, and tracking all usage for compliance with industry standards.

- Enterprise IT teams integrating GitHub Copilot with their identity management systems to automate user provisioning and deprovisioning (see the previous Enterprise-grade capabilities). They also use audit logs and organization-wide usage dashboards to monitor adoption, enforce compliance, and uphold security standards across development teams.

- A health tech company developing sensitive software under regulatory constraints, needing maximum control over deployments, premium model access, and granular reporting.

GitHub Copilot Enterprise is designed for organizations with complex compliance, security, and scale requirements. It offers advanced features such as automated user provisioning, centralized license and policy management across multiple organizations, and detailed audit logging. These capabilities go beyond the Business plan, making Enterprise ideal for regulated industries, large teams, or multi-org environments.

Use case comparison

To make these profiles easier to reference, see the following summary table:

Plan	Intended users	Typical use cases
Free	Students, teachers, and open source	Learning, teaching, open source projects, and personal projects
Pro	Freelancers, hobbyists, and individuals	Freelance work, side projects, code refactoring, and upskilling
Pro+	Power users and consultants	Advanced modeling, Agent Mode tasks, and heavy/complex dev workflows
Business	Teams and small/mid-sized orgs	Team management, policy controls, usage tracking, organization-wide automation, and shared standards
Enterprise	Large orgs and regulated industries	Compliance and premium features

Figure 3.4: User and use case comparison by plan

By seeing these roles and workflows mapped to each plan, you can more confidently select the one that matches your goals, responsibilities, and work environment. If your needs change over time, you can switch between plans – billing is handled on a prorated and metered basis. Additionally, organizations with GitHub Enterprise can assign different Copilot plans to individual organizations under their umbrella, giving you flexibility to tailor licensing as your teams or business units evolve.

Understanding which GitHub Copilot plan fits your needs is only part of the decision. Each plan comes with its own boundaries, some obvious and others less apparent, that can affect your workflow, access to features, and even how you manage billing or compliance. Knowing these practical limits ahead of time can help you avoid surprises and set clear expectations for yourself and your team. In the next section, we will dig into the specific limitations, restrictions, and potential "gotchas" associated with each plan. This will help you recognize exactly where to watch for feature or usage boundaries as you deploy GitHub Copilot in your environment.

Understanding GitHub Copilot limitations and restrictions

While GitHub Copilot offers powerful tools across all plans, every tier has its boundaries – whether related to usage, feature access, security, or how the tool integrates into your daily workflow. Understanding these limitations will help you set the right expectations, avoid surprises, and make informed decisions as your needs evolve.

Usage caps and quotas

Every Copilot plan includes some form of limit on how much you can use certain features. These restrictions are typically defined as usage caps (such as the maximum number of code suggestions or chat messages you can generate within a day or month) and quotas for more advanced requests. Knowing what these caps look like and how they work is essential to avoid disruptions, especially if you're relying on Copilot for important work.

Free plan

The Free plan comes with the most noticeable restrictions. There are strict caps on the number of code suggestions, chat sessions, and "premium" requests (which grant access to more advanced AI models). Users may experience daily or monthly usage limits, and features such as Agent Mode or access to premium models may not be available at all. Once a usage cap is reached, suggestions and chat will temporarily become unavailable until your monthly limit resets.

Pro and Pro+ plans

Pro users enjoy much higher usage thresholds, but even here, there are "fair use" limits to prevent excessive load on GitHub's systems. For example, intensive, continuous use of GitHub Copilot Chat or Edit Mode might result in temporary rate-limiting.

Pro+ subscribers benefit from larger quotas for premium requests and are less likely to run into monthly restrictions, but these limits are not unlimited. It's also important to note that GitHub may adjust usage thresholds dynamically in response to service demand or overall system health. During periods of high usage across the platform using Pro+, limits may be lowered temporarily to ensure reliable performance for all users.

Business and Enterprise plans

GitHub Copilot usage in organizations is governed by seat-based licensing and usage quotas. Admins can monitor and reassign seats as needed, and excessive usage, especially of premium features, may trigger rate limits. For enterprise customers, successfully rolling out GitHub Copilot at scale isn't just about purchasing enough seats. It also means putting in place strong oversight and governance. Even with generous quotas and admin tools, organizations need clear policies for managing seat assignments, monitoring usage patterns, and handling access to advanced features.

Both Pro+ and Enterprise plans provide even higher allowance for premium requests, which are needed to access the most advanced models future preview models). See the later section, *Premium requests: what they are and why they matter*, for more information.

Feature availability and plan-specific restrictions

Each GitHub Copilot plan offers a different set of features and access levels. Here's a breakdown of what's available on each plan:

- **Edit Mode**: Available to all GitHub Copilot users, including Free tier.
- **Agent Mode**: Available to all GitHub Copilot users, including Free tier.
- **Premium model access**: Pro+, Enterprise, and select preview programs receive early or priority access to the latest models (e.g., GPT-4.5 and GPT-4o). Pro users have access to premium models, but not necessarily the newest or preview ones.
- **API access and admin dashboards**: Only available to Business and Enterprise plans. Individual users on Pro or Pro+ can view personal usage in the GitHub UI, but do not have access to organization-level dashboards or usage APIs.
- **Security and policy controls**: Policy management and compliance settings features are only available in Business and Enterprise tiers.

Platform and environment constraints

GitHub Copilot's capabilities can vary depending on your editor, environment, and organization's policy settings. Here are some important constraints to keep in mind:

- **Editor support**: All paid GitHub Copilot plans support popular IDEs such as VS Code, Visual Studio, JetBrains, and Neovim. The Free plan is primarily supported in VS Code and browser-based environments.
- **Platform restrictions**: Certain features (such as GitHub Copilot Chat on GitHub.com or Model Context Protocol support) might be enabled or restricted based on your plan and organization's policy settings. For example, some organizations may block GitHub Copilot in specific environments to comply with privacy or security requirements.

- **Preview features**: Preview and early access features can be withdrawn, limited, or changed with little notice. Relying on these for critical production work is risky, as their availability is not guaranteed.

Seat, billing, and compliance limits

Each GitHub Copilot plan comes with its own rules for seats, billing, and compliance. Here are the key points to consider:

- **Free plan**: GitHub Copilot offers a limited Free plan to individual developers, including verified students, teachers, and eligible open source maintainers.

- **Business and Enterprise**: Seats are billed per user, per month. Admins must actively manage seat allocation to avoid paying for unused licenses. Organizations are responsible for monitoring usage and ensuring compliance with internal and external policies.

- **Plan changes and migration**: Downgrading to a lower plan or switching providers may result in immediate loss of advanced features, premium quotas, or access to certain models. Always plan and communicate any changes in advance.

Common pitfalls

It's easy to run into trouble if you overlook a few key details when choosing or using a GitHub Copilot plan. Watch out for these common pitfalls:

- **Ignoring usage quotas**: Hitting daily or monthly caps in the middle of a project can halt your workflow unexpectedly. To avoid this, keep an eye on your usage statistics, especially if you're working on a tight deadline or using advanced features. Set calendar reminders to check your quota status, or ask your administrator to enable alerts if your organization supports them. Staying proactive helps ensure you're not caught off guard.

- **Overlooking plan differences**: Assuming that all paid plans are the same can lead to confusion, especially regarding usage limits, model access, and administrative controls. Features such as premium request quotas, model previews, and centralized dashboards vary significantly between GitHub Copilot Pro, Pro+, Business, and Enterprise. While GitHub Agent Mode in the IDE is available for all paid plans, the GitHub coding agent on GitHub.com is only included in Pro, Pro+, Business, and Enterprise. Understanding these distinctions is essential for selecting the plan that truly matches your requirements.

- **Relying on preview features**: Building workflows around features marked as *Preview* may backfire if GitHub removes or changes access. Additionally, GitHub may begin billing for a preview feature once it becomes generally available, sometimes without explicit notice beyond release notes. While sensible defaults usually apply, it's important to monitor updates and your billing statements to avoid unexpected charges if you continue to use a feature that transitions from free preview to a paid add-on.

- **Underestimating compliance needs**: Teams in regulated industries should confirm that their plan supports all required policy controls and security integrations.

> For the most current details on GitHub Copilot features and plan differences, refer to the Copilot feature comparison table mentioned earlier.

After exploring the feature sets and limitations of each GitHub Copilot plan, it's just as important to understand how these options affect your budget and ongoing usage. Pricing isn't always straightforward, especially as new features such as premium requests and model tiers have been introduced, so in the next section, we'll take a practical look at how GitHub Copilot pricing and billing work for each plan.

Pricing structure and billing considerations

Selecting the right GitHub Copilot plan isn't just about features – it's also a financial decision. Understanding how each plan is priced, what's included, and how usage is billed can save you from unexpected charges and help you make the most of your investment. This section explains how pricing works as of October 2025, including key concepts such as premium requests and the factors that can influence your monthly bill.

How GitHub Copilot plans are priced

GitHub Copilot offers several pricing tiers to fit different needs and team sizes. Here's a quick overview of how each plan is structured and billed:

- **Free plan**: The Free tier is available at no cost to everyone.
- **Pro and Pro+ plans** (10 USD/month per user and 19 USD/month per user, respectively): Both are billed per user, per month. The Pro plan is priced to be affordable for individuals and freelancers, while Pro+ carries a premium for power users who want higher usage caps, advanced model access, and new features such as Agent Mode.
- **Business plan** (19 USD/month per user): Designed for teams and organizations, the Business plan is billed per seat, per month, or annually, with management features, security controls, and centralized billing. Seat management is handled through the organization's GitHub account, and admins can add or remove seats as needed.

- **Enterprise plan** (39 USD/month per user): The Enterprise tier provides the most advanced features and administrative controls, designed to meet complex organizational, security, and compliance requirements. Pricing for Enterprise is typically negotiated based on volume, support needs, and any additional requirements your organization may have.

> With Business and Enterprise plans, organizations can set monthly Copilot budgets to control usage and keep costs predictable. When usage gets close to the budgeted amount, admins receive alerts so they can review and adjust before going over.

> The prices referenced here are correct as of October 2025. Always refer to `https://github.com/features/copilot` for the most current pricing, eligibility, and feature definitions, as these details can change frequently.

Premium requests: what they are and why they matter

As GitHub Copilot evolves, premium requests have become a central billing concept, especially for users who want access to the latest or most powerful models (future previews). Premium requests are a limited resource, counted separately from standard suggestions or chat messages. Each time you use features powered by advanced models or access certain preview capabilities, you consume premium requests.

These are often capped per month, depending on your plan.

A **premium request** is a higher-cost operation that typically involves using GitHub Copilot with an advanced model or accessing features that require more compute resources (Agent Mode). Every time you initiate a "chat turn" with a premium model or use certain advanced capabilities, one premium request is deducted from your monthly quota.

Premium requests are included (with higher quotas) in Pro+ and Enterprise plans. Free, Pro, and Business users either have a very limited quota or none at all for these requests. When you exceed your quota, GitHub Copilot will either revert to a standard model or restrict access to premium features until your quota resets.

If you regularly use advanced models or features, running out of premium requests can mean a sudden drop in performance or feature availability. It's important to monitor your usage via usage dashboards and plan accordingly. To help with this, see the later section, *Usage dashboards and monitoring*.

Billing models and considerations

When it comes to billing, there are a few important factors to keep in mind with GitHub Copilot plans. Here's what you should know:

- **Monthly billing**: GitHub Copilot plans are billed per user, per month, with charges calculated on a metered and prorated basis. This means you only pay for active seats during the billing period, and any changes in seat count are reflected in your monthly invoice.

- **Seat management**: Business and Enterprise customers must manage seats proactively. Removing inactive users promptly can prevent unnecessary charges. If you add or remove seats mid-billing cycle, charges are typically prorated.

- **Trial periods**: Some plans offer a 30-day trial, after which billing will begin automatically unless canceled.

- **Plan upgrades and downgrades**: Upgrades take effect immediately, granting instant access to new features. Downgrades or cancellations may result in immediate loss of premium features or quotas, so always plan changes with your workflow in mind.

Avoiding billing surprises

To avoid unexpected charges or disruptions, it's important to stay on top of your GitHub Copilot usage and billing details. Here are a few practical tips:

- **Monitor usage**: Make use of usage dashboards and billing pages to track both standard and premium request usage. This helps prevent unexpected rate limiting or overages.

- **Understand model changes**: GitHub occasionally updates which models are considered "standard" or "premium." When in doubt, consult the official documentation to see which features may result in additional usage or costs.

- **Billing support**: Business and Enterprise customers have access to priority billing support for resolving discrepancies or addressing questions about seat allocation, premium request usage, or invoice details.

By understanding how GitHub Copilot's plans and premium requests are billed, you can set expectations with your team, avoid unpleasant surprises, and ensure that your investment in this tool delivers maximum value.

Up until now, you've seen just how many variables go into picking the right GitHub Copilot plan – feature sets, usage limits, premium requests, and administrative controls, to name just a few. With so many factors to weigh, it's natural to wonder how to make the best choice for yourself, your team, or your organization. In the next section, we'll break down the decision process into clear, actionable steps.

Choosing the right plan

With several GitHub Copilot plans and a constantly evolving feature set, selecting the best option can feel overwhelming, especially when requirements span everything from solo coding projects to enterprise-scale adoption. To make this choice easier, this section provides a practical, scenario-driven approach for evaluating your needs and narrowing down your options.

Start with your primary goals

First, clarify what you want to achieve with GitHub Copilot:

- Are you learning, exploring, or contributing to open source?
- Do you need to support freelance or side projects?
- Are you managing a team or responsible for organizational security and compliance?
- Is access to the latest models or advanced features (such as Agent Mode) essential for your work?

Being honest about your goals will help you quickly zero in on the plans most likely to deliver value.

Decision flowchart: which plan fits your needs?

To help visualize your decision, see the following flowchart, which guides you through questions about usage, environment, and feature needs:

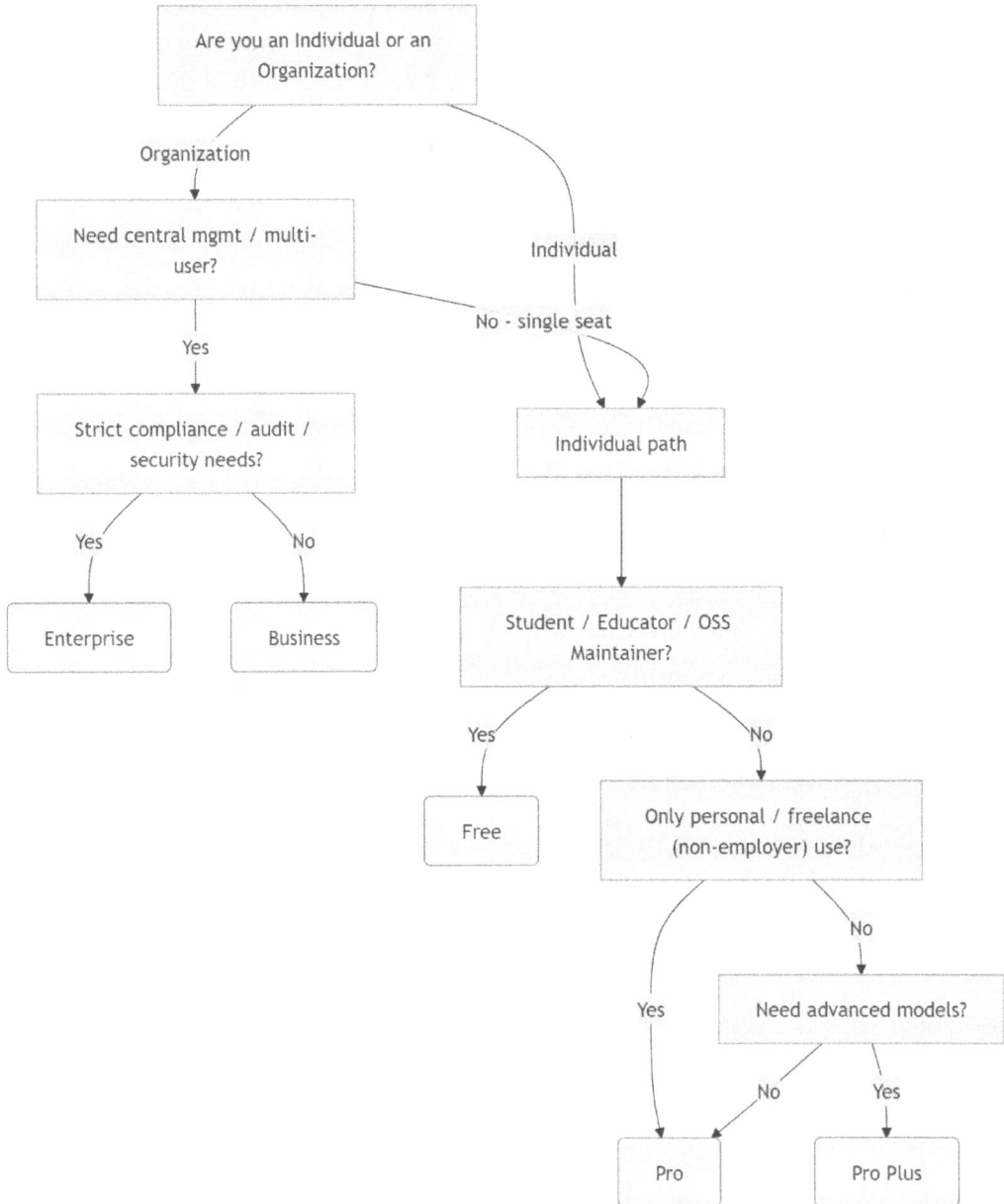

Figure 3.5: Plan decision flowchart

For a quick reference, see the following table:

Scenario/requirement	Recommended plan
Learning, teaching, or open source work	Free
Individual developer, personal/freelance use	Pro
Need premium models or Agent Mode	Pro+
Team management and policy controls	Business
Org-wide automation, compliance, and audit	Enterprise

Figure 3.6: Table mapping scenarios to plans.

Best practices for choosing

Selecting the right GitHub Copilot plan is easier when you take a thoughtful, flexible approach. Consider these best practices:

- **Review needs annually**: As GitHub Copilot evolves, your requirements may change. Revisit your plan choice to ensure ongoing value.

- **Test with a pilot group**: Organizations may start with a handful of users to validate fit before scaling up.

- **Stay up to date**: Feature sets and plan boundaries shift over time. Regularly consult GitHub's Copilot documentation (https://github.com/features/copilot) before renewing or expanding licenses.

- **Factor in future growth**: If you anticipate growth, select a plan that allows easy upgrades without workflow disruptions. For example, a small start-up might begin with a Business plan for 10 developers, but as the team expands, choosing a plan that supports seamless seat additions and quick upgrades ensures that everyone can access Copilot without delays or administrative headaches.

By starting with your goals and working through these scenarios, you can confidently select the plan that fits your needs, and be ready to adjust as your usage or organization evolves. But selecting a GitHub Copilot plan is just the first step – your needs and priorities may evolve as your team grows, your projects expand, or your organization's security requirements change. Switching plans or adjusting seat counts doesn't have to be disruptive, but it does require a thoughtful approach to ensure everyone retains access to the right features and you avoid unnecessary costs.

Next, we will show simple ways to handle upgrades, downgrades, and plan migrations, so access stays steady and costs stay in check.

Staying up to date with recent and upcoming changes

GitHub Copilot is a rapidly evolving product. As new AI models, features, and security requirements emerge, plans and capabilities are updated frequently. What's available today may expand or change tomorrow. To get the most out of your subscription and avoid unexpected limitations or billing changes, it's important to stay informed about recent updates and what's on the horizon. We'll discuss how to stay connected to the GitHub Copilot community and keep up with new developments in a later chapter.

Where to find the latest information

Because GitHub Copilot's capabilities and licensing details can shift rapidly, the best way to stay current is to check official sources regularly:

- **GitHub Copilot feature comparison table** (`https://github.com/features/copilot`): This page is updated with each major feature or plan change, providing the most reliable overview of what's included in each plan.

- **Release notes and GitHub Changelog** (`https://github.blog/changelog/`): The GitHub Changelog includes updates on new features, model changes, and preview program announcements.

- **GitHub Copilot updates site by Xebia** (`https://github-copilot.xebia.ms/`): This resource offers curated updates, tips, and guides tailored for real-world teams.

- **In-product notifications** (`https://github.com/features/copilot`): Watch for notifications in GitHub.com, the GitHub Copilot sidebar, or your IDE, as GitHub often announces new features or changes directly in the tools.

- **GitHub Next** (`https://githubnext.com/`): GitHub Next is an innovation lab within GitHub that explores and prototypes new ideas for the future of software development. This initiative brings together engineers, researchers, and designers to experiment with emerging technologies, develop cutting-edge tools, and share concepts that could shape the next generation of developer workflows.

Staying prepared for upcoming features

As GitHub Copilot grows, you can expect a steady flow of new capabilities, often accompanied by changes to plan requirements, usage limits, or billing. The following will help you stay prepared:

- **Opt into previews**: If your work would benefit from early access, join GitHub preview or beta programs, or ensure that your plan (Pro+ or Enterprise) is eligible

- **Engage with admin dashboards**: For organizations, monitoring usage dashboards can reveal when new features roll out and help spot potential adoption blockers

- **Communicate changes**: Assign a point of contact (or "GitHub Copilot champion") to monitor changes and communicate key updates to your team, so users aren't caught off guard

- **Review policies regularly**: Especially in enterprise and regulated environments, review GitHub Copilot and GitHub security/compliance policies each quarter to make sure your setup remains compliant as options change

Common pitfalls

It's easy to run into issues if you're not staying current with GitHub Copilot updates. Here are a few pitfalls to avoid:

- **Relying on outdated info**: Making decisions based on blog posts or documentation that's even a few months old can lead to missing out on important new features.

- **Assuming preview features are permanent**: Preview or early access features may change, move to higher tiers, or even be discontinued. Build workflows that are resilient to change.

- **Overlooking communication**: Not all changes are highlighted in newsletters or announcements. Actively monitoring official sources is the only way to be sure you're up to date.

> Bookmark the GitHub Copilot feature page (`https://github.com/features/copilot`) and check it before making any major purchasing, adoption, or workflow decisions.

Staying up to date ensures that you're making the most of this tool – maximizing value, minimizing risk, and taking advantage of the latest AI-driven development capabilities. Now, let's take a look at the considerations when upgrading or downgrading your plan.

Upgrading, downgrading, and change management

As your needs change, whether you're growing a team, seeking advanced features, or looking to control costs, you may need to adjust your GitHub Copilot plan. Licensing is flexible, but it's important to manage transitions thoughtfully to avoid interruptions, loss of access, or confusion among users. This section explains how upgrades and downgrades work, outlines best practices for managing change, and highlights common pitfalls to help you maintain a smooth experience.

Upgrading your GitHub plan

Upgrading typically unlocks new features, increases usage quotas, or extends access to premium models and automation tools. Here's how the upgrade process works and what you can expect when moving to a higher GitHub Copilot plan:

- **Instant access**: Most upgrades (e.g., moving from Pro to Pro+ or from Business to Enterprise) take effect immediately. As soon as the upgrade is processed, users gain access to new features such as higher premium request quotas and advanced models.

- **Billing adjustments**: Upgrading may trigger a prorated charge for the remainder of your billing cycle. If you upgrade mid-month, you'll only be billed for the time remaining.

- **Admin controls**: For organizations, admins can bulk upgrade seats through the GitHub organization settings. Always communicate with your team before rolling out new features to avoid confusion.

Downgrading or canceling your plan

Downgrading to a lower-tier plan or canceling entirely is possible at any time, but it's important to understand the immediate effects. Here's what happens when you downgrade or cancel your GitHub Copilot plan, so you know what to expect:

- **Feature loss**: Downgrading will result in the immediate loss of premium features not included in your new plan. For example, moving from Pro+ to Pro reduces premium request quotas and limits the availability of advanced models. These changes take effect right away, and users may notice the difference immediately.

- **Quota resets**: Any unused premium requests or admin dashboard features will no longer be available after the downgrade.

- **Billing**: Downgrades often take effect at the end of your current billing period, but some features are removed immediately. Always check your organization's billing portal for specifics.

As a best practice, notify users ahead of a planned downgrade, especially if workflows rely on advanced features. Provide clear communication and, if possible, a support channel for any transition issues.

Migrating between individual and organizational plans

Sometimes, users start with individual licenses and later migrate to an organizational (Business or Enterprise) plan, or vice versa. Here are some tips on migration:

- **License transfer**: When moving users from personal to organizational plans, ensure that seats are allocated correctly in the GitHub organization. Personal licenses should be canceled to avoid double-billing.

- **Data continuity**: While GitHub Copilot suggestions and settings are tied to your GitHub account, organizational policies and usage analytics are managed centrally. No user code is lost, but access to admin dashboards or compliance settings may change.

- **Seamless onboarding**: Use bulk invite and user provisioning tools to streamline large-scale migrations.

Change management best practices

Changing plans, especially at scale, can cause confusion if not managed carefully. Here are some best practices:

- **Plan ahead**: Schedule plan changes during periods of low activity or outside of critical project deadlines

- **Communicate clearly**: Inform all affected users of what's changing, when it will happen, and what features may be gained or lost

- **Offer training**: If new features are being introduced, provide training or resources to help users make the most of them

- **Monitor usage**: After any change, keep an eye on usage dashboards to spot issues early and gather feedback for further adjustments

Common pitfalls

Downgrading or changing plans can introduce a few common problems if you're not careful. Watch out for these pitfalls:

- **Sudden feature loss**: Downgrading without warning can interrupt ongoing work, especially if users depend on features such as more premium requests or advanced models

- **Double-billing**: Forgetting to cancel individual plans when moving to an organizational license can result in paying twice for the same users

- **Seat mismanagement**: Not reclaiming unused seats after organizational changes wastes budget

- **Inadequate communication**: Users caught off guard by feature or policy changes are more likely to experience frustration or productivity dips

> Document your licensing policies internally and make sure both admins and users know how to request changes or report issues. GitHub's official docs are always the best place to check for process updates and plan-specific details.

Handled well, plan changes and migrations are a routine part of scaling GitHub Copilot use. By taking a structured approach, you can ensure a smooth transition and continued productivity.

As you settle into your chosen GitHub Copilot plan, it is important to remember that both the product and its licensing options are always evolving. New features are introduced, model access and quotas may change, and pricing structures can be updated as GitHub responds to user needs and developments in AI technology. Keeping yourself informed is the best way to make sure your team continues to benefit from Copilot and avoids any surprises or disruptions.

In the next section, we will explore the practical dashboards and key metrics available for tracking usage.

Usage dashboards and monitoring

Once GitHub Copilot is deployed, visibility into how it's being used is essential. Monitoring usage helps you understand adoption, uncover opportunities for training or optimization, and ensure that you're not running into quota or billing surprises. In this section, we introduce several dashboards and monitoring tools, explain what insights they provide, and show how to leverage them for better outcomes.

All of the data shown in these dashboards comes from the **GitHub Copilot Metrics API**, which you can query directly to build your own custom views or integrate usage data into internal reporting systems.

Consumption Metrics dashboard

The Consumption Metrics dashboard is an example of Xebia-developed tooling that demonstrates how GitHub Copilot usage metrics can be displayed in a clear and actionable way. While this dashboard is especially valuable for organization administrators and team leads, it can also help individuals understand their own engagement with GitHub Copilot. Keep in mind that these metrics focus on how often and in what ways users interact with GitHub Copilot, not direct measures of productivity. The dashboard is best used to visualize adoption trends and patterns, offering insights into how GitHub Copilot fits into your team's overall workflow rather than attempting to quantify output or performance.

Here's what you can expect to find on the Consumption Metrics dashboard and how to interpret the key metrics:

- **Lines not accepted versus lines accepted**: A key metric for understanding impact is the comparison between lines suggested and accepted versus lines suggested but not accepted. This data reveals not just how often GitHub Copilot is helping, but also where its suggestions may be missing the mark.

- **Lines accepted**: Shows the number of GitHub Copilot-suggested lines that developers chose to keep in their code. High acceptance often means its output is aligned with coding standards and user intent. Keep in mind that this metric only shows complete acceptances of suggestions, so when there are 10 lines suggested by GitHub Copilot and the user accepts only 3, this metric will show 0.

- **Lines not accepted**: Reflects suggestions that were dismissed, skipped, or overwritten by the developer. High numbers here can highlight opportunities for prompt improvement, misalignment with project patterns, or areas where it's less effective.

Regularly reviewing both accepted and not accepted lines helps teams pinpoint where the tool excels and where there may be friction. If a particular file, project area, or language shows consistently low acceptance rates, it might be time to revisit prompt engineering strategies or provide targeted training.

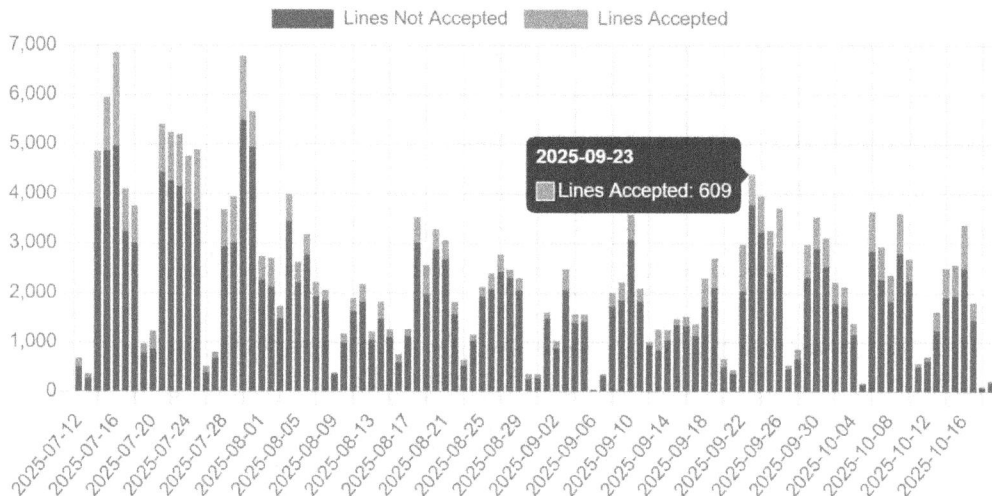

Figure 3.7: Lines not accepted versus lines accepted

To view this image in color

Use the free color PDF edition included with your purchase. Refer to the *Free Benefits with Your Book* section in the Preface for details.

- **Lines suggested per language**: Shows which programming languages are seeing the most GitHub Copilot-generated suggestions. This helps teams identify where it's making the biggest impact and which languages may benefit from further training.
- **Percentage lines accepted per language**: Measures how often users accept GitHub Copilot's suggestions, broken down by language. High acceptance rates may indicate that the tool is well-calibrated to your code base and practices, while lower rates might suggest a need for prompt refinement or additional training.

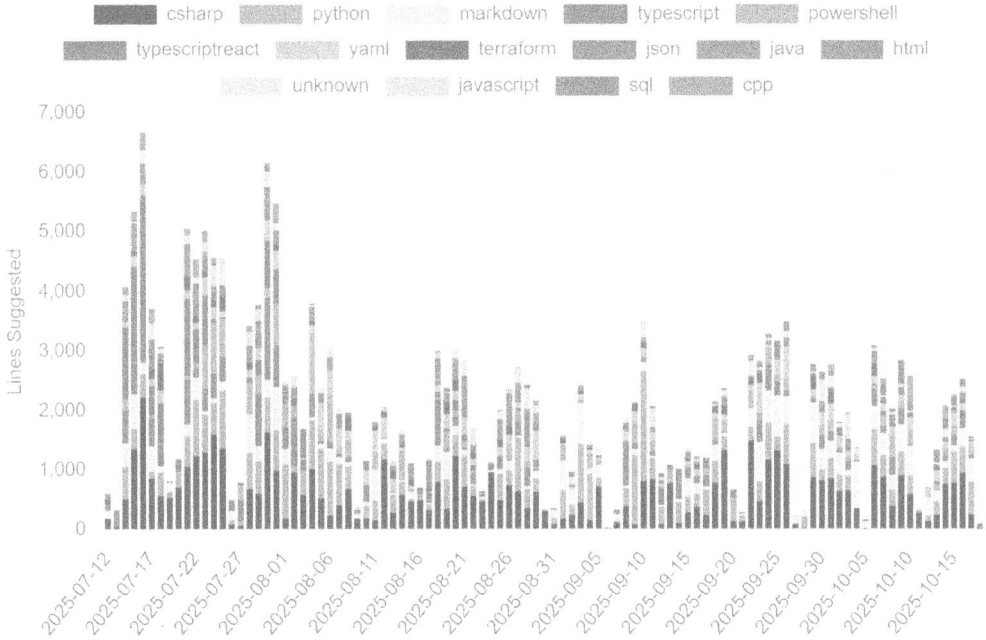

Figure 3.8: Lines accepted per language

- **IDEs used per day**: Tracks which **integrated development environments (IDEs)** are active each day. This data can highlight adoption trends, help troubleshoot onboarding issues, and reveal which environments are most popular among your users.

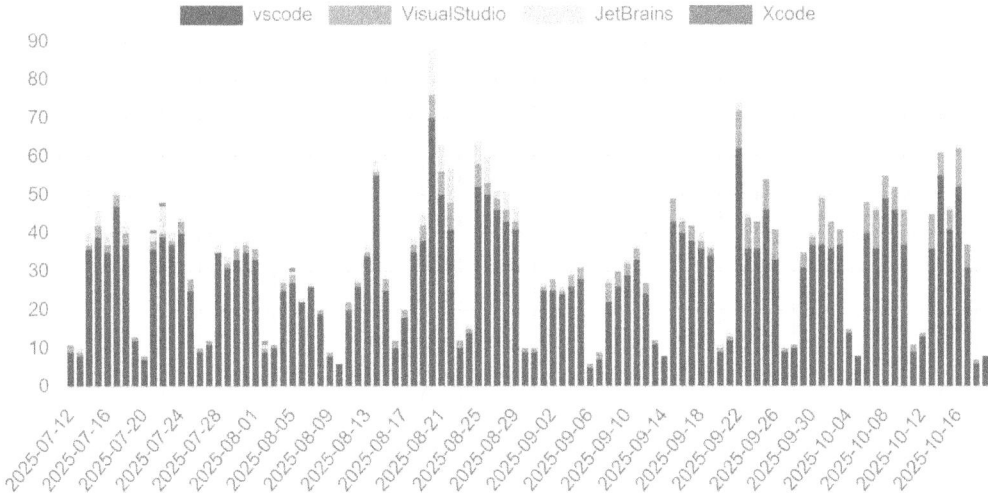

Figure 3.9: IDEs used per day

- **Total engaged users for IDE ask**: Shows how many users are actively engaging with GitHub Copilot's **ask** feature, providing insight into how conversational AI is being adopted as part of your development workflow.

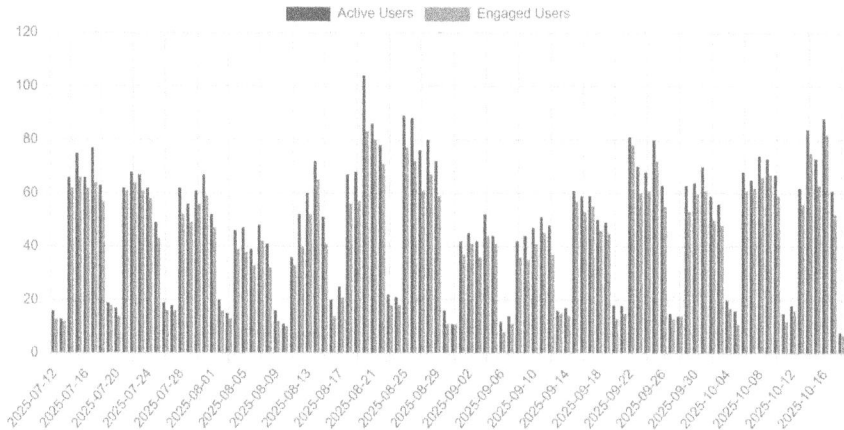

Figure 3.10: Total active versus engaged users per day

To view this image in color

Use the free color PDF edition included with your purchase. Refer to the *Free Benefits with Your Book* section in the *Preface* for details.

Regularly reviewing this dashboard can help you spot adoption gaps, optimize onboarding, and identify where GitHub Copilot is delivering the most value or where additional support or training may be needed.

It's tempting to treat dashboard stats, such as lines suggested or acceptance rates, as a direct measure of developer productivity, but it's rarely that simple. Writing more code does not always mean writing better code, and high Copilot usage does not guarantee faster or higher-quality results. These dashboards are best used to spot adoption trends, identify coaching opportunities, and make sure people are not running into limits or blockers. For meaningful productivity insights, look beyond the raw numbers and focus on the stories behind the data. Are developers shipping valuable features? Is Copilot making repetitive tasks easier? Are teams collaborating more effectively? For a broader framework on measuring and improving engineering outcomes, see the *GitHub Engineering System Success Playbook*: `https://resources.github.com/engineering-system-success-playbook`. Use the dashboards as a conversation starter rather than a final verdict on performance.

Premium Requests Usage Analyzer

As premium requests become central to GitHub Copilot's billing and advanced feature access, tracking their consumption is crucial for organizations and power users.

The **Premium Requests Usage Analyzer** is a dashboard developed by Xebia to give organizations and power users a transparent view of how premium requests are being consumed within GitHub Copilot. By surfacing usage data across users, teams, and entire organizations, this tool helps you keep track of advanced feature consumption, identify trends, and make informed decisions about licensing and workflow optimization. For more details or to try it yourself, visit the dashboard online at `https://xebia.github.io/github-copilot-premium-reqs-usage/`.

Here's what the Premium Requests Usage Analyzer tracks and how it can help you manage advanced Copilot features:

- **Premium requests usage by user, team, or org**: It provides detailed statistics on how many premium requests have been used, who's using them, and which features or models are driving that consumption.

- **Chat turn analytics**: Every interaction with a premium model (a "chat turn") deducts from your monthly premium request quota. The analyzer helps you understand usage patterns and forecast when quotas may be reached.

- **Trends and anomalies**: It spots spikes in usage that might indicate a shift in workflow or possible misuse, enabling proactive management of your investment.

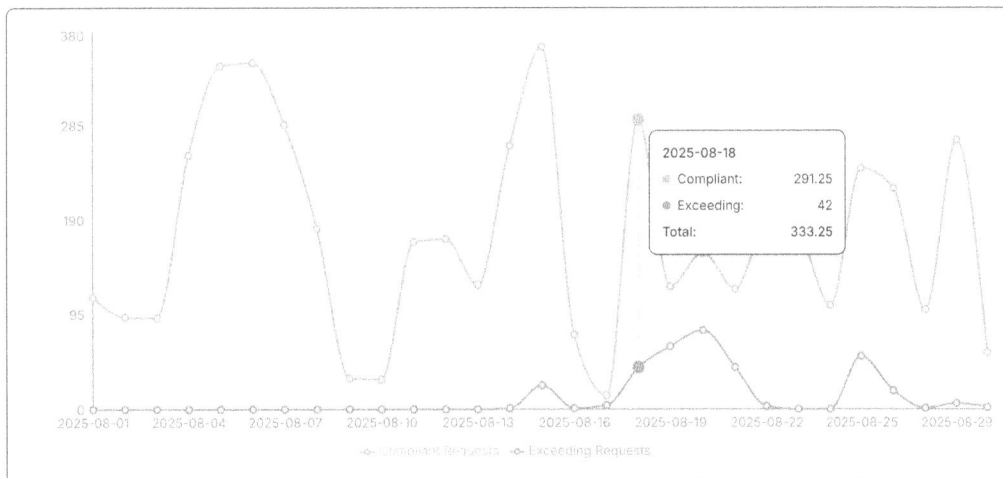

Figure 3.11: Premium Requests Usage Analyzer dashboard

Before you can use the GitHub Copilot Premium Requests Usage Analyzer dashboard, you must first export your organization's usage data to a CSV file. To do this, navigate to **Organization | Settings | Billing and Licensing | Usage | Get Usage Report**. From there, select **Copilot Premium Requests Usage Report** to download the required CSV. Once you have this file, upload it to the analyzer dashboard to visualize and track your premium request consumption. Keep in mind that this export only shows the current billing period, so you need to store it for longer-term trend analysis.

Regular monitoring helps you avoid running out of premium requests mid-cycle, and historical data supports better decisions around upgrading, downgrading, or reallocating seats.

Updates site by Xebia

For organizations or admins wanting a curated view of all the latest GitHub Copilot features, known issues, and real-world tips, the updates site by Xebia (`https://github-copilot.xebia.ms/`) offers a valuable supplement to GitHub's official dashboards.

This site tracks feature releases, previews, bug fixes, and practical usage guidance. It's an excellent resource for "GitHub Copilot champions" who manage rollouts or training and want to keep teams updated without having to sift through changelogs. You should

bookmark the link as a quick reference for feature rollouts, major migrations, or onboarding sessions.

Best practices for dashboard use

To get the most value from your usage dashboards, keep these best practices in mind:

- **Set up regular reviews**: For teams and organizations, review usage dashboards at least monthly to catch trends and address issues early
- **Share insights**: Use data from the dashboards to celebrate wins (e.g., high acceptance rates), identify GitHub Copilot champions, and target training where adoption lags
- **Integrate with onboarding**: Use IDE and *ask* activity data to help new users get started and spot those who may need extra help
- **Watch for bottlenecks**: Premium request dashboards can help avoid the surprise of running out of advanced model access during a critical sprint or demo

Common pitfalls

It's easy to overlook important signals when using dashboards. Watch out for these common pitfalls:

- **Not monitoring at all**: Without regular dashboard reviews, it's easy to miss low adoption, overuse of premium requests, or missed opportunities for workflow improvement
- **Focusing only on totals**: Dig into the details – per language, per team, and per feature – to identify where it's most and least effective
- **Ignoring trends**: Sudden drops in usage or acceptance may signal an onboarding issue, prompt changes, or technical blockers that need immediate attention

> Don't wait until users complain about quotas or missing features. Use dashboards proactively to spot and address issues before they disrupt development.

By leveraging these dashboards and monitoring tools, you can maximize the value of GitHub Copilot, provide targeted support to your teams, and ensure a smooth, cost-effective AI-powered development experience.

Summary

In this chapter, you learned how GitHub Copilot licensing works as of October 2025 across Free, Pro, Pro+, Business, and Enterprise. You saw what each plan includes, how premium requests and model access differ by tier, where limits and restrictions apply, how pricing and prorated billing work, and how to choose a plan using real scenarios and a practical decision guide. You also reviewed upgrade and downgrade paths and learned how to track adoption with usage dashboards.

By understanding the licensing landscape, you can select the right plan, maximize your return on investment, and keep your team or organization working efficiently. As GitHub Copilot continues to grow, return to this chapter and the resources linked here to ensure that you're always making informed, up-to-date decisions.

As you've seen, selecting the right plan is only the beginning. How you use the tool in your daily workflow is just as important. Now that you have a clear understanding of licensing, it's time to explore what GitHub Copilot can actually do inside your favorite development environments.

In the next chapter, we'll take a closer look at the essential features that make GitHub Copilot a powerful coding companion. From code completions and inline suggestions to natural language edits and Agent Mode, you'll learn how these tools work within popular IDEs and how to make the most of them in your everyday development.

Frequently asked questions

Q: Which plan is right for me or my team?

A: If you're a student, educator, or OSS maintainer, start with the Free plan. For individual professional use, Pro is usually sufficient. Upgrade to Pro+ for premium models and a higher premium requests quota. For teams needing policy controls, dashboards, and centralized billing, Business is best. Enterprise is the clear choice for organizations requiring top-tier security, compliance, and automation.

Q: What are the main trade-offs between plans?

A: Higher-tier plans offer more generous premium request quotas, enhanced security controls, and usage monitoring tools, ideal for large teams or regulated environments. Lower-tier plans include core features such as Agent Mode but may have reduced request limits and delayed access to preview models or advanced capabilities.

Q: How do I avoid unexpected billing or quota issues?

A: Monitor usage regularly via the Metrics dashboard and Premium Requests Usage Analyzer. Understand how premium requests work for your plan and review billing settings after any upgrades or downgrades.

Q: What happens if I hit a usage or premium request cap?

A: If you exceed your monthly premium request quota, you may temporarily lose access to certain advanced features, such as Copilot Extensions, code review, or previews of newer models (e.g., Claude or GPT-4.5). However, you'll still have access to standard models such as GPT-4.1 and GPT-4o, and core features such as Copilot Chat, Agent Mode, and code completions will continue to work. Your quota resets monthly, and higher-tier plans offer more generous limits.

Q: Can I upgrade, downgrade, or migrate plans easily?

A: Yes. Upgrades typically take effect immediately and add features/prorated charges. Downgrades often apply at the end of the billing cycle and may remove features right away. Communicate changes to your team and plan transitions outside of critical project windows.

Q: Where do I find the latest information about GitHub Copilot features and plans?

A: Always check the GitHub Copilot feature comparison table at `https://github.com/features/copilot`, GitHub's official changelog at `https://github.blog/changelog/`, and trusted community resources. Preview features and plan details may change frequently.

Get This Book's PDF Version and Exclusive Extras

UNLOCK NOW

Scan the QR code (or go to `packtpub.com/unlock`). Search for this book by name, confirm the edition, and then follow the steps on the page.

Note: Keep your invoice handy. Purchases made directly from Packt don't require one.

Part 2

Getting Started with GitHub Copilot

The second part of the book will go into the main features in the different supported editors in depth: we start with suggestions while you type and take you to the chat interface with its different modes (Ask, Edit, and Agent Mode). You'll learn what the differences between these modes are, and when to use them for different types of tasks.

After getting to know the main features, we take things a step further by showing additional functionalities that extend the editor experience, especially during debugging. You'll see how GitHub Copilot integrates with the terminal to make fixing runtime errors and debugging issues even easier. We then close off by looking at advanced collaboration features in editors, such as the pull request extension in VS Code, where GitHub Copilot can assist with writing PR titles and descriptions and even help with the initial review, all directly within your editor environment.

This part of the book includes the following chapters:

- *Chapter 4, Mastering GitHub Copilot in Your IDE: Inline Suggestions, Chat, and Agent Mode*
- *Chapter 5, Going Beyond Code: Debugging, Terminal, and Collaboration with GitHub Copilot*

4

Mastering GitHub Copilot in Your IDE: Inline Suggestions, Chat, and Agent Mode

GitHub Copilot does more than provide access to different subscription plans. Once enabled in your IDE, Copilot becomes an active part of your daily workflow. It can suggest code in real time, respond to natural language comments, help explain complex sections of code, and even automate large-scale changes. Understanding how these features work inside your development environment is the key to using Copilot effectively and responsibly.

In this chapter, we will explore Copilot's IDE functionalities step by step. You will learn how completions speed up routine coding, how comments can be turned into real implementations, and how inline suggestions adapt to the context of your project. We will also cover Copilot Ask Mode for conversational help, Copilot Edit Mode for refactoring and improvements, and Copilot Agent Mode for automating multi-step tasks across your repository. Along the way, you will see practical examples ranging from JavaScript functions to infrastructure-as-code templates, and we will highlight common pitfalls so you can avoid mistakes as you bring Copilot into your workflow.

By the end of this chapter, you will have a clear, hands-on understanding of how Copilot integrates into the IDE to support your entire development process, from writing a single line of code to managing large-scale changes across multiple files. You will also have seen how to apply these features across application code, infrastructure templates, CI/CD workflows, and documentation.

In this chapter, we will cover the following topics:

- A copilot, not an autopilot
- Code completions: the core experience
- Comments to code: turning natural language into working code
- Inline suggestions and context awareness: real-time predictions as you type
- GitHub Copilot Ask Mode: conversational assistance in the IDE
- GitHub Copilot Edit Mode: instantly refactoring and improving code
- GitHub Copilot Agent Mode: automating multi-step tasks
- Combining features for real workflows
- GitHub Copilot in different IDEs: what's the same, what's unique

Technical requirements

As discussed in *Chapter 1*, GitHub Copilot integrates seamlessly with multiple editors, such as **Visual Studio Code (VS Code)**, **Visual Studio**, **JetBrains** IDEs (such as **PyCharm** and **IntelliJ IDEA**), **Neovim**, **Eclipse**, and **Xcode**. While some features will arrive in VS Code first, core functionalities, including code completions, inline suggestions, and Copilot Ask, are available across all of these environments. This ensures you can work with GitHub Copilot in the editor that best matches your workflow and programming language preferences.

A copilot, not an autopilot

Before going any further, it's worth reinforcing the core philosophy: you are always the pilot. GitHub Copilot is there to assist, accelerate, and inspire, but you decide what code to write, accept, or modify. Think of GitHub Copilot as a helpful teammate who can suggest the next step, explain a complex snippet, or generate a test, but the final decision always belongs to you.

After installing and activating GitHub Copilot in your IDE, you'll notice it starts suggesting code almost immediately as you type. Whether you're working in C#, Python, JavaScript, or dozens of other languages, GitHub Copilot can do the following:

- Predict and complete lines or blocks of code
- Turn natural language comments into real code
- Offer documentation or explanations for tricky sections
- Refactor or improve existing functions on request

- Answer "how do I..." questions right in the editor
- Automate multi-step changes with Agent Mode

You'll see GitHub Copilot's "ghost text" suggestions appear in real time, and you can interact with the GitHub Copilot sidebar or Chat panel for deeper assistance. As an example, suppose you're starting a new Python function for data processing. As soon as you write a descriptive comment, GitHub Copilot proposes a relevant code block. If you get stuck, you can open the Chat window in the sidebar and ask for an explanation, a test case, or a quick refactor, without breaking your flow.

However, while using Copilot, try to avoid these common pitfalls:

- **Treating Copilot as a black box**: Accepting suggestions blindly can lead to subtle bugs or code that doesn't fit your style.
- **Forgetting feature availability may differ by IDE**: Not every editor supports every GitHub Copilot feature on day one. Double-check the documentation if you're missing a feature.
- **Assuming GitHub Copilot will always "just work"**: GitHub Copilot relies on the context it sees. If your code is incomplete or ambiguous, suggestions may be less accurate. Providing clear comments and writing code in small increments improves results.

As discussed earlier, Copilot works across popular IDEs. In the next section, we move from a general overview to a closer look at how its features work inside the editor. You will see how Copilot integrates with your coding environment by providing completions, turning comments into code, assisting with inline suggestions, and supporting Agent Mode.

Code completions: the core experience

GitHub Copilot's most foundational feature is code completion. As you type, it analyzes the surrounding context, such as variable names, function signatures, comments, and nearby code, to predict what you will likely need next. These predictions appear as faint, gray "ghost text" directly in your editor, offering the next word or line, or even an entire block of code. This seamless integration allows you to move more quickly through everyday development tasks while keeping your focus in the editor.

For example, if you are writing in C# and you want to loop through numbers and display them, you might start with a simple for loop like this:

```
for (int i = 0; i < 100; i++)
```

Based on the loop structure you began, Copilot predicts that you may want to output each value of i and suggests the `Console.WriteLine(i);` statement. This not only saves time but also reduces the chance of small mistakes, such as off-by-one errors or missed property references.

You can see the result in *Figure 4.1*.

```
for (int i = 0; i< 100; i++)
{
    Console.WriteLine(i);
}
```

Figure 4.1: Ghost text suggestion in action; code completion suggestion in C# for a for-loop

These completions help you maintain flow, especially for repetitive structures, standard library calls, or code patterns you use frequently.

Accepting, cycling, and rejecting suggestions

Copilot provides several ways to interact with code suggestions:

- **Accept**: Press *Tab* (or the equivalent in your editor) to accept a suggestion and insert it into your code
- **Cycle**: Use keyboard shortcuts such as *Alt + [* or *Alt +]* (VS Code default) to scroll through multiple suggestions when available
- **Reject**: Press *Esc* to dismiss the current suggestion if it doesn't fit your needs, or just keep on typing

These options allow you to quickly test alternatives, find the most suitable code, or return to writing your own implementation if none are quite right.

Taking an example, type the `squareAll(nums)` stub with the three `Option` comments, then pause. Copilot proposes `return nums.map(n => n * n);` as the first completion, and when you press *Alt +]* to cycle, a second style appears as a ghost line, `return nums.reduce((acc, n) => { … })`, as shown in *Figure 4.2*. Press *Tab* to accept the version you want, press *Alt + [* to go back, or press *Esc* and keep writing if neither fits.

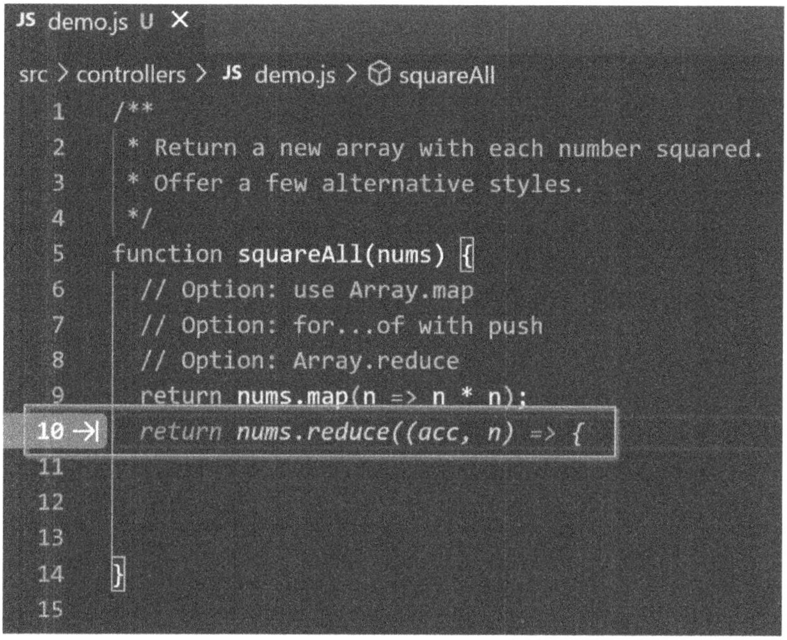

Figure 4.2: Cycling to a reduce alternative in VS Code

Best practices for completions

To get the most value from Copilot's code completions, keep the following practices in mind:

- **Review every suggestion**: GitHub Copilot's predictions are fast but not always perfect. Always double-check suggested code for correctness, security, and suitability.

- **Use for routine patterns**: Code completions shine for repetitive or boilerplate code such as logging, data parsing, or test scaffolds.

- **Context matters**: The more relevant your surrounding code and comments, the more accurate Copilot's suggestions.

Common pitfalls to avoid

While Copilot completions can accelerate your workflow, there are a few common pitfalls to watch out for:

- **Accepting unverified suggestions**: Trusting a completion without reviewing it can introduce logic bugs, security vulnerabilities, or code that doesn't match your team's standards

- **Missing better alternatives**: Accepting the first suggestion without cycling through options may cause you to overlook a better or more idiomatic implementation

- **Overusing completions in unfamiliar code**: Relying on GitHub Copilot to generate code in a language or code base you don't understand can lead to confusion or mismatched patterns

> GitHub Copilot's code completions are a productivity booster, not a replacement for your own judgment. Use them to keep momentum, but always take a moment to check the details.

By practicing how to cycle through, accept, and reject suggestions, you build confidence in shaping Copilot's output to match your project's needs. With these mechanics in place, we can now move beyond simple completions and see how Copilot can generate code directly from natural language comments.

Comments to code: turning natural language into working code

One of GitHub Copilot's standout features is its ability to turn natural language comments directly into draft implementations. By describing what you want in a comment, just as you would explain an idea to a colleague, you can prompt GitHub Copilot to generate complete code snippets, functions, or even entire classes. You can see this feature in action in *Figure 4.3*.

```javascript
// Load plane data from a JSON file
// Filter out planes where "isActive" is false
// Sort the planes by "year" in descending order
// Print the top 5 planes with the highest "rangeInKm"
router.get('/top5', (req, res) => {
    const fs = require('fs');
    const planesData = JSON.parse(fs.readFileSync('planes.json', 'utf8'));
    const activePlanes = planesData.filter(p => p.isActive);
    const sortedPlanes = activePlanes.sort((a, b) => b.year - a.year);
    const top5Planes = sortedPlanes.slice(0, 5);

    res.status(200).json(top5Planes);
});
```

Figure 4.3: A comment-to-code transformation in JavaScript

This approach speeds up your workflow and makes it easier to implement ideas, even in areas where you might not recall the exact syntax or best practices.

Writing natural language prompts

To get the most out of comments to code, keep these guidelines in mind:

- **Be clear and direct**: Be specific. Write comments such as `// Convert Celsius to Fahrenheit`, not vague notes such as `// Convert the temperature`.

- **Mention edge cases or requirements**: If you want error handling or a specific library, mention it in the comment. See the following example:

```
// Parse a JSON string into an object
// If parsing fails, return an empty object instead of throwing an
error
```

Copilot will recognize the need for error handling and suggest a try-catch block in JavaScript.

- **Use context**: Surrounding variable names and function signatures help produce better results. See the following example:

```
def calculate_discount(price, discount_rate):
# Apply discount only if rate is between 0 and 1
```

Here, Copilot can see the function name and parameters and is more likely to generate correct logic, such as clamping invalid rates or applying the formula properly.

Let's look at two quick examples to make this concrete. For example, if you need a function that returns the maximum number in an array, add a clear comment above the function, like this:

```
// Find the maximum value in an array
function getMax(arr) {


}
```

GitHub Copilot uses this comment, along with surrounding code context, to suggest a relevant implementation:

```
// Copilot suggests:
return Math.max(...arr);
```

Here's another example for working with dates:

```
// Format a date as YYYY, MM, DD
function formatDate(date) {
    // Copilot suggests:
    return date.toISOString().split('T')[0];
}
```

The clearer and more precise your comment, the more helpful the generated code will be.

Common pitfalls to avoid

When writing natural language comments for Copilot, keep in mind that some approaches reduce the quality of suggestions. Watch out for these common issues:

- **Vague comments**: Comments such as `// process data` result in generic or unrelated code
- **Omitting important details**: Not mentioning input types or expected results can lead to incomplete suggestions
- **Too many requirements in one comment**: Overloading a comment with multiple tasks can make Copilot's suggestions less accurate

> Always review and test GitHub Copilot's generated code. Treat each suggestion as a starting point, not a finished solution. We recommend adding integration or unit tests that validate the correct working of the code, and executing those tests locally before pushing your code upstream.

By following these guidelines, your comments give Copilot the clarity and context it needs to generate more accurate draft implementations.

Now that we've seen how natural language prompts shape Copilot's output, let's look at how inline suggestions work in real time as you type.

Inline suggestions and context awareness: real-time predictions as you type

GitHub Copilot doesn't just respond to comments; it also watches what you type and offers real-time suggestions based on the surrounding context. This **inline suggestion** feature is like having a knowledgeable co-worker quietly anticipating your next step, saving you keystrokes and surfacing solutions you might not have considered.

Inline suggestions appear as faint, gray "ghost text" directly in your editor. Copilot analyzes not only what you're typing but also nearby variables, function names, data structures, and even filenames, so its suggestions are tailored to your current task.

Context awareness is what makes Copilot's inline suggestions feel relevant instead of random. For example, if you are working in a Dockerfile, Copilot may propose valid FROM and RUN instructions, while in a SQL file, it might suggest a SELECT query template. By grounding suggestions in context, Copilot helps you move forward without breaking focus to look up syntax or boilerplate code.

What makes inline suggestions powerful is that they're not limited to completing a single line. GitHub Copilot can often generate multi-line code snippets or full blocks, such as function bodies, configuration sections, or even chained API calls. See the following examples:

- In JavaScript, if you start defining a loop, Copilot may propose the entire loop structure, including initialization, condition, and increment logic
- In Terraform, typing the beginning of a resource block can prompt Copilot to draft the whole section with providers, arguments, and variable references pre-filled
- In Python, beginning a function that processes a list could result in Copilot suggesting a complete function body with iterations, conditionals, and a return statement

These suggestions accelerate repetitive or boilerplate-heavy work while nudging you toward best practices in the process. By blending context awareness with multi-line completions, GitHub Copilot acts less like an autocomplete tool and more like a partner who sees where your code is going and helps you get there faster.

For example, in JavaScript, if you start typing a function, GitHub Copilot predicts the body based on the function name and parameter:

```
function calculateAverageRange(scores) {
    const sum =
}
```

Here, it inferred your intent from the function name (calculateAverageRange) and the parameter (planes), as we can see in *Figure 4.4*.

```
function calculateAverageRange(planes) {
    const sum = planes.reduce((acc, plane) => acc + plane.rangeInKm, 0);
    return planes.length ? sum / planes.length : 0;
}
```

Figure 4.4: Inline suggestion completing the body of a function

Alternatively, if you want to calculate the sum of an array, you could begin with a simple function outline like this:

```
// Calculate the sum of an array
function sum(arr) {
```

As you type, GitHub Copilot predicts the likely implementation and suggests the following code to complete it:

```
    return arr.reduce((a, b) => a + b, 0);
}
```

GitHub Copilot's context awareness also extends beyond immediate lines – if you've declared a variable or resource previously, GitHub Copilot may reference or use it in a subsequent suggestion.

How inline suggestions differ from comments to code

It's easy to confuse inline suggestions with comments to code, but they are different tools for different moments in your workflow:

- With comments to code, you explicitly describe your intent with natural language comments, and Copilot generates code based on your description. See the following example:

```
// Load data from a JSON file
// Filter out inactive users
// Return top 5 by last login
```

- With inline suggestions, Copilot predicts your next step while you are typing code using function names, parameters, nearby variables, and file context. For example, you might type the following:

```
for (const user of users)
```

Copilot might suggest the following:

```
console.log(user.name);
```

Think of comments to code as you telling Copilot what you want in plain language, while inline suggestions are Copilot predicting the natural next step as you write. Used together, they form a powerful pair: one is explicit guidance, the other is predictive assistance.

Best practices

To make the most of Copilot's inline suggestions, consider the following practices when writing code:

- **Leverage context**: Define variables and function signatures first. GitHub Copilot's suggestions become more relevant as it learns from your immediate context.
- **Small steps work best**: Write code incrementally. GitHub Copilot produces more precise suggestions when the structure and intent of the code are clearly expressed.
- **Use for patterns**: Inline suggestions are most effective when applied to repetitive structures such as loops, filters, resource blocks, and configuration sections that follow well-established patterns.

Common pitfalls to avoid

Even though Copilot's inline suggestions can be a big time-saver, there are a few limitations and risks you should watch out for:

- **Overlooking project standards**: GitHub Copilot might suggest code that doesn't fully align with your project's naming conventions or style guides, so always review before accepting.
- **Large or generic suggestions**: Multi-line suggestions are helpful, but may introduce extra code or assumptions that don't fit your needs.
- **Context confusion**: In highly complex or ambiguous files, GitHub Copilot's guesses may be off. Consider simplifying code or adding comments for clarity.

> Treat GitHub Copilot's inline suggestions as accelerators for your own ideas. Accept what fits, edit as needed, and discard what doesn't feel right for your context. Keep on testing the new code to make sure it works as intended. Adding automated tests (with GitHub Copilot) can help with this.

By understanding how Copilot offers inline suggestions and adapts to the context of your code, you can take advantage of its ability to anticipate your next steps and accelerate everyday tasks.

With this foundation in place, we can now look at how Copilot goes beyond silent predictions and provides conversational assistance through Ask Mode.

GitHub Copilot Ask Mode: conversational assistance in the IDE

Not every IDE implements GitHub Copilot Chat. Editors such as VS Code, JetBrains IDEs, and Visual Studio provide a dedicated panel for conversational interactions, while others, such as Neovim, do not, since they lack a user interface to display a chat window.

Where it is supported, **GitHub Copilot Ask Mode** allows you to use natural language questions to interact with your code base. You can request explanations of complex logic, generate tests, draft documentation, or even get guidance on configuration files, all without breaking your workflow. Copilot Ask Mode is particularly useful when you need context-aware help, want to understand unfamiliar code, or need to automate repetitive documentation and test-generation activities.

How Copilot gathers context

When you use GitHub Copilot Chat features, the IDE shares relevant parts of your workspace with the service to help generate meaningful responses. This may include the file you're working on, recent edits, or references to nearby code. Each IDE integration handles this slightly differently, but the goal is the same: provide enough context so Copilot can generate answers and suggestions that align with your project.

For instance, in VS Code or JetBrains IDEs, Copilot Chat can use the open file plus selected text as a grounding point. In editors without a chat panel, such as Neovim, this integration is not available since there's no interface for Copilot to surface conversational results.

Using GitHub Copilot Ask Mode

GitHub Copilot Ask Mode brings the capabilities of conversational AI into your coding workflow. You simply type a question or request into the Chat panel, and it responds with explanations, code samples, or actionable suggestions tailored to your code, as you can see in *Figure 4.5*.

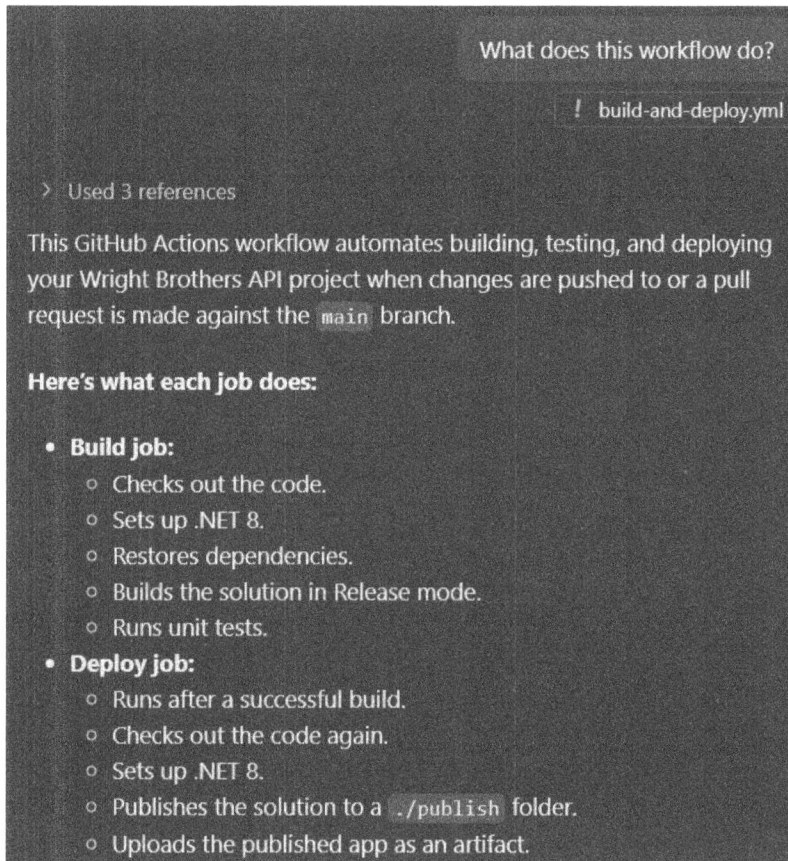

Figure 4.5: Copilot Chat answering "What does this workflow do?" in a GitHub Actions YML file

This works for code, scripts, configuration files, and even CI/CD YAML definitions, making it a flexible resource for developers, DevOps engineers, and cloud professionals. For example, suppose you encounter a tricky regular expression and aren't sure what it does. You can highlight the following code:

```
const pattern = /^(\d{3}), (\d{2}), (\d{4})$/;
```

You can then ask GitHub Copilot the following:

```
// What does this regex match?
```

Copilot would respond with the following:

```
This matches a string in the format of a US Social Security Number (e.g.,
123, 45, 6789).
```

Alternatively, maybe you're looking at the following workflow file and want to know what it accomplishes:

```
# .github/workflows/deploy.yml
name: Deploy Application
on:
  push:
    branches: [ main ]
jobs:
  deploy:
    runs, on: ubuntu, latest
    steps:
      , uses: actions/checkout@v3
      , name: Deploy to Azure
        uses: azure/webapps, deploy@v2
```

You could ask GitHub Copilot the following:

```
// Summarize what this workflow does and if there are any best practices
missing.
```

It might respond with the following:

```
This workflow deploys your application to Azure on every push to the
main branch. Consider adding steps for testing or environment, specific
deployments for more robust automation.
```

You can also request code snippets, explanations of configuration settings, or quick documentation in plain language. The response appears with controls such as **Apply in Editor**, **Copy**, and **Insert**, so you can use the suggestion immediately.

Corrected & Improved Example

Adjust build steps/tooling as needed (Node/.NET/etc.). Replace placeholders with real values and secrets.

```
name: Deploy Application

on:
  push:
    branches: [ main ]
    paths:
      - 'src/**'
      - 'package.json'
      - '.github/workflows/deploy.yml'
  workflow dispatch:
```

Apply in Editor

Figure 4.6: Copilot Chat summarizing a GitHub Actions workflow and highlighting missing best practices, with options to copy or insert the suggested text directly into the editor

Getting the most out of GitHub Copilot Ask Mode

To make your conversations with Copilot more productive, keep these approaches in mind:

- **Be specific and contextual**: The more context you give, the better the answers. Reference code snippets, filenames, or even specific lines.

- **Use follow-up questions**: Treat Copilot Ask Mode like a conversation. Clarify your goal, ask for alternatives, drill down on details, and remember it uses your recent chat and nearby code as context.

- **Request explanations, tests, or improvements**: Don't hesitate to ask for unit/integration tests, security reviews, or suggestions to optimize code or configs.

In practice, you might ask Copilot a focused question while giving it clear context, as suggested in the previous list. For instance, if you have a Node.js project, you might ask the following:

```
In .github/workflows/deploy.yml, add a step to run tests before the deploy
job runs, use npm test.
```

GitHub Copilot will propose inserting a job step that runs the project's test command before the deployment step, such as the following:

```
- name: Run tests
  run: npm test
```

Then, as a follow-up question, ask Copilot, "What important checks are we still missing in this workflow, for example, caching dependencies, uploading coverage, or adding an audit step?"

Using slash commands and @participants

GitHub Copilot Chat supports more than plain natural language questions. To make requests more precise, you can use slash commands and @participants. These features act as shortcuts, steering Copilot toward a specific type of response or narrowing its focus to a particular context in your workspace.

Slash commands are keywords you type at the beginning of a message to instruct GitHub Copilot on how to handle your request. The following are some examples:

- `/explain`: Breaks down what a piece of code does
- `/fix`: Suggests a correction for an error or bug in your code
- `/tests`: Generates unit tests for the file or function you are viewing
- `/doc`: Creates documentation comments for your code

These commands save time by eliminating the need to phrase requests in full sentences. Instead of typing "Can you explain this function?" you can simply type `/explain` while the function is open.

Meanwhile, **@participants** keywords let you direct GitHub Copilot to draw information from a specific context. Examples include the following:

- `@workspace`: Gives Copilot access to the entire project, so it can consider multiple files when answering
- `@file`: Restricts Copilot's attention to the current file only
- `@terminal`: Allows Copilot to generate commands suited for a terminal session

By combining slash commands and @participants, you can craft highly targeted prompts. See the following example:

```
@workspace /tests
Generate integration tests that cover login and logout flows.
```

Here, Copilot will both recognize that tests are requested and know to scan across the full workspace for relevant code paths.

However, when using both features, keep these points in mind:

- If you leave out an @participant keyword, GitHub Copilot may only consider the current file, leading to incomplete answers.
- Slash commands are shortcuts, not replacements for natural language, so try not to rely on them. If GitHub Copilot misunderstands, try rephrasing instead of repeating the command.

- Not all IDEs expose the chat interface where these commands are available. For example, Neovim has no built-in UI panel for GitHub Copilot Chat, so slash commands and @ participants cannot be used there.

Adding context with #keywords

In addition to slash commands and @participants, GitHub Copilot Chat also recognizes inline context handles that provide a sharper focus for your request. These begin with the # symbol and tell Copilot what part of your environment to consider, such as the following:

- `#file`: Refers to the entire contents of the current file
- `#symbol`: Focuses on the function, class, or symbol currently under your cursor
- `#terminalLastCommand`: Passes along the most recent command run in your integrated terminal

As an example, you can use `/explain #symbol` to ask for an explanation of only the function or symbol under your cursor, not the entire file. This is handy when you want a quick read before editing.

Alternatively, you can use `/explain #terminalLastCommand` to ask for a plain-English explanation of the last command you ran in the terminal. This helps when a script fails or a build step is unclear.

These context handles are especially powerful when combined with slash commands and @ participants, giving you layered control over how GitHub Copilot interprets your request.

> Use GitHub Copilot Ask Mode to turn confusion into momentum. If you're ever stuck, ask for a summary, a test, or a best practices review. Treat GitHub Copilot as a knowledgeable, always available teammate.

Common pitfalls to avoid

Even though Copilot Ask Mode can provide quick explanations and useful suggestions, there are a few common mistakes that can limit its effectiveness:

- **Being too vague**: Asking "Is this good?" without context will lead to generic responses. Always specify what you want to know or improve.
- **Not reviewing suggestions**: GitHub Copilot's explanations are often helpful, but always verify accuracy, especially for config files or scripts that impact deployment.
- **Assuming GitHub Copilot knows all context**: GitHub Copilot only sees what's in your editor. For questions about related files, open them or paste relevant sections into the chat.

By using Ask Mode effectively, you can get targeted explanations, generate supporting tests, and improve your understanding of complex code without leaving the editor.

With this conversational support in place, the next step is to see how Copilot can go beyond advice and directly transform your code through Edit Mode.

GitHub Copilot Edit Mode: instantly refactoring and improving code

GitHub Copilot Edit Mode takes the concept of AI-powered coding a step further, allowing you to instruct GitHub Copilot to modify, refactor, or improve your existing code and configuration files using natural language prompts. Instead of manually rewriting a function, reformatting SQL, or updating infrastructure code, you simply tell GitHub Copilot what you want changed.

The result? Faster improvements and more time focused on logic rather than rote edits.

Edit Mode is geared toward immediately implementing the changes you are asking for, in the files that are relevant to the question at hand. This makes it a lot easier to apply these changes compared to when in Ask Mode, where you have to copy and paste the changes yourself.

Scenarios for edits

Edits can be applied across programming languages, scripts, SQL, and infrastructure-as-code files, making this feature useful no matter what type of project you are working on. Here are some example scenarios:

- **Refactoring functions**: Make code more modular, readable, or idiomatic. See the following example: `"Convert this function to async/await syntax."`

- **Improving queries**: Clean up SQL or NoSQL statements. See the following example: `"Simplify this SQL query and ensure it uses proper JOIN syntax."`

- **Optimizing infrastructure code**: Parameterize, add tags, or apply best practices in Bicep or Terraform. See the following example: `"Update this Bicep template to add required tags and use parameters for region and SKU."`

- **Documentation updates**: Update or generate README sections or inline comments. See the following example: `"Update this markdown section to use a numbered list instead of bullets."`

- **Scripting adjustments**: Add error handling or improve automation scripts. See the following example: `"Add error handling to this PowerShell script so it retries on network failure."`

Using GitHub Copilot Edit Mode

GitHub Copilot Edit Mode is typically activated by selecting a block of code and issuing a command or prompt, either through a dedicated panel (such as "GitHub Copilot: Edit with prompt..." in VS Code) or by right-clicking and choosing GitHub Copilot options. You describe what you want changed, and the tool generates the refactored or transformed version, as you can see in *Figure 4.7*.

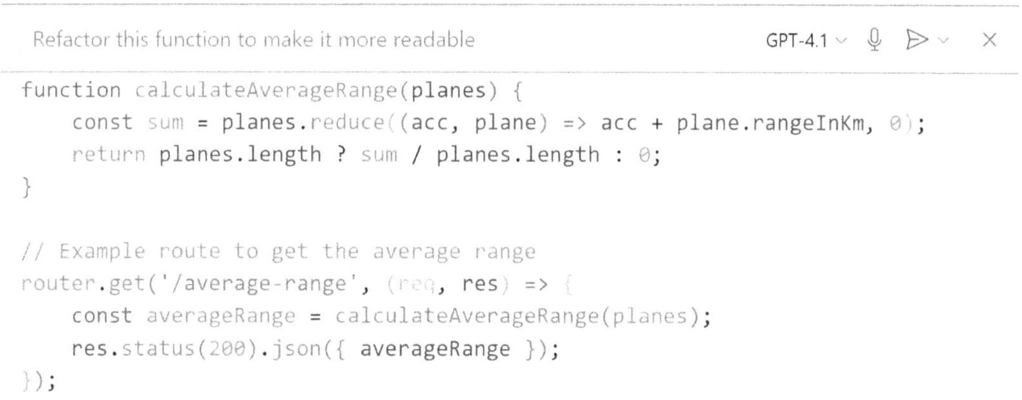

```
Refactor this function to make it more readable                    GPT-4.1 ⌄  🎤  ▷⌄   ✕

function calculateAverageRange(planes) {
    const sum = planes.reduce((acc, plane) => acc + plane.rangeInKm, 0);
    return planes.length ? sum / planes.length : 0;
}

// Example route to get the average range
router.get('/average-range', (req, res) => {
    const averageRange = calculateAverageRange(planes);
    res.status(200).json({ averageRange });
});
```

Figure 4.7: Copilot Edit Mode refactoring a function for readability

Let's look at a couple of examples. Suppose you have a complex SQL query that's hard to read:

```
SELECT id, name, salary, department FROM employees WHERE salary > 70000
AND (department = 'IT' OR department = 'Engineering') ORDER BY salary
DESC;
```

You could prompt GitHub Copilot with the following:

```
 Reformat for readability and add aliases for columns.
```

It could suggest the following:

```
SELECT
    id AS employee_id,
    name AS employee_name,
    salary,
    department
FROM
    employees
WHERE
    salary > 70000
```

```
    AND (department = 'IT' OR department = 'Engineering')
ORDER BY
    salary DESC;
```

Alternatively, let's say you want to add tags and parameterize a resource in a Bicep template:

```
resource storageAccount 'Microsoft.Storage/storageAccounts@2022, 09, 01' =
{
  name: 'myuniquestorage'
  location: 'eastus'
  sku: {
    name: 'Standard_LRS'
  }
  kind: 'StorageV2'
}
```

You could prompt GitHub Copilot with the following:

```
Parameterize the name and location, and add a 'Project' tag.
```

It might generate something like this:

```
param storageAccountName string
param location string = 'eastus'

resource storageAccount 'Microsoft.Storage/storageAccounts@2022, 09, 01' =
{
  name: storageAccountName
  location: location
  sku: {
    name: 'Standard_LRS'
  }
  kind: 'StorageV2'
  tags: {
    Project: 'MyProject'
  }
}
```

You can use similar edit prompts for updating documentation, improving variable names, or optimizing Bash scripts and configuration files.

Best practices

To use Copilot Edit Mode effectively and get results you can trust, keep the following practices in mind:

- **Review every change**: Treat GitHub Copilot's edits as suggestions – always review, test, and validate before committing.

- **Use specific, actionable prompts**: The clearer your request (e.g., "extract this logic to a new function named `getSalary`"), the better the results.

- **Work iteratively with edits**: Break down large or complex changes into smaller steps instead of asking for one big transformation at once. For example, first request that Copilot extract a block of logic into its own function, then issue a second edit to rename variables or improve formatting. Chaining small edits in sequence gives you more control, reduces the risk of incomplete or incorrect refactors, and makes it easier to verify each step before moving on.

Common pitfalls to avoid

While Copilot Edit Mode can save significant time, there are a few risks and limitations to watch out for when applying changes:

- **Unintended changes**: GitHub Copilot may adjust more than you expect. Double-check for subtle logic shifts, especially in SQL or infrastructure files.

- **Incomplete refactors**: Large or complex prompts may result in partial edits. Break down requests for more reliable results.

- **Losing context**: If you edit code that relies on nearby definitions, make sure GitHub Copilot sees enough context to do the job correctly.

> Use Copilot Edit Mode as a "smart pair of hands" for routine improvements, saving you time on repetitive edits and letting you focus on what matters most.

By learning how to use Edit Mode, you can direct Copilot to make focused improvements and transformations right inside your editor. These edits help with everyday refactoring, query cleanups, infrastructure adjustments, and script improvements, keeping you productive without leaving your workflow.

With Edit Mode as the foundation, the next step is to explore Agent Mode, where Copilot can coordinate multi-step changes and apply updates across multiple files or even your entire project.

GitHub Copilot Agent Mode: automating multi-step tasks

As projects grow, so do the demands for automating repetitive or large-scale code changes across multiple files and technologies. **GitHub Copilot Agent Mode** takes AI-driven development to the next level, helping you orchestrate multi-step tasks that would otherwise require time-consuming, manual work.

What is Agent Mode?

Agent Mode enables GitHub Copilot to reason about multi-step tasks. Instead of working line by line, you define a goal or describe a project-wide change. GitHub Copilot analyzes your code base, determines the steps, and proposes changes in context. You review, approve, or modify each step, retaining full control.

Agent Mode can span code, documentation, and configuration updates in a single workflow, making it especially useful when a change needs to touch multiple parts of a project. For example, it can update code references, documentation links, and configuration files together, ensuring consistency across the repository.

With this capability, Copilot goes beyond generating snippets and can carry out end-to-end tasks. It checks the changes it makes either through AI reasoning or by executing local scripts and tests its findings in your project. This makes Agent Mode especially valuable in DevOps, CI/CD, and cloud engineering scenarios.

Common uses include updating API endpoints, renaming resources, modernizing scripts, and adjusting CI/CD workflows. Agent Mode is available in supported IDEs (with the richest experience often found in VS Code) and is best suited to complex refactoring, automation, and bulk updates.

When and how to use Agent Mode

Agent Mode is most effective when you are working on broad or repetitive changes that affect multiple parts of your project. Agent Mode shines in the following cases:

- You need to make consistent changes across multiple files or directories
- Refactoring impacts both application code and configuration
- Automating repetitive DevOps, CI/CD, or infrastructure updates is a priority

To get started with Agent Mode, do the following:

1. In your IDE, open the **Copilot Chat** panel. From the drop-down menu at the top of the panel, select **Agent**.

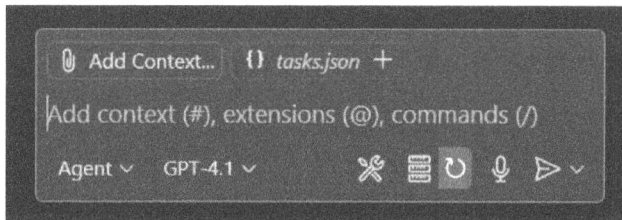

Figure 4.8: Agent Mode in VS Code IDE Chat panel

2. Next, describe your goal. For example, you could type "Update all deployment pipelines to use `ubuntu, latest` instead of `ubuntu, 20.04`," or "Replace `Invoke WebRequest` with `Invoke RestMethod` in PowerShell scripts."

3. GitHub Copilot will then scan your project, list proposed changes, and allow you to accept or adjust each one.

Reviewing and accepting changes in Agent Mode

When Agent Mode proposes edits, you stay in control by reviewing the diffs and deciding whether to accept, adjust, or reject each change. Let's walk through a concrete example.

Suppose your organization is standardizing on a new deployment environment across all CI/CD pipelines. In this example, here is the existing pipeline snippet that still targets the old Ubuntu 20.04 image:

```
pool:
  vmImage: 'ubuntu-20.04'
```

To apply the new image across your repositories with one request, ask GitHub Copilot Agent Mode per the following example:

```
Update all Azure Pipelines YAML files to use 'ubuntu-latest' as the
vmImage.
```

The Agent scans your repository, finds every YAML file with this pattern, and proposes an update:

```
pool:
  vmImage: 'ubuntu-latest'
```

The proposed changes appear in a diff view, where you can do the following:

- **Keep** the changes if they look correct
- **Adjust** your prompt (e.g., "only apply this to release pipelines") and rerun
- **Undo** the suggestion if it does not fit your needs

Nothing is committed until you approve it, and Copilot can optionally run local unit or integration tests to validate the results before you merge.

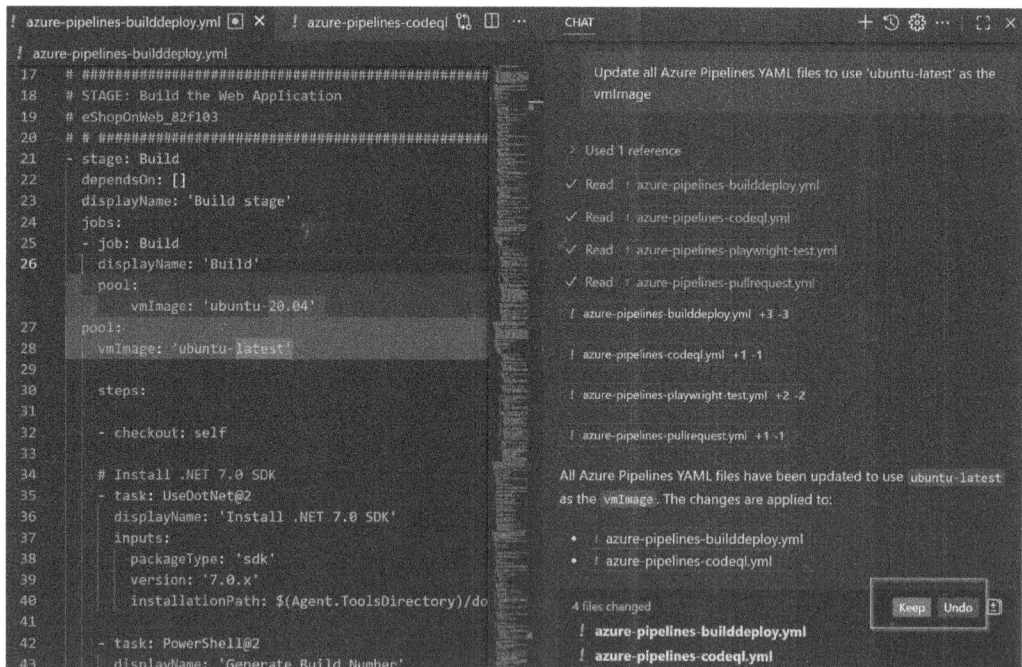

Figure 4.9: Reviewing proposed edits in Agent Mode using a CI/CD YAML update

Best practices

To get reliable results with Agent Mode and avoid unnecessary rework, keep these practices in mind:

- **Start with a clear goal**: Be specific in your prompt. For instance, "update all pipeline files to add a code scanning step" gives better results than "improve my CI/CD."
- **Review every change**: Don't blindly accept sweeping updates. Use the review/approve workflow to catch errors or unnecessary modifications.
- **Test after applying**: Run builds, deployments, or scripts after Agent Mode changes to confirm nothing is broken.

Common pitfalls to avoid

While Agent Mode can save significant time on large-scale updates, there are a few risks to watch out for when applying its suggestions:

- **Over-automation**: Large, automated changes can introduce subtle bugs or configuration drift. Review carefully, especially in production repos.
- **Unintended scope**: Vague prompts may lead GitHub Copilot Agent Mode to update files you didn't intend – always check the file list.
- **Missed edge cases**: Complex or custom code patterns may be missed. Combine Agent Mode with manual reviews for the best coverage.

> GitHub Copilot Agent Mode is your virtual assistant for repetitive or sweeping project changes, but you're always in charge. Take time to review and test before merging large-scale updates. Run the changed code locally if possible, and execute (unit) tests as well.

By learning how to use Agent Mode, you have a way to direct Copilot through larger, multi-step changes across your code base. This complements the earlier features, such as completions, comments to code, inline suggestions, Ask Mode, and Edit Mode, by giving you a tool for project-wide automation.

With these capabilities in place, the next section will show how you can combine all of these features into real workflows, chaining them together to handle practical development tasks from start to finish.

Combining features for real workflows

GitHub Copilot's greatest value emerges when you combine its features, code completions, comments to code, Ask Mode, Edit Mode, and Agent Mode into seamless workflows that mirror how real developers and engineers work. By chaining these tools, you can move from idea to implementation, review, and automation with greater speed and confidence, regardless of the code, script, or config file you're working in.

This section shows how GitHub Copilot's capabilities support you through a realistic task, from writing new code to improving it, automating bulk changes, and documenting, all in a single, productive flow.

Workflow example 1: from comment to complete solution (JavaScript)

This example shows Copilot's core features working in sequence, starting with a plain comment and finishing with tests, a small refactor, and a documentation update:

1. **Comment to code**: Start a new file named password.js. Add a short, specific comment and the empty function, then pause to let Copilot suggest the body:

   ```
   // Generate a random password of given length
   function generatePassword(length) {
     // Copilot completes with a full implementation
   }
   ```

   Accept the suggested implementation with *Tab*. You can use *Alt +]* or *Alt + [* to cycle alternatives, or press *Esc* to dismiss and keep typing.

2. **Inline completion**: As you type inside the function, Copilot proposes an inline completion that returns a random string. Review the suggestion, then accept it if it matches your intent:

   ```
   return Array.from({length}, () =>
     String.fromCharCode(Math.floor(Math.random() * 94) + 33)
   ).join('');
   ```

3. **Ask Mode**: Open GitHub Copilot Ask Mode in VS Code, then write the test in full sentences so the request is unambiguous:

   ```
   Write a simple Jest unit test for generatePassword that checks the
   returned length.
   ```

Here is the response:

```
test('generates password of correct length', () => {
  expect(generatePassword(10)).toHaveLength(10);
});
```

Then run the test to confirm the basic behavior.

4. **Edit Mode**: Select only the generatePassword function, then use GitHub Copilot Edit Mode to request a targeted change:

```
Refactor to exclude ambiguous characters like O and 0, and keep the
rest of the printable ASCII range.
```

GitHub Copilot updates the logic to filter out those characters.

5. **Agent Mode**: Use Copilot Agent Mode to make a small repository change that reinforces the new feature:

```
Update all README.md files in this repository to document the
generatePassword(length) function, add a short usage example, and
include a note about excluding O and 0.
```

Agent Mode proposes the edits and a summary of changes. Inspect the changes, then commit if they look correct.

That is the full loop, starting with a clear comment, accepting or adjusting inline code, asking for tests, refining with an edit, then applying a small repo-wide update with Agent Mode.

Workflow example 2: infrastructure and CI/CD (Terraform, YAML, PowerShell)

This example shows Copilot features working across an end-to-end scenario, from infrastructure code to a pipeline step, a deployment script, and finally a small bulk change across the repository:

1. **Comment to code**: Open a Terraform file, then write a short, specific comment and start the block. Pause to let Copilot complete the resource:

```
Create an S3 bucket with versioning enabled
resource "aws_s3_bucket" "logs" {
Copilot will fill in the bucket config with versioning
}
```

Accept the suggestion. You will usually see a full bucket resource with a `versioning {` `enabled = true }` block and a few useful tags.

2. **Inline completion**: Begin a pipeline step that will run your deployment script. Copilot proposes the missing fields and a sensible inline script:

```
- task: AzureCLI@2
  inputs:
    scriptType: bash
    scriptLocation: inlineScript
    inlineScript: |
        Initialize and apply Terraform
  ..terraform init -input=false
  terraform plan -out=tfplan
  terraform apply -input=false -auto-approve tfplan
```

Review the commands, then accept or edit to match your workflow.

3. **Ask Mode**: Open GitHub Copilot Ask Mode, then request a clear security improvement to the pipeline:

```
Add a security scan step before the Terraform apply, prefer
Microsoft Security DevOps or a simple Trivy file system scan.
```

Copilot proposes an additional task using a tool such as Trivy or Azure Security Center.

4. **Edit Mode**: Select your deployment script, then use GitHub Copilot Edit Mode to request better logging and error handling:

```
Add detailed logging and error handling.
```

GitHub Copilot edits the script, improving robustness and traceability. Review the diff, then keep or tweak the pattern to match your standards.

5. **Agent Mode**: Use GitHub Copilot Agent Mode to roll out a consistent update across the repository with the following prompt:

```
Update all Azure Pipelines YAML files to use ubuntu-latest for the
build agent. Show me a summary of files changed before creating a
pull request.
```

Agent Mode finds each pipeline, updates `vmImage`, and presents a summary so you can review before committing.

That is the full flow: generate a resource with a clear comment, add a pipeline step with inline completion, ask for a security check, tighten your script with an edit, and apply a safe bulk change with Agent Mode.

Best practices for combining Copilot features

When using Copilot features together in a single workflow, a few best practices will help you get the most reliable results and avoid unnecessary rework:

- **Move iteratively**: Start with completions and comments to generate initial code, then use Ask Mode to clarify or create tests, follow with Edit Mode for targeted refactoring, and finish with Agent Mode for repository-wide changes.

- **Mix code and config**: GitHub Copilot works across code, pipelines, infrastructure, and documentation, which means you can use the same workflow to update all of these together instead of treating them as separate tasks.

- **Review at each step**: Don't skip manual review between features. Each GitHub Copilot tool accelerates your work, but you're the final check.

Common pitfalls to avoid

While combining Copilot features can streamline development, there are a few pitfalls to watch out for to ensure accuracy and maintain control over your code base:

- **Skipping validation:** Chaining features can make it easy to move fast, but always test code, scripts, and configs after GitHub Copilot changes, especially after Agent Mode bulk edits.

- **Over-automation without review**: Combining Agent Mode and Edit Mode without reviewing intermediate steps can introduce issues across multiple files.

- **Losing track of changes**: Use version control tools to track GitHub Copilot's multi-step changes. Review diffs before merging to main branches.

> Think of GitHub Copilot's features as modular building blocks. Use them together for a streamlined, end-to-end workflow, but always steer the process and check the results.

By walking through these workflow examples, you have seen how Copilot's individual features can be chained together to handle practical development, infrastructure, and automation tasks from start to finish. These scenarios demonstrate the flexibility of Copilot within the IDE, but the experience can vary depending on which editor you are using.

In the next section, we will explore GitHub Copilot in different IDEs, highlighting what remains consistent across environments and what unique capabilities each editor provides.

GitHub Copilot in different IDEs: what's the same, what's unique

GitHub Copilot is available across the most popular development environments, including VS Code, Visual Studio, and JetBrains IDEs (such as IntelliJ IDEA, PyCharm, and WebStorm). While the core experience is consistent, each editor has its own set of capabilities and nuances. Knowing what's possible in your chosen environment helps you get the most from GitHub Copilot and avoids confusion when features differ between tools.

Differences and unique features

While the foundation is the same, each IDE offers slightly different GitHub Copilot experiences. Some advanced features may appear in one editor before others. You can see a breakdown of the main IDEs and their features in this table:

Feature	VS Code	Visual Studio	JetBrains IDEs
Inline Completions	✓	✓	✓
Comment to Code	✓	✓	✓
Copilot Ask/Chat	✓ Sidebar/Panel	✓ Panel	✓ Panel
Copilot Edit Mode	✓ (Full)	✓ (Full)	✓ (Full)
Agent Mode	✓ (Richest)	✓ (Full)	✓ (Full)
Multi-file/Project Refactoring	✓ (Agent Mode)	✓ (Agent Mode)	✓ (Agent Mode)

Feature	VS Code	Visual Studio	JetBrains IDEs
Markdown/Config File Support	✓	✓	✓
Frequent Feature Updates	✓ (First)	✓ (After VS Code	✓ (After VS)

Figure 4.10: Comparison table of Copilot features by IDE

GitHub Copilot is available across several major IDEs, and while the core experience remains similar, each editor offers a slightly different set of capabilities. Here is an overview of what you can expect in the most commonly used environments:

- **VS Code**: Often gets new GitHub Copilot features first, including Edit Mode and Agent Mode. The open ecosystem makes it a showcase for new AI-driven workflows and supports the widest range of file types. The Chat extension has been made open source so that other editors can replicate the same mechanisms in their environment.

- **Visual Studio**: Supports completions, comments to code, and GitHub Copilot Ask/Chat for .NET and other supported languages. Copilot Edit Mode is available but may have limitations compared to when used in VS Code, especially for bulk or multi-file changes.

- **JetBrains IDEs**: Provide solid inline suggestions, comment-to-code translations, and conversational chat within the editor. As of now, Copilot Edit Mode is available, enabling interactive code refactoring across multiple files. Agent Mode is also generally available, supporting automated multi-step updates using natural language tasks.

- **Neovim**: Offers inline code suggestions, enabling real time completions as you type.

- **Eclipse IDE**: Supports both inline suggestions and Copilot Chat (Ask Mode) directly within the editor.

- **Xcode**: Provides inline suggestions and includes Copilot Chat functionality, delivering conversational assistance within the IDE.

Best practices

To make the most of GitHub Copilot in your preferred IDE, keep the following practices in mind:

- **Check the GitHub Copilot extension page for your IDE**: Features change quickly. Review the docs or release notes to stay current. Here are direct links:

    - **VS** Code: `https://marketplace.visualstudio.com/items?itemName=GitHub.copilot`

    - **JetBrains**: `https://plugins.jetbrains.com/plugin/17718-github-copilot`

    - **Visual** Studio: `https://learn.microsoft.com/visualstudio/ide/visual-studio-github-copilot-install-and-states?view=vs-2022`

- **Leverage the right tool for the job**: If you need the newest features, such as Agent Mode, try VS Code for bulk refactoring or DevOps automation tasks.

- **Sync shortcuts**: Customize keyboard shortcuts so Copilot actions fit naturally into your workflow.

Common pitfalls to avoid

Working with GitHub Copilot across different IDEs is powerful, but there are a few challenges that can trip you up if you are not prepared:

- **Expecting feature parity**: Not all editors support every GitHub Copilot feature at the same time. Adjust your expectations if you don't see a feature available in your IDE.

- **Missing updates**: Failing to update the GitHub Copilot extension may leave you without the latest improvements.

- **Inconsistent UX**: Minor UI differences (such as the location of the chat panel or edit commands) can cause confusion. Explore your IDE to discover where GitHub Copilot features are accessed.

> If you're ever in doubt about what GitHub Copilot can do in your editor, check the docs or the extension marketplace. Updates are frequent, and features roll out regularly across the ecosystem. You can find the marketplace by visiting `https://github.com/marketplace`.

Summary

In this chapter, you learned how GitHub Copilot works inside the IDE across core features such as code completions, comments to code, inline suggestions, Ask, Edit, and Agent Mode, and how to combine them into practical workflows that cover application code, infrastructure definitions, CI/CD files, and documentation. You saw why this matters for day-to-day development, since these tools can reduce repetitive work, surface reasonable starting points, and speed up refactoring while still requiring you to review, test, and keep changes aligned with project standards. You also learned that the core experience is consistent across major editors, with some differences in advanced capabilities, so checking your IDE's Copilot extension for updates is worthwhile.

In the next chapter, we shift from feature mechanics to IDE integrations such as the terminal, command-line interface, and debugging support, so you can apply GitHub Copilot beyond the editor pane and streamline more of your workflow.

Get This Book's PDF Version and Exclusive Extras

UNLOCK NOW

Scan the QR code (or go to `packtpub.com/unlock`). Search for this book by name, confirm the edition, and then follow the steps on the page.

Note: Keep your invoice handy. Purchases made directly from Packt don't require one.

5

Going Beyond Code: Debugging, Terminal, and Collaboration with GitHub Copilot

GitHub Copilot has grown far beyond a simple code completion tool. Modern development workflows need more than snippets and suggestions; they need context-aware assistance built into every part of the IDE. Whether you are scripting infrastructure, reviewing code changes, or tracking down a bug, these integrations help you move from idea to implementation with less friction.

This chapter looks at the IDE features that make that possible. You will see how Copilot works in the terminal and Command Palette, extends its reach through the command line, and provides help during debugging. We will also explore how it can summarize local changes, draft manual pull request notes, and assist with other small but important tasks that keep projects moving.

If you have ever wanted to get help with a tricky shell command, receive suggestions while reviewing a diff, generate a summary of staged changes without leaving the IDE, or analyze and fix errors as you debug, then the sections ahead will be useful. The examples go beyond completions and show how Copilot integrates into the everyday flow of coding, scripting, and testing across different languages and stacks.

Finally, while this chapter focuses on IDE workflows, some features only exist on GitHub.com, such as automated pull request summaries and web-based review tools. You will see more about those in *Chapter 6*.

In this chapter, we will cover the following topics:

- Terminal and Command Palette integration
- GitHub Copilot CLI features
- Debugging support
- Other IDE-integrated tools
- Real-world workflow scenarios

Terminal and Command Palette integration

As modern development moves beyond just editing files, the terminal becomes a central part of the workflow. Whether you're running build scripts, launching tests, or managing cloud resources, the terminal is often where real work happens. GitHub Copilot brings AI-powered assistance into this space, making it available in both the terminal window and your IDE's Command Palette.

Using the terminal

In supported IDEs such as Visual Studio Code, GitHub Copilot offers direct integration within the built-in terminal. This means you can do the following:

- Ask for help crafting shell commands or PowerShell scripts
- Get explanations for cryptic commands or errors
- Generate one-off scripts to automate routine tasks
- Quickly fix typos or suggest alternatives on the fly

You don't have to leave your flow to look up flags, syntax, or best practices; just use GitHub Copilot to boost your productivity right in the terminal.

For example, suppose you need to find all .log files larger than 50 MB and archive them. You can open GitHub Copilot Chat (or use the Command Palette) and type the following:

```
Write a PowerShell command to find all .log files over 50MB in the current
directory and compress them as .tar.gz.
```

Copilot would then suggest something like the following:

```
Get-ChildItem -Path . -Filter *.log | Where-Object { $_.Length -gt 50MB }
| ForEach-Object {
    $tarName = "$($_.Name).tar.gz"
    tar -czf $tarName }
```

You can then copy, adjust, or run the command directly. The button shown in *Figure 5.1* lets you insert the generated command straight into your terminal with a single click:

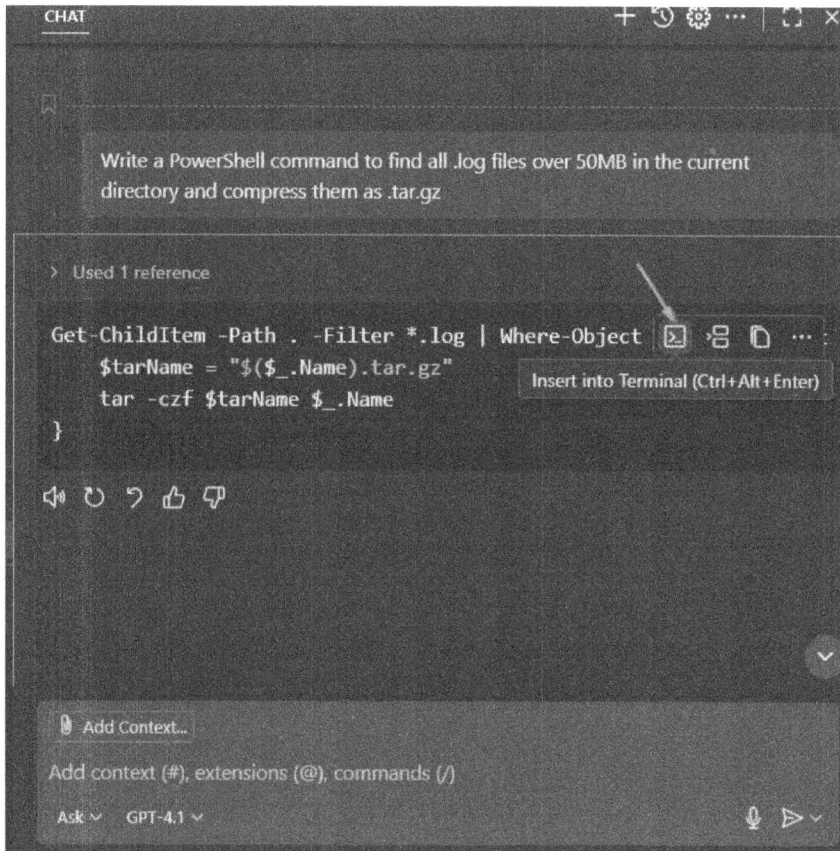

Figure 5.1: The VS Code terminal, showing a prompt and a generated command showing Insert into Terminal

Using the Command Palette

The Command Palette is another way GitHub Copilot surfaces its capabilities inside the IDE. This integration is specific to **Visual Studio Code (VS Code)**. Other IDEs, such as Visual Studio or JetBrains products, don't expose Copilot through a Command Palette in the same way.

Using the Command Palette, you can do the following:

- Trigger GitHub Copilot to generate, explain, or refactor commands and scripts
- Use keyboard shortcuts to launch Copilot Chat or code actions while in the terminal
- Search for Copilot-specific commands (such as **Copilot: Explain Last Terminal Command** or **Copilot: Generate Script**) directly from the palette

Using the Command Palette in this way is great for jumping between editing code and running commands, all without breaking your workflow.

Taking an example, imagine you've just run a complex PowerShell command in the terminal and aren't sure what it does. Instead of searching online, highlight the command, open the Command Palette, and select **GitHub Copilot: Explain Terminal Selection**. The explanation appears in plain language, describing what the command is doing—in this case, finding all .log files larger than 50 MB and compressing them into a .tar.gz archive.

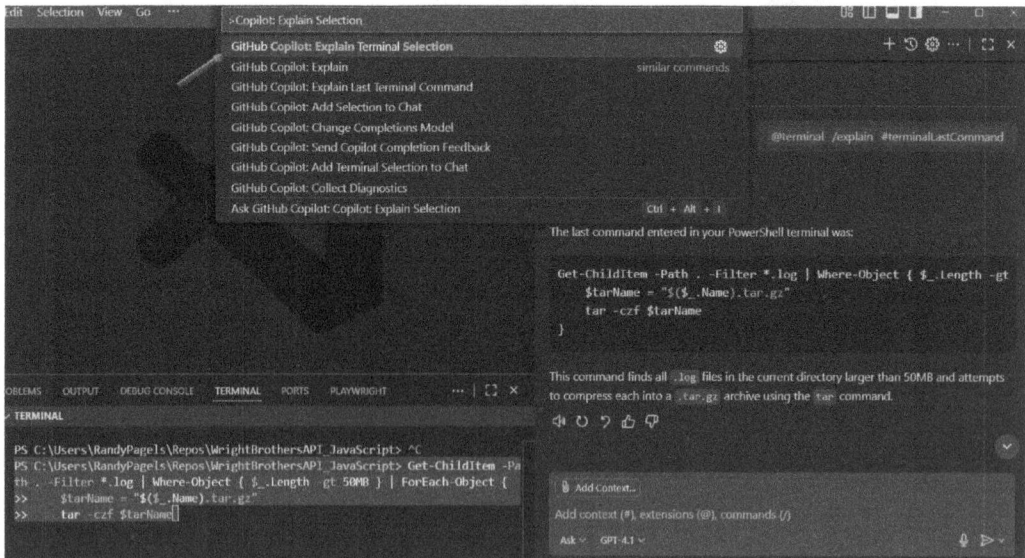

Figure 5.2: Command Palette open in VS Code, explaining PowerShell

Best practices

To get the most reliable results when working with commands or scripts, keep these best practices in mind:

- **Keep prompts specific:** The clearer your terminal or Command Palette prompt, the better Copilot's suggestions. If you want a one-liner, mention it; if you want a script, say so.

- **Use inline explanations:** When using a command you don't fully understand, let GitHub Copilot explain it before you run it, especially when dealing with file deletions or administrative actions.

- **Chain commands safely:** GitHub Copilot can help chain multiple commands (e.g., in Bash or PowerShell), but always review suggestions before executing anything with broad impact.

Common pitfalls to avoid

While these integrations can save time, there are also a few traps that developers should watch for. Keep these common pitfalls in mind to avoid problems down the line:

- **Trusting suggestions without review:** Always check proposed commands, especially those that delete files or change system state.

- **Ambiguous prompts leading to weak suggestions:** Vague requests (such as `clean up logs`) might miss important details. Be clear about directories, file types, or date ranges.

- **Overreliance for sensitive scripts:** Don't rely solely on GitHub Copilot for production scripts or commands involving sensitive data. Always add an extra review step.

The terminal and Command Palette bring AI assistance directly into your day-to-day shell and script work inside the IDE. They are best for quick commands, explanations, and edits that stay within the editor environment. Sometimes, however, you need the same support outside the IDE in standalone scripts, pipelines, or broader automation. This is where GitHub Copilot CLI comes in, extending these capabilities to any terminal session and making them available for integration into your CI/CD workflows.

GitHub Copilot CLI features

Most developers start with GitHub Copilot in an IDE, but you can also work with it directly from the terminal. GitHub Copilot CLI brings the coding agent into your shell so you can generate scripts, explain commands, refactor files, and reason about your repo without leaving the command line. This fits naturally into day-to-day automation and operations work.

What is GitHub Copilot CLI?

GitHub Copilot CLI opens an interactive session with the coding agent inside your terminal. From that session, you can do the following:

- Generate shell commands and complete scripts from natural language
- Explain or summarize commands, diffs, and snippets
- Propose edits or refactors to files in your working directory (you approve before anything runs)
- Ask about your GitHub work, such as open pull requests or assigned issues, when authenticated

Setting up the GitHub Copilot CLI extension

To get started, make sure you have the following:

- An active GitHub Copilot subscription
- A supported environment (macOS, Windows, or Linux) with Git installed
- Node.js 22+, npm 10+

Then, follow these steps:

1. First, enter this command to install the CLI globally :

   ```
   npm install -g @github/copilot
   ```

2. Next, launch the CLI:

   ```
   copilot
   ```

3. Authenticate using your GitHub account. If you are not logged in, you will be prompted to use the in-session slash command:

   ```
   /login
   ```

4. After that, the CLI prints a short code and opens your browser to `github.com`. In the browser, you'll see a page asking you to enter the code shown in your terminal. Enter it.

5. After that, GitHub shows an **Authorize** screen for GitHub Copilot. Click **Authorize**.

6. Now, return to the terminal. The CLI confirms that you are signed in and the session is ready.

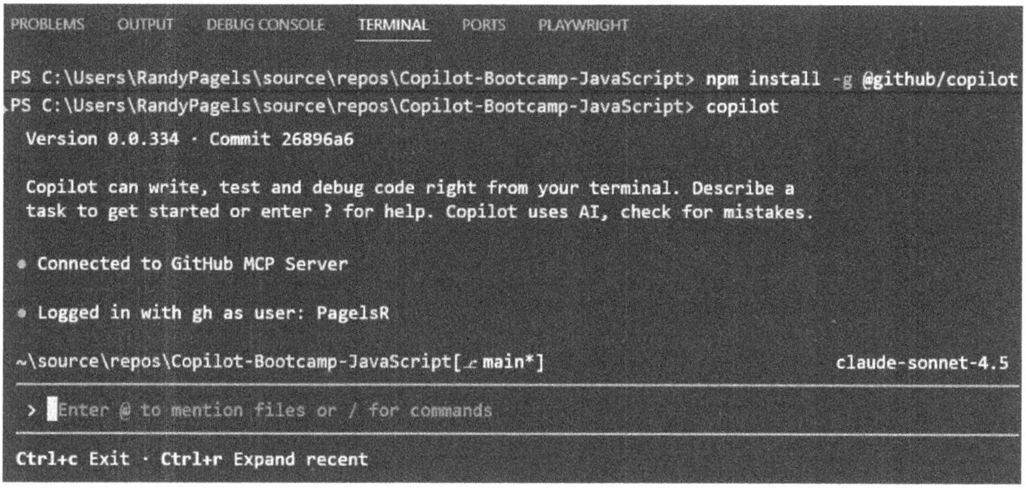

```
PROBLEMS    OUTPUT    DEBUG CONSOLE    TERMINAL    PORTS    PLAYWRIGHT

PS C:\Users\RandyPagels\source\repos\Copilot-Bootcamp-JavaScript> npm install -g @github/copilot
PS C:\Users\RandyPagels\source\repos\Copilot-Bootcamp-JavaScript> copilot
  Version 0.0.334 · Commit 26896a6

  Copilot can write, test and debug code right from your terminal. Describe a
  task to get started or enter ? for help. Copilot uses AI, check for mistakes.

● Connected to GitHub MCP Server

● Logged in with gh as user: PagelsR

~\source\repos\Copilot-Bootcamp-JavaScript[ main*]                        claude-sonnet-4.5

>  Enter @ to mention files or / for commands

Ctrl+c Exit · Ctrl+r Expand recent
```

Figure 5.3: Terminal window open, showing a Copilot CLI prompt

Alternatively, if you cannot use the browser flow, you can provide a fine-grained **personal access token (PAT)**. This is a token you generate on GitHub to let tools authenticate as you, without using your password. To create a fine-grained PAT with the correct permission, follow these steps:

1. Go to `https://github.com/settings/personal-access-tokens/new`.

2. Give the token a name and (optionally) an expiration.

3. Under **Permissions**, click **Add permissions**, then select **Copilot Requests**.

    The **Copilot Requests** permission lets the CLI send prompts to GitHub Copilot and receive responses on your behalf. It does not grant repository, organization, or code write access unless you add other permissions. Only this permission is required for Copilot CLI in this context.

4. Generate the token and copy it.

5. Provide the token to the CLI and set an environment variable – either GH_TOKEN or GITHUB_TOKEN. We recommend that you set GH_TOKEN, as this is what the CLI looks for first. If that is not set, the CLI will look for GITHUB_TOKEN instead.

    Here are some examples of setting the GH_TOKEN environment variable:

    ```
    # macOS/Linux (bash/zsh)
    export GH_TOKEN=ghp_yourFineGrainedTokenHere
    copilot
    # Windows PowerShell
    ```

```
$env:GH_TOKEN="ghp_yourFineGrainedTokenHere"
copilot
```

Note that if you set both GH_TOKEN and GITHUB_TOKEN, GH_TOKEN takes precedence.

Also, note that GH_TOKEN and GITHUB_TOKEN are environment variables, not buttons.

6. Now, launch Copilot.

7. As an optional step, choose a model. By default, the CLI uses Claude Sonnet 4.5, but to switch models, type /model. Then, select from the available options, such as Claude Sonnet 4 or GPT-5.

8. Finally, verify that everything is working. You can do this by either of the following:

    - Typing help
    - Asking for something simple, such as Explain this command: ls -la

You should see a response that describes the command and flags. If you do not, check that you are signed in and that GH_TOKEN or GITHUB_TOKEN is set correctly.

> For the latest list of what GitHub Copilot CLI can do, including its available commands, features, and optional command-line flags (such as --explain, --json, or --file, which change how a command runs), visit the official documentation at https://docs.github.com/en/copilot/concepts/agents/about-copilot-cli.

Real-world examples of Copilot CLI in action

GitHub Copilot CLI shines in two everyday situations: it generates the scripts you need and explains commands you want to verify. It can also query your GitHub work when authenticated.

Example 1: Automating CSV backup and cleanup

GitHub Copilot CLI is especially helpful for automating small but repetitive tasks. Imagine you want to back up all CSV files in your ~/downloads folder to the ~/archive folder to clean up old files that are no longer needed. Instead of writing the script by hand, you can ask Copilot CLI to generate it:

```
Write a bash script that moves all .csv files from ~/downloads to ~/
archive and then deletes files older than 30 days in ~/archive.
```

Copilot responds with a ready-to-use Bash script:

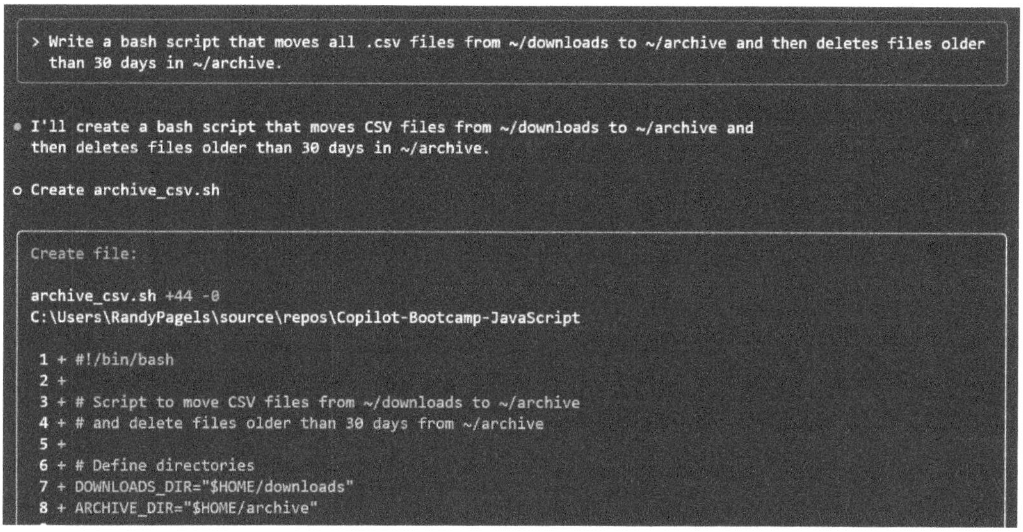

```
> Write a bash script that moves all .csv files from ~/downloads to ~/archive and then deletes files older
  than 30 days in ~/archive.

• I'll create a bash script that moves CSV files from ~/downloads to ~/archive and
  then deletes files older than 30 days in ~/archive.

o Create archive_csv.sh

  Create file:

  archive_csv.sh +44 -0
  C:\Users\RandyPagels\source\repos\Copilot-Bootcamp-JavaScript

  1 + #!/bin/bash
  2 +
  3 + # Script to move CSV files from ~/downloads to ~/archive
  4 + # and delete files older than 30 days from ~/archive
  5 +
  6 + # Define directories
  7 + DOWNLOADS_DIR="$HOME/downloads"
  8 + ARCHIVE_DIR="$HOME/archive"
```

Figure 5.4: Using GitHub Copilot CLI to generate a Bash script for archiving and cleaning up CSV files

At this point, choose how you want to use the script. In the session UI, you can copy it to the clipboard or ask GitHub Copilot to write the file for you. When you choose to write, the CLI shows a confirmation prompt (see *Figure 5.5*) asking whether to edit the file now, approve all file operations for the rest of the session, or decline and give new instructions. Confirm the write, then review the saved file, make it executable, and run or schedule it as needed. You can also ask GitHub Copilot to explain the script before you execute it:

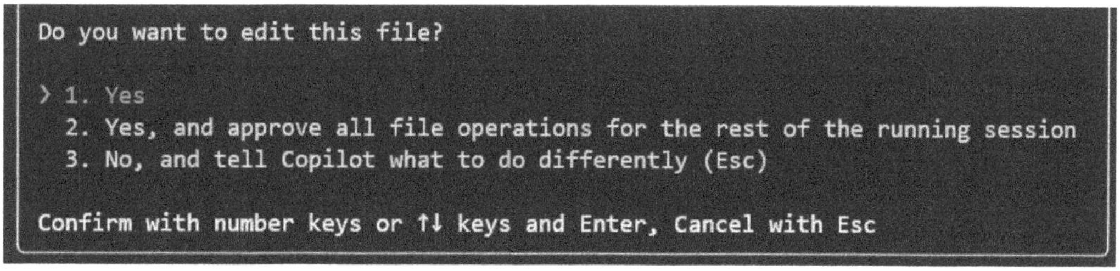

```
Do you want to edit this file?

> 1. Yes
  2. Yes, and approve all file operations for the rest of the running session
  3. No, and tell Copilot what to do differently (Esc)

Confirm with number keys or ↑↓ keys and Enter, Cancel with Esc
```

Figure 5.5: GitHub Copilot CLI asks for confirmation before writing or editing files

Example 2: Explaining a Git command

Another common use case for GitHub Copilot CLI is understanding commands you come across in scripts or documentation. Instead of searching online or guessing, you can ask GitHub Copilot CLI to break them down into plain language. For instance, you see a compact history command in a script or review note and want to be sure what it shows before you run it:

```
Explain this command: git log --graph --oneline --decorate origin/main..
HEAD
```

As you can see in *Figure 5.6*, Copilot explains each part of the command clearly. GitHub Copilot explains that `git log` prints commit history, `--graph` draws a simple branch graph in the left margin, `--oneline` shows each commit on a single line with a short commit hash and subject, and `--decorate` displays references such as branch names and tags. The `origin/main..HEAD` range limits the output to commits that are on your current branch but not on `origin/main`, which is handy when you want to review what your branch adds before opening a pull request or writing a summary:

```
> Explain this command: git log --graph --oneline --decorate origin/main..HEAD

• This git log command shows you the commits that exist in your local branch but
  haven't been pushed to the remote yet. Let me break down each part:

  git log - The base command to view commit history

  --graph - Displays an ASCII graph showing the branch and merge history on the
  left side, making it easy to visualize how commits relate to each other

  --oneline - Condenses each commit to a single line showing just the short commit
  hash and the commit message, making the output much more compact and readable

  --decorate - Shows reference names (branch names, tags, HEAD) next to commits,
  so you can see where branches point

  origin/main..HEAD - This is the range specification and the key part:

    * origin/main is the remote tracking branch (what main looked like the last time you fetched/pulled)
    * HEAD is your current local position
    * The .. syntax means "show commits reachable from HEAD but not from origin/main"

  In practical terms, this command answers the question: "What commits have I made
  locally that I haven't pushed yet?" It's extremely useful before pushing to see
  exactly what you're about to send to the remote repository.
```

Figure 5.6: GitHub Copilot CLI explaining Git commands and clarifying how each flag and the commit range work

This is especially helpful when working with infrastructure scripts or automation you didn't write yourself. Rather than searching online or taking risks with unfamiliar commands, GitHub Copilot breaks them down in plain language, helping you understand exactly what each part does before executing it.

Example 3: Interacting with GitHub.com

You can also use the CLI to query GitHub directly. Once signed in, ask about your open pull requests, assigned issues, and other work without leaving the terminal.

To get a quick snapshot of your active work across repositories, ask the following:

```
List my open pull requests
```

GitHub Copilot returns your open pull requests. To narrow the scope, include a repository:

```
List all open issues assigned to me in octocat/Hello-World
```

You can then use the results to jump to reviews or triage tasks without leaving the terminal.

Integrating Copilot CLI with automation

Imagine that you have a small housekeeping task that keeps returning: archiving CSVs and pruning older files. Rather than hand-write and maintain a script, you can ask GitHub Copilot CLI to draft it, review the result, check it into your repo, and let GitHub Actions run it on a schedule. This shows the full loop from a quick local prompt to reliable, repeatable automation. Here's how:

1. Generate the script with GitHub Copilot CLI. After starting a session, request and review it:

   ```
   Write a bash script named archive_csvs.sh that moves all .csv files
   from ~/downloads to ~/archive and deletes .csv files older than 30
   days.
   Add basic error handling and simple logging.
   ```

2. Save the file as `./.github/scripts/archive_csvs.sh`:

   ```
   #!/usr/bin/env bash set -euo pipefail SRC_DIR="${SRC_DIR:-$HOME/
   downloads}" DST_DIR="${DST_DIR:-$HOME/archive}" LOG="${LOG:-archive_
   csvs.log}" ... mv "$SRC_DIR"/.csv "$DST_DIR"/ 2>/dev/null || echo
   "No CSVs to move" find "$DST_DIR" -type f -name '.csv' -mtime +30
   -delete -print echo "[$(date -Iseconds)] Done" | tee -a "$LOG" ...
   ```

3. Next, make the script executable and commit it to your repository so that it becomes part of your version-controlled workflow. Run the following commands in your terminal:

```
chmod +x .github/scripts/archive_csvs.sh
git add .github/scripts/archive_csvs.sh
git commit -m "Add archive_csvs.sh generated with GitHub Copilot CLI"
git push
```

4. Add it into a GitHub Actions workflow that runs nightly, called `.github/workflows/archive-csvs.yml`:

```
...
name: Nightly CSV Archive
  on:
    schedule:
      - cron: "5 1 * * *"
    workflow_dispatch:

jobs:
  archive:
  runs-on: ubuntu-latest
  steps:
  - uses: actions/checkout@v4
  - name: Run archive script
    run: ./.github/scripts/archive_csvs.sh
  ...
```

You use GitHub Copilot CLI once to draft the task, keep the result under version control, and let GitHub Actions run it on a schedule. The work remains visible in reviews, and the behavior is consistent run after run.

Best practices

To make the most of Copilot CLI in everyday work and automation, keep these best practices in mind:

- **Be specific**: `Bash script to deploy a Docker container with error handling` is clearer than `Write a deployment script`
- **Review before running**: Be careful with changes to files, services, or credentials

- **Ask for explanations**: If unsure, request a breakdown before execution
- **Adopt gradually**: Use the CLI for small local tasks first, then standardize what works

Common pitfalls to avoid

Even with automation, the CLI is not foolproof. Be aware of these common pitfalls so you can avoid mistakes and keep your workflows safe:

- **Vague prompts**: Ambiguity leads to incomplete results
- **Skipping review**: Do not paste output straight into sh or pwsh without reading it
- **Over-automation**: Keep a human in the loop for critical infrastructure steps

GitHub Copilot CLI brings the coding agent to your terminal so you can generate scripts, explain commands, and get a quick view of your GitHub work. Used with review and a few careful habits, it fits naturally alongside your IDE and helps keep work moving without extra context switching.

Next, we shift focus back into the IDE itself. Beyond writing and automation, Copilot can also assist when things go wrong. In the following section, you will see how Copilot supports debugging sessions by explaining stack traces, suggesting fixes, and even generating diagnostic code to help identify root causes.

Debugging support

Debugging is a critical phase in the development cycle and often one of the most time-consuming. GitHub Copilot's IDE integrations are designed to help you not just write code but also understand and fix it. GitHub Copilot assists throughout the debugging process: analyzing stack traces, suggesting fixes, explaining errors, and even generating diagnostic scripts. This section shows how Copilot's presence in your IDE can make troubleshooting less painful and more productive.

What can GitHub Copilot do in the debugger?

In supported IDEs (such as Visual Studio Code), GitHub Copilot can be invoked during active debugging sessions or while inspecting error logs and stack traces. Some common workflows include the following:

- **Explaining error messages and stack traces**: Highlight an error or stack trace and ask GitHub Copilot for a plain-language explanation
- **Suggesting fixes for bugs**: Prompt GitHub Copilot to recommend code changes based on a failing test, exception, or runtime error

- **Generating diagnostic code**: Request scripts or functions to help isolate and reproduce bugs (e.g., extra logging or input validation)
- **Assisting with test debugging**: Get suggestions for test assertions, edge cases, or how to reproduce a failure

Example 1: JavaScript stack trace analysis

Consider a scenario where your Node.js app crashes during execution. In VS Code's terminal, you see an error like this:

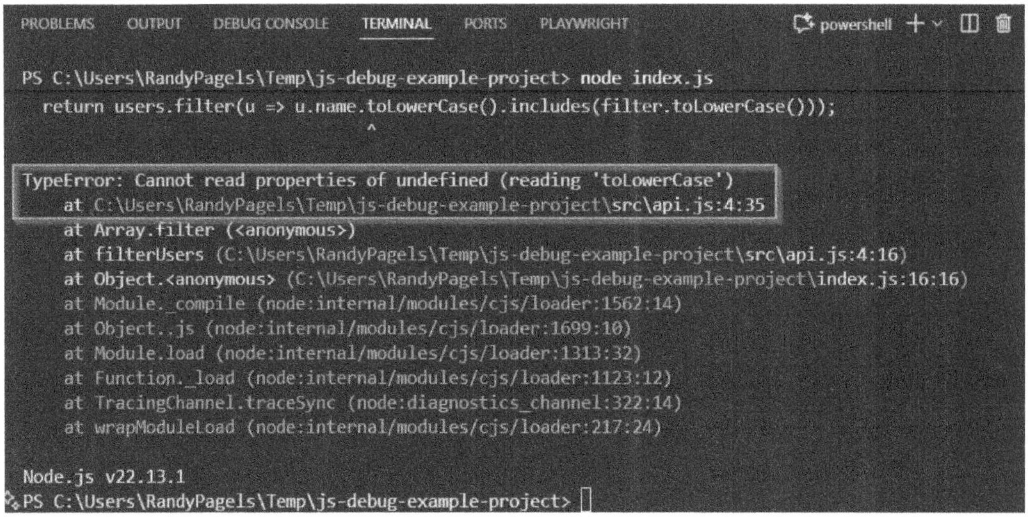

Figure 5.7: Error shown in the VS Code terminal during a Node.js run. The stack trace is selected for explanation, then pasted into Copilot Chat to get a diagnosis and fix

At first glance, the message is not very helpful. You know toLowerCase is being called on undefined, but it is not obvious why. To investigate with Copilot, do the following:

- If available in your setup, select the stack trace text in the terminal, open the Command Palette, and run **GitHub Copilot: Explain Terminal Selection**.
- If the command is not available, copy the stack trace from the terminal and paste it into Copilot Chat, then use the following prompt:

```
Explain this error and suggest a fix.
```

Copilot explains that the filter argument is sometimes undefined, so calling `toLowerCase()` throws an error. It then proposes a safer version of the function:

```
// ...existing code...

// You can ask Copilot: "Suggest a safe version of filterUsers that avoids
// crashing when user.name or filter is missing." It would typically add
// guards like shown below.
function safeFilterUsers(users, filter) {
  if (!Array.isArray(users)) return [];
  if (typeof filter !== 'string') return users;
  const f = filter.toLowerCase();
  return users.filter(u => typeof u.name === 'string' && u.name.
toLowerCase().includes(f));
}


// ...existing code...
```

After applying the change, run the program again. The error is gone, and the behavior is correct, with or without a filter value.

This example demonstrates how GitHub Copilot can act as a real-time debugging companion. By analyzing stack traces and explaining the root cause in plain language, it bridges the gap between a confusing error message and a clear path to resolution. Instead of guessing why a crash occurred, you can quickly understand the failure, apply a targeted fix, and verify the outcome, all without leaving your IDE.

Example 2: SQL error assistance

Consider a situation where you are writing a query against an employees table and the execution fails with the following message:

```
ERROR: column "employeeid" does not exist
LINE 1: SELECT employeeid, name FROM employees;
```

At this point, you know the query failed, but the error message alone does not tell you the exact cause. To investigate, you highlight the error message and prompt Copilot with the following:

```
Explain and fix this SQL error.
```

Copilot explains that the error occurs because the `employeeid` column does not exist in the employees table. It identifies two possible reasons:

- The column name is misspelled (e.g., should be `employee_id` or `id`)
- The column does not exist in the table schema

Plus, it provides the steps to fix it:

1. Check the actual column names in the employees table.
2. Update your query to use the correct column name.

Figure 5.8 shows the full Copilot response and further details to resolve the SQL error:

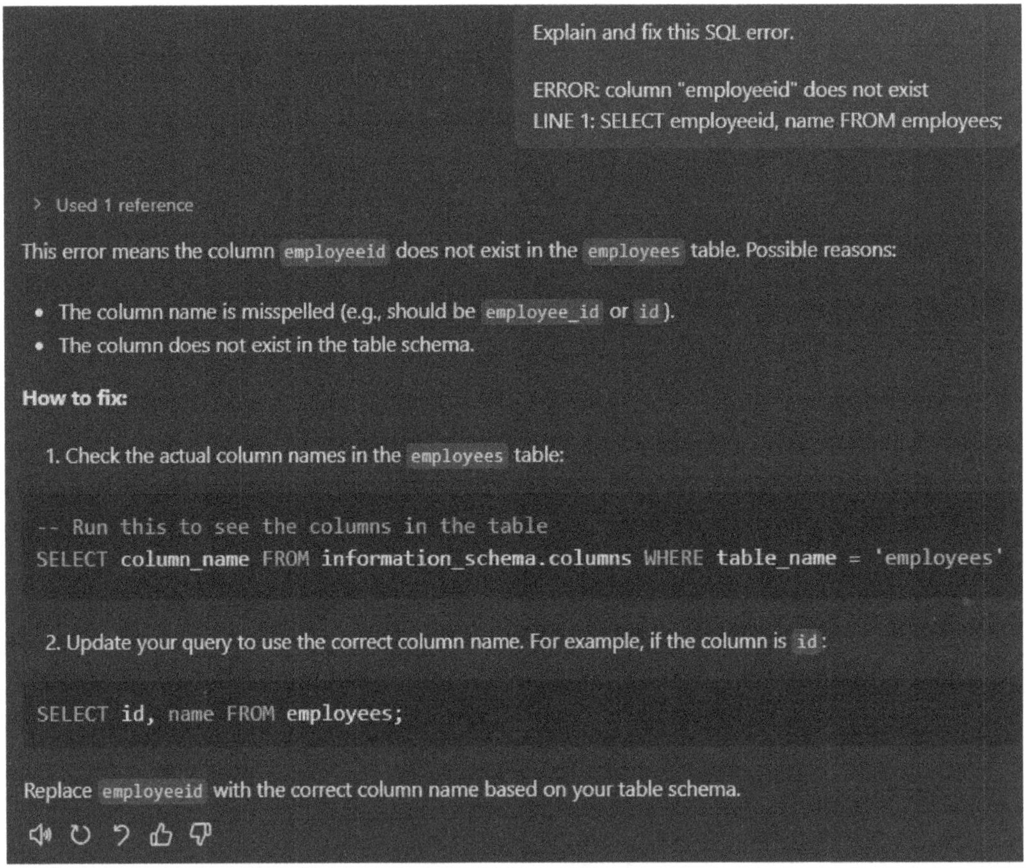

Figure 5.8: Terminal window explaining and resolving a SQL error

This example demonstrates how GitHub Copilot provides more than a simple correction. It not only identifies the likely issue but also guides you through verifying the schema before applying a fix. This structured workflow, which explains the error, checks the environment, and then updates the code, shows why GitHub Copilot is an effective debugging partner, reducing guesswork and helping you resolve issues more confidently.

Supported languages and scenarios

Copilot's debugging help is not limited to a single language or environment. It works across a wide range of programming languages, scripting tools, and configuration formats, including the following:

- JavaScript/TypeScript (Node.js, web apps)
- Python
- C#/F#
- SQL (T-SQL, PostgreSQL, etc.)
- PowerShell, Bash, and other scripting languages
- Infrastructure as Code (Bicep, YAML, Terraform, etc.)
- CI/CD pipeline definitions

You can mix and match these technologies in a single project. Copilot will offer debugging suggestions for whatever you highlight or request, as long as the relevant context is available in your editor.

Best practices

To make Copilot's debugging assistance both reliable and safe, keep these best practices in mind when asking for help with errors or stack traces:

- **Be specific with error context**: The more details you provide (full stack trace, failing input, or test scenario), the more precise GitHub Copilot's assistance
- **Prompt for both explanation and fix**: Sometimes, the best approach is to ask Copilot to first explain, then recommend a fix—this helps you understand, not just patch
- **Validate all suggestions**: Always test GitHub Copilot's code in your debug environment before moving to production

Common pitfalls to avoid

While Copilot can be a valuable debugging partner, there are also risks to be aware of. Watch out for these common pitfalls to avoid creating new problems as you troubleshoot:

- **Blindly applying suggested fixes**: Always understand why GitHub Copilot is recommending a change—some suggestions may only mask underlying issues.

- **Omitting full context**: GitHub Copilot works best when it "sees" the relevant code, configuration, and error output. Include as much as you can in your prompt.

- **Relying on Copilot for all debugging**: AI is great at pattern-matching and suggesting common fixes, but don't skip root cause analysis for complex issues.

Debugging is one of the most time-consuming parts of development, and Copilot's ability to explain errors, propose fixes, and generate diagnostic code shows how AI can speed up that process without replacing human judgment. Once errors are resolved, however, development often continues into reviews, tests, and quality checks. In the next section, we will look at other IDE-integrated tools where GitHub Copilot helps with code reviews, manual pull request summaries, test runners, and analysis workflows that keep projects healthy and maintainable.

Other IDE-integrated tools

Beyond editing and debugging, modern IDEs serve as the nerve center for code review, testing, and quality checks. GitHub Copilot extends its reach into these areas, helping you review code, draft summaries, and work more efficiently, even if your team doesn't use GitHub.com for pull requests.

Manual pull request summaries and local code review

Teams review code in different ways. Some use hosted pull request workflows on GitHub.com, while others prefer to keep reviews entirely within the IDE. GitHub Copilot supports both approaches by helping you summarize, analyze, and comment on code changes, whether you are working locally or through the **GitHub Pull Requests** extension.

There are two main ways to take advantage of this:

- **Manual local review**: In this workflow, you highlight diffs, stage changes, or paste snippets into the Chat interface. Copilot then generates summaries or review comments tied directly to the code under review.

- **Integrated review with the GitHub Pull Requests extension**: In this workflow, you use the GitHub Pull Requests extension in VS Code to generate commit messages or review notes automatically from staged changes. This keeps everything inside the IDE without requiring manual copy-paste.

The subsections that follow show each method in detail, highlighting how Copilot ties its assistance to the current change set and how the integrated extension workflow can streamline reviews even further.

> Use Copilot Chat for broad explanations (e.g., pasting in a multi-file diff for context) and local code review for focused analysis of the current change set. Together, they give you both the big picture and the precise detail.

Manual local review

When working locally, stage your changes, then click **Generate Commit Message** in the **SOURCE CONTROL** panel (see the button highlighted by the red arrow in *Figure 5.9*). GitHub Copilot creates a summary from the staged diff that you can edit before committing or reuse in a review note.

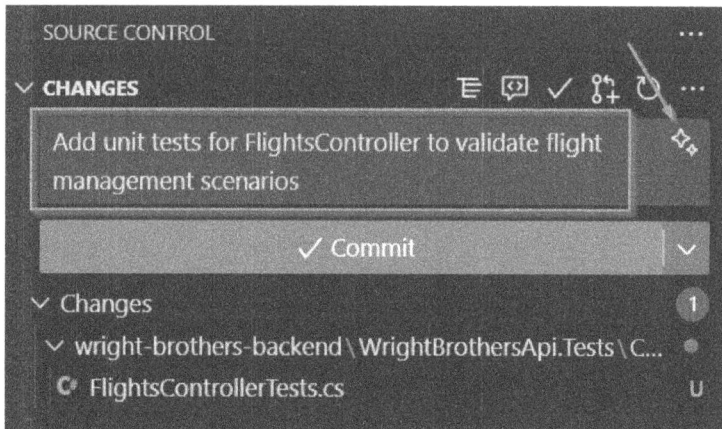

Figure 5.9: The SOURCE CONTROL panel in VS Code showing the Generate Commit Message button

GitHub Copilot analyzes the staged diff and produces a natural-language commit message suggestion. You can review the text, cycle through alternatives if offered, or refine it before committing. This ensures that your commit message explains the purpose of the change, not just what files were modified. You can then finalize the commit directly, or reuse the summary as a review note to share with others, regardless of which source control system your team uses.

In addition to generating commit messages, you can also request targeted review assistance on specific lines of code. Highlight the new or modified lines in your editor and prompt GitHub Copilot to review them for potential issues or edge cases. GitHub Copilot may point out missing null checks, opportunities for input validation, or style inconsistencies. This gives you lightweight feedback without needing to open a full pull request, making it useful for quick iterations or solo projects.

Integrated review with the GitHub Pull Requests extension

For a streamlined workflow in VS Code, use the **GitHub Pull Requests** and **Issues** extensions. As shown back in *Figure 5.9* (the red arrow again), the **SOURCE CONTROL** panel includes **Generate Commit Message**, which drafts a summary from your staged diff. When you are ready to open a pull request, switch to the **Create Pull Request** view shown in *Figure 5.10*. There, you can review the generated text, adjust the title and description, and click **Create**. The screen also includes **Copilot Code Review** so you can run an AI review before submitting:

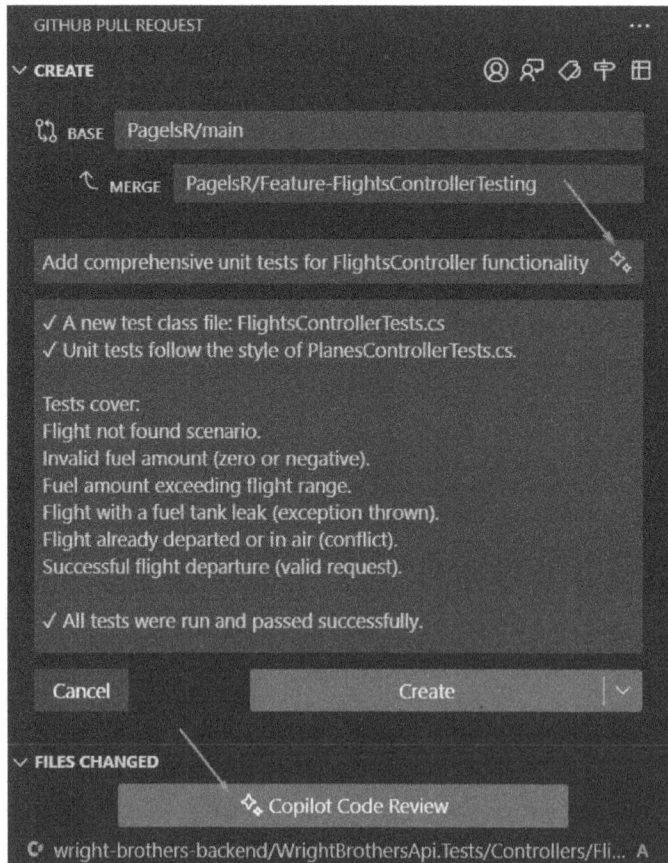

Figure 5.10: VS Code PR extension generating a commit summary

When creating or updating a pull request in VS Code with the same extension, you'll also notice the **Copilot Code Review** button. Clicking it runs an AI-powered review on the staged or pending changes. The tool provides inline comments, points out test weaknesses, and suggests improvements, just like a teammate leaving review notes. You can see an example in *Figure 5.11*:

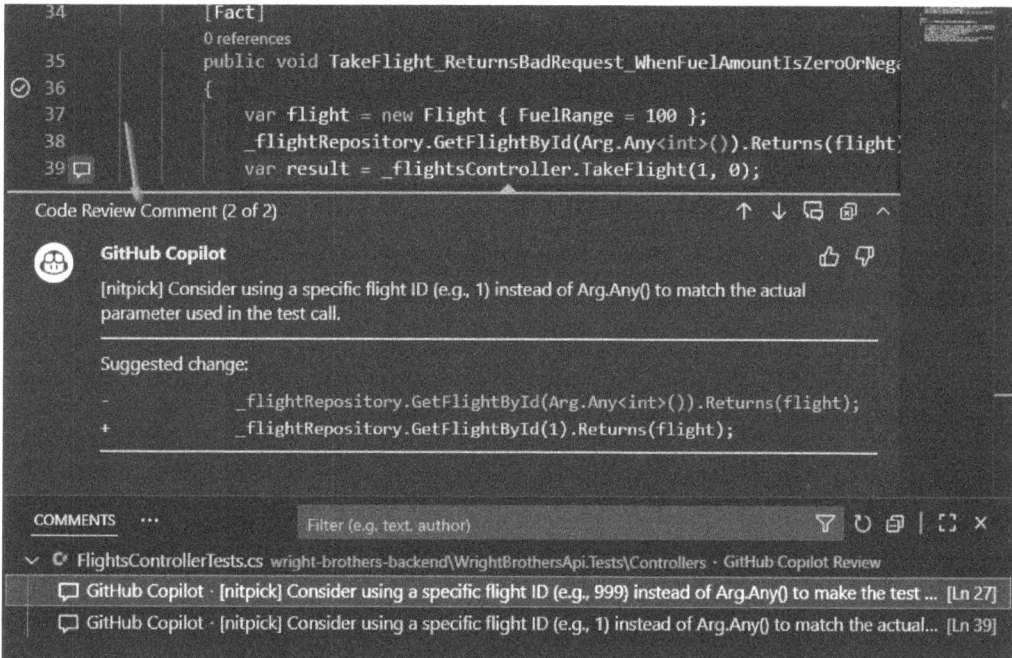

Figure 5.11: Code Review in the PR extension, showing suggested changes with inline comments

Use GitHub Copilot's feedback as a starting point, then refine or adjust based on your team's standards. This balances automation with human oversight.

Best practices

To get the most value from Copilot's IDE-integrated tools and to ensure that the results are both useful and safe, consider the following best practices:

- **Paste only relevant diffs**: For best results, keep the diff or code changes focused and targeted

- **Request both a summary and review**: Try prompts such as `Summarize these changes and list possible risks`

- **Integrate into local workflow**: Use GitHub Copilot alongside your preferred Git GUI, terminal, or IDE diff tools

Common pitfalls to avoid

While Copilot can streamline reviews and summaries, there are a few common pitfalls that can reduce its effectiveness. Keep these in mind to avoid frustration and get more accurate results:

- **Overly broad diffs**: Large, multi-file diffs can overwhelm GitHub Copilot. Break changes into smaller chunks for better summaries.
- **Missing context**: If GitHub Copilot can't "see" related files or dependencies, ask more targeted questions or review those areas manually.

Test runners and code analysis

Testing and analysis are critical parts of ensuring that software remains reliable, maintainable, and secure. GitHub Copilot can support these tasks inside the IDE by helping you generate test cases, strengthen existing coverage, and make sense of the often overwhelming output from test runs or static analysis tools. Rather than replacing these processes, GitHub Copilot speeds them up and provides context so that you can focus on the decisions that matter.

One of the most common uses is generating tests from code. If you highlight a function and prompt Copilot with a request such as `"Write unit tests for this function using Jest"` or `"Generate tests for this function using pytest"`, it produces a scaffolded test file tailored to your chosen framework. This is especially helpful when you are starting fresh or when you want to quickly cover basic cases before refining with more specific scenarios.

Example 1: Generating a test case

Suppose you have added a new function to a Python module. By selecting the function in your editor and prompting `Write unit tests for this function using pytest`, Copilot produces a draft test file. The generated tests may include assertions for common inputs, boundary conditions, and expected failures. You can then refine these tests to fit your project's requirements. This saves time by avoiding the blank-page problem and gives you a quick starting point to expand upon.

GitHub Copilot also helps when dealing with analysis output. Static analysis tools such as ESLint or Pylint are excellent at finding issues, but they often generate long lists of warnings that are difficult to prioritize. Instead of reading through every line, you can paste the output into Copilot Chat and request a focused summary.

Example 2: Summarizing analysis results

After running ESLint on a JavaScript project, you might paste the results into Copilot Chat and prompt Summarize these findings and recommend the top three fixes. Copilot identifies the most significant issues, such as unused variables, a function with poor performance, or inconsistent style, and returns a concise set of actionable recommendations. Instead of being buried in warnings, you have a prioritized list of changes to address first.

Together, these scenarios illustrate how Copilot can enhance both testing and analysis. It accelerates the process of writing tests, suggests improvements you might not have considered, and helps you extract meaningful insight from dense output. By integrating directly into your IDE, Copilot supports the quality-focused side of development, ensuring that new features are not only delivered quickly but also tested and validated effectively.

Best practices

To get the most out of Copilot when working with tests and analysis tools, consider these best practices:

- **Pair Copilot with your existing tools**: Use Copilot to fill in gaps that your linter, test runner, or analyzer doesn't cover. For example, if your linter flags a recurring pattern, Copilot can propose a refactoring to address it consistently.
- **Ask for specifics**: Direct prompts such as Suggest additional test assertions for this function in pytest produce better results than broad requests such as Improve these tests.
- **Use Copilot to prioritize**: When static analysis produces dozens of warnings, ask Copilot to identify the top three issues to focus on first. This keeps your workflow manageable and action-oriented.

Common pitfalls to avoid

While Copilot can be a helpful partner in testing and analysis, overreliance or vague prompting can undermine its usefulness. Be mindful of these common pitfalls:

- **Relying solely on generated tests**: GitHub Copilot's test scaffolds are only a starting point and rarely provide full coverage. Always expand and adapt them to meet your project's needs.
- **Using generic prompts**: Broad requests such as Make these tests better often lead to unhelpful results. Be clear about the language, framework, and the kind of improvements you want.

- **Treating Copilot as a replacement for analysis**: GitHub Copilot can summarize linter results, but you should still review the full report for minor issues that could accumulate over time.

Extension points

An extension point is a feature in an IDE that lets you customize or extend the way a tool behaves. In the context of GitHub Copilot, extension points allow you to connect Copilot's capabilities to other tools or to streamline how you interact with it inside the editor. This flexibility makes Copilot feel less like a separate add-on and more like a native part of your daily workflow.

Extension points are useful because they let you do the following:

- Adapt Copilot to your habits. For example, you can create a keyboard shortcut for `Explain Diff` so that instead of opening the Command Palette each time, you can trigger Copilot with a single keystroke while reviewing changes.

- Integrate with other extensions. Many developers already rely on tools such as GitLens for Git history or Docker for container workflows. By combining these with Copilot, you can use prompts such as `Summarize this file's history` while viewing GitLens annotations, keeping review and analysis in one place.

- Reduce context switching. Instead of copying logs or diffs into Copilot Chat manually, you can use shortcuts or connected tools that send the content directly into Copilot for explanation or summarization.

As an example, suppose you frequently use GitHub Copilot to summarize failing test output. In VS Code, you can add a key binding that maps *Ctrl + Alt + T* (or any shortcut you prefer) to the **GitHub Copilot: Explain Selection** command. Now, whenever a test fails, you simply highlight the error in the terminal and press the shortcut. Copilot immediately provides a plain-language explanation without breaking your flow.

> Some capabilities, such as automatic pull request summaries and web-based review tools, are exclusive to GitHub.com. We'll explore these in detail in *Chapter 6*.

The IDE is more than just a code editor. It is also where reviews, tests, and analyses happen. GitHub Copilot's ability to generate commit summaries, review code locally or through the Pull Requests extension, and assist with test and analysis workflows shows how it integrates into many parts of the development environment. These features help developers stay focused, reduce context switching, and provide useful feedback directly where the work happens.

The next section looks at how these features work together in practice. We will step through concrete examples that combine terminal commands, CLI automation, debugging support, and integrated tools to show how GitHub Copilot supports the full flow of everyday development from start to finish.

Real-world workflow scenarios

The real strength of GitHub Copilot's IDE integrations shines when you use them together in daily tasks. This section brings together terminal assistance, GitHub Copilot CLI, debugging, local code review, and testing support into hands-on, practical flows, so you can see how these features combine to save time and reduce context-switching.

Scenario 1: From bug discovery to fix and review

Imagine that you're running integration tests in your IDE's terminal and see a failing test. What do you do?

Begin by investigating the bug. You can do either of the following:

- Highlight the error message or failing line and use the inline prompt `Explain this error and suggest a fix`. This option provides an explanation and suggests updated code directly in context.

- Click the **Fix Test Failure** icon next to the failing test. This option analyzes the failure automatically and proposes a direct fix without requiring a typed prompt.

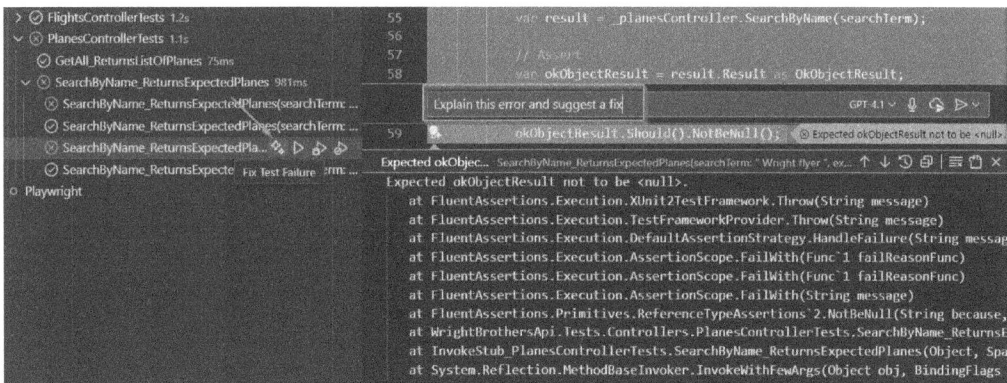

Figure 5.12: When debugging a failing test, choose between inline help to explain and fix the error, or the one-click Fix Test Failure option

Next, use GitHub Copilot's inline suggestion to update the function under test. Once the code is modified, rerun your test suite in the terminal. This time, the tests pass successfully.

To finish, copy your local Git diff into GitHub Copilot Chat and prompt `Summarize this change for my commit message`. Copilot generates a natural-language summary that you can adapt and include in your commit. This keeps the history clear and improves transparency for your team.

This workflow shows how Copilot can streamline the debugging process end-to-end. It explains vague error messages, suggests targeted fixes, and even drafts commit summaries that clearly describe the change. By reducing the manual steps between failure and resolution, it keeps development moving forward with less context-switching.

Scenario 2: Infrastructure automation and CI/CD improvements

Imagine you are maintaining a service that generates large log files, and you want to automate both cleanup and security checks in your pipeline. How do you proceed?

To start, generate a reusable script for log management from the terminal using GitHub Copilot CLI. In the session, enter the following prompt:

```
Create a Bash script to compress and delete .log files older than 14 days.
```

GitHub Copilot returns a draft script that compresses older logs and removes files beyond your retention window. Review the output, make any edits you need, and save the script for use in your environment:

```
> Create a Bash script to compress and delete .log files older than 14 days.


X Create bash script for compressing and deleting old log files
   $ @'
   #!/bin/bash

   # Script to compress and delete .log files older than 14 days

   # Define log directory (default to current directory or pass as argument)
   LOG_DIR="${1:-.}"

   # Check if directory exists
   if [ ! -d "$LOG_DIR" ]; then
       echo "Error: Directory $LOG_DIR does not exist"
       exit 1
   fi
```

Figure 5.13: Script generation using GitHub Copilot CLI for automated log cleanup

Next, you want to strengthen your GitHub Actions pipeline with a security scan. In VS Code, open your workflow YAML file, highlight the relevant section, and prompt Copilot as follows:

```
Insert a step before deploy to scan code with Trivy.
```

Copilot proposes a properly structured YAML block that runs the Trivy scanner. You insert the new step, adjust parameters for your environment, and commit the change.

Before pushing upstream, you run the updated workflow locally (using a runner that supports local execution). The new security scan step surfaces a dependency warning. You paste the output into Copilot Chat and ask for a summary. Copilot explains the issue in plain language and suggests actions, such as updating the affected library.

This workflow shows how Copilot supports infrastructure automation end-to-end. It generates the scripts you need, assists in updating your CI/CD definitions, and helps you interpret the results, all within the same development loop.

Scenario 3: Reviewing and documenting a feature branch

Imagine you are working on a feature branch and want to prepare it for team review and documentation.

Begin by checking out the branch and staging your changes. With those changes ready, highlight the diff or key files in your IDE and prompt GitHub Copilot with the following:

```
Summarize the main purpose and risks of this feature update.
```

Copilot generates a natural-language summary that captures the intent of the changes, along with potential risks, such as performance impacts or areas where additional testing may be needed.

Next, adapt GitHub Copilot's draft into a review-ready summary. You can use it as the basis for a manual pull request description, add it to your commit history, or include it in project documentation. This ensures your work is clearly communicated, even if your team is not using GitHub.com for pull requests.

Finally, share Copilot's summary and risk notes with your team. This gives reviewers a clear starting point, highlights important concerns, and improves the quality of feedback. Even teams working outside hosted pull request workflows benefit from having concise, consistent documentation of what a feature branch introduces.

This workflow shows how Copilot helps with the often time-consuming process of documenting and reviewing changes. It summarizes the purpose of a feature, identifies potential risks, and generates review-ready notes that can be shared with teammates. Even outside of hosted pull request workflows, this makes feature reviews faster, clearer, and easier to communicate.

Scenario 4: End-to-end testing workflow

Imagine you are building and validating an API endpoint and want to make sure it is thoroughly tested.

Begin by writing the function for the add() endpoint. From there, highlight the code in your IDE and prompt GitHub Copilot as follows:

```
Generate pytest tests for this endpoint.
```

Copilot produces a draft test file with a fixture for the client and assertions to check that new tasks are added correctly. This gives you a starting point that can be refined as your feature evolves:

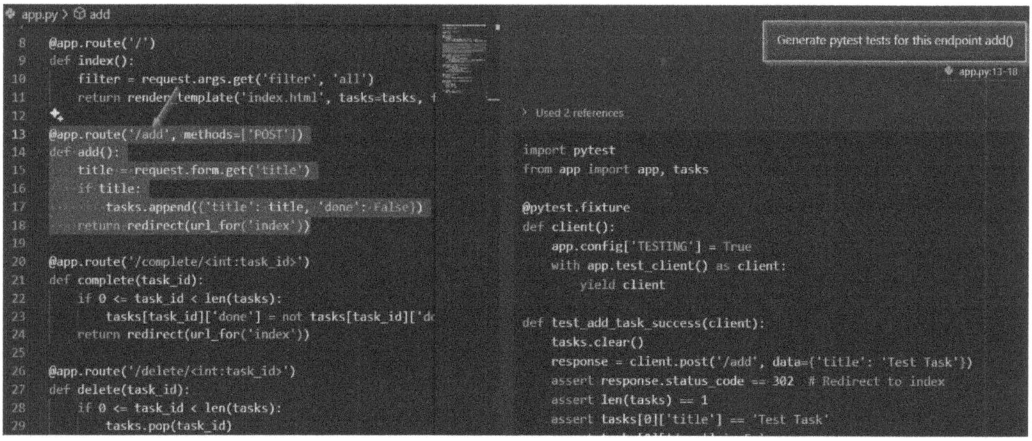

Figure 5.14: Generate unit tests

Next, run the generated tests. When a failure occurs, copy the error output into GitHub Copilot Chat and prompt as follows:

```
Explain why this test failed and suggest a fix.
```

Copilot analyzes the failure, explains the cause in plain language, and suggests specific adjustments to the code or test. You apply the advice, rerun the tests, and repeat the process until they all pass.

This workflow shows how Copilot supports the full test cycle. It helps generate initial test cases, clarifies failures, and suggests fixes, reducing the time it takes to move from implementation to reliable end-to-end validation.

Best practices for workflow integration

The preceding scenarios show how GitHub Copilot can support every phase of development, from debugging and testing to automation and reviews. To keep that flow consistent, apply these best practices when integrating GitHub Copilot into your daily workflow:

- **Move seamlessly**: Use GitHub Copilot in your editor, terminal, and code review steps, keeping everything in one place
- **Prompt for each phase**: Start with explanation, move to fix, then summarize and review
- **Mix and match languages**: Copilot handles JavaScript, Python, Bash, PowerShell, YAML, SQL, Bicep, and more—use the right tool for each task

Common pitfalls to avoid

By combining Copilot's IDE integrations for editing, scripting, debugging, reviewing, and automation, you can move faster and keep your focus on solving problems, not juggling tools. But no tool is perfect. These are the most common pitfalls to watch out for and how to avoid them:

- **Skipping reviews**: Moving fast is great, but always check Copilot's output for errors or risky changes before committing.
- **No testing**: Run generated code in a safe environment first, so you catch problems before they hit production.
- **Vague prompts**: `Fix this code` is too broad. Be specific so Copilot can give precise, useful results.
- **Missing context**: Include relevant code, diffs, or error output so Copilot can see the full picture.
- **Ignoring standards**: Even if the code works, make sure it matches your team's naming, formatting, and security rules.

Quick reference checklist

Before accepting GitHub Copilot's suggestions, ask yourself the following:

- Does this output do what I actually want?
- Is it safe to run, commit, or share?

- Can I test and validate the changes locally?
- Have I reviewed the logic, commands, or scripts for edge cases?
- Is the style and approach consistent with my team/project?
- Have I provided enough context to get a high-quality suggestion?

When in doubt, treat GitHub Copilot as your copilot, not the pilot. Review, revise, and test. If something feels off, ask for clarification or break the problem down further.

Summary

You learned how GitHub Copilot works inside the IDE and terminal to support real work, not just completions: prompting from the terminal and Command Palette, using GitHub Copilot CLI to generate and explain scripts, asking for help while debugging to interpret stack traces and suggest fixes, and running local reviews to produce clear commit messages and manual pull request summaries. You also saw test runners and code analysis in action, along with practical scenarios that tie these pieces together. This matters because it keeps you in one flow. You can script, review, test, and debug with less context switching, clearer documentation, and safer execution when you review suggestions before running them.

In the next chapter, you'll see how GitHub Copilot extends beyond local development to enhance collaboration on GitHub.com itself, where it summarizes pull requests, assists with code reviews, and streamlines web-based automation to help teams work more efficiently together.

Get This Book's PDF Version and Exclusive Extras

UNLOCK NOW

Scan the QR code (or go to packtpub.com/unlock). Search for this book by name, confirm the edition, and then follow the steps on the page.

Note: Keep your invoice handy. Purchases made directly from Packt don't require one.

Part 3

Exploring GitHub Copilot Integrations

Outside of all the features integrated in the editor, there are a lot of extension points with other systems as well. GitHub shows its industry strengths with its platform, which handles all different software development lifecycle steps in a single integrated platform, layering GitHub Copilot functionality on top of it: you can start a conversation with the AI right from github.com, create an issue with all the context you need to define the changes that you want to have implemented, and then hand that off to the Coding Agent to create the pull request and changes for you. Even better: for incoming PRs, GitHub Copilot can already do the first PR review for you!

As well as those features integrated into the web interface, we also take a deep look at how the Model Context Protocol (MCP) is revolutionizing the integration with other systems to bring even more context into your AI experience. From adding requirements from an external system (Jira, Azure DevOps – you name it) to letting the Agent Mode write back to external systems as well. You'll see how powerful it is to bring in the requirements right from where you define them into your chat conversation, and let Agent Mode make the necessary changes!

This part of the book includes the following chapters:

- *Chapter 6, Collaborating with Copilot on GitHub.com: Issues, PRs, Reviews, and Coding Agent*
- *Chapter 7, Extending GitHub Copilot with the Model Context Protocol (MCP)*

6

Collaborating with Copilot on GitHub.com: Issues, PRs, Reviews, and Coding Agent

GitHub Copilot has become a core part of the modern developer's toolkit, offering much more than just code suggestions in your editor. Over the past couple of years, GitHub Copilot has expanded directly onto GitHub.com, bringing intelligent assistance right where developers collaborate, on issues, **pull requests (PRs)**, and discussions. With these web-based features, GitHub Copilot moves beyond individual productivity and starts to shape how teams communicate, review code, and automate routine project tasks across the entire development life cycle.

While earlier chapters focused on GitHub Copilot's experience inside IDEs, code completions, conversational chat, automated edits, and agent-driven changes, this chapter zooms in on what happens when you work in the browser. Here, GitHub Copilot isn't just a sidekick for writing code, but also a helpful assistant for reviewing, summarizing, and moving work forward in the context of GitHub-hosted repositories.

You'll see how GitHub Copilot can help with the following:

- Drafting and summarizing issues and discussions
- Suggesting fixes and generating PR summaries
- Reviewing and commenting on code directly in PRs
- Automating changes using Coding Agent features

- Answering questions, explaining diffs, and even taking on delegated tasks when assigned issues
- Explaining and addressing workflow failures in GitHub Actions
- Fixing security alerts

In practice, developers who treat GitHub Copilot as a collaborator, asking clear questions, reviewing its suggestions, and letting it take care of repetitive work, tend to get the most value from these features. GitHub Copilot on GitHub.com works best when there's enough context to guide its output and when suggestions get a quick review before being merged or shared.

In this chapter, you will cover the following topics:

- GitHub Copilot Chat on GitHub.com
- Issue and discussion support
- PR support
- Coding Agent on GitHub.com
- Additional GitHub.com Copilot features

GitHub Copilot Chat on GitHub.com

GitHub Copilot Chat is a conversational interface built directly into GitHub.com. It lets you interact with GitHub Copilot right where collaboration happens, in issues, PRs, and workflow logs. Instead of switching back to your IDE, you can open a chat panel in the browser to ask questions, request explanations, or generate content in the context of your repository.

Unlike the IDE version, where chat history is tied to your local editor, conversations on GitHub.com are saved to your GitHub account. This means context and history carry across sessions and devices, providing continuity whether you log in from your desktop, laptop, or mobile app.

When you are viewing a PR on GitHub.com, click the Copilot Chat icon next to the search bar in the repository header to open the chat panel:

Figure 6.1: Opening Copilot Chat from the repository header while viewing a PR on GitHub.com

Once the panel is open, ask Copilot to summarize the proposed changes. This gives reviewers a quick technical overview of the code without needing to read through every file diff or commit message:

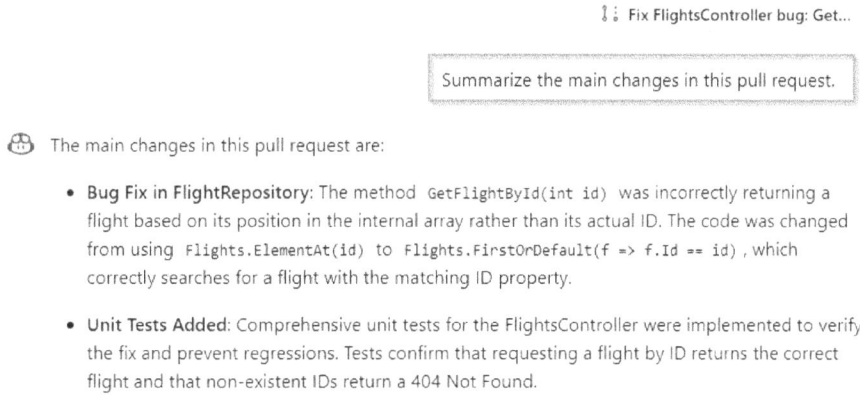

⇅ Fix FlightsController bug: Get...

Summarize the main changes in this pull request.

The main changes in this pull request are:

- **Bug Fix in FlightRepository:** The method `GetFlightById(int id)` was incorrectly returning a flight based on its position in the internal array rather than its actual ID. The code was changed from using `Flights.ElementAt(id)` to `Flights.FirstOrDefault(f => f.Id == id)`, which correctly searches for a flight with the matching ID property.

- **Unit Tests Added:** Comprehensive unit tests for the FlightsController were implemented to verify the fix and prevent regressions. Tests confirm that requesting a flight by ID returns the correct flight and that non-existent IDs return a 404 Not Found.

Figure 6.2: Copilot Chat summarizing the main code changes in a PR on GitHub.com

GitHub Copilot Chat can generate a plain-language summary of the changes in a PR, helping reviewers quickly understand what is being proposed.

Reviewing a SQL migration in a PR

One of the most common uses of GitHub Copilot Chat on GitHub.com is clarifying code changes during review. When reviewing a PR, you can ask GitHub Copilot to explain a code change without typing a prompt. In the diff file, click the down arrow in the upper-right corner and select **Copilot | Explain**. GitHub Copilot then generates a plain-language explanation of the selected change directly in the panel.

```
61  + -- ================================================
62  + -- Table: Flight
63  + -- Represents historical flights with relationships to Pilot, Plane, and
       Airfield
64  + -- ================================================
65  +  CREATE TABLE Flight (
66  +     FlightId INT IDENTITY(1,1) PR
67  +     FlightNumber VARCHAR(20) NOT
68  +     PilotId INT NOT NULL,
69  +     PlaneId INT NOT NULL,
70  +
71  +
72  +
73  +
74  +
75  +     Distance
76  +     Weather
77  +     Notes VA
78  +     CreatedD
79  +
80  +     -- Forei
81  +     CONSTRAI
        Pilot(PilotI
82  +     CONSTRAI
```

+ Add comment on lines R61-R78   Alt N

⊕ Suggest change on lines R61-R78

Ask about this diff

Explain

Attach to current thread

🐙 Copilot   >

Copy   ^ C

Select all   ^ A

Copy link   Alt ^ Y

Explain

🐙 **Explanation of the Selected Change**

The selection creates the `Flight` table in the `AviationDB` database. This table is designed to store historical flight records and includes the following columns:

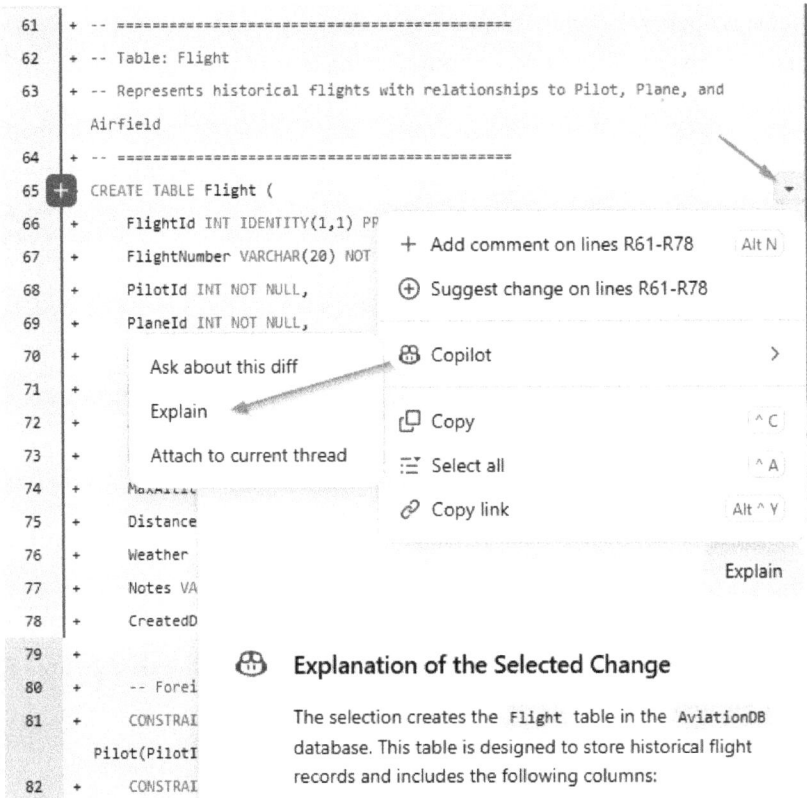

Figure 6.3: Copilot providing a plain-language explanation of a SQL migration in a PR diff

GitHub Copilot responds in plain language, breaking down schema changes or updates. This saves reviewers time and helps contributors focus discussions on design rather than deciphering the basics.

Explaining a CI failure in GitHub Actions

GitHub Copilot Chat is not limited to PRs. It also integrates directly with GitHub Actions, so you can investigate failing workflow runs without leaving the logs view.

When a job fails, you can expand the step, scroll to the error message, and click **Explain error**. Copilot then generates a plain-language breakdown of what went wrong and suggests how to fix it.

An example of a response might be the following:

```
This job failed because the build step is missing a dependency on Node.
js 18. You can fix this by adding a setup-node action before running your
build command.
```

This keeps troubleshooting close to the source of the problem without copying logs into another tool or asking teammates for help.

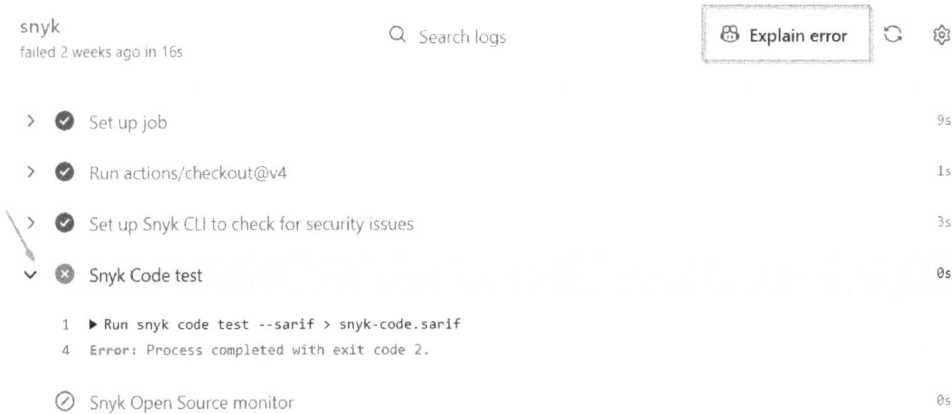

Figure 6.4: Chat explaining a failed workflow step in GitHub Actions

Onboarding and documentation

In long-running issues or discussions, GitHub Copilot Chat can quickly condense the thread into a structured summary. Instead of scrolling through dozens of comments, you can ask for the key decisions made so far and any open questions that remain. This is especially valuable for new contributors or teammates joining midstream who need to get up to speed fast.

An example prompt might look like this:

```
Summarize the main points of this actual discussion in this thread and
list any open questions.
```

GitHub Copilot will then generate a short, structured summary, highlighting what decisions have already been made and what remains unresolved. This helps newcomers orient themselves in active projects and ensures discussions stay accessible over time.

> Summarize the main points of this actual discussion in this thread and list any open questions

Here is a summary of the main points of the discussion in this pull request thread:

Main Points:

- The PR proposes a comprehensive test suite for FlightsController.
- 58 new tests were added, resulting in 59 total tests passing.
- Achieved 100% code coverage for FlightsController (exceeding the target of 85%).
- All five controller endpoints are covered with thorough validation.
- All flight status transitions and business logic are tested.
- Edge cases, including boundary values and error conditions, are handled.
- The tests utilize NSubstitute for mocking and FluentAssertions for validation.
- The test patterns follow those established in PlanesControllerTests.
- Repository interaction calls and exception handling are validated.
- Summary: The test suite provides robust validation of all endpoints, status transitions, fuel management, and error scenarios.

Open Questions:

- There are no explicit open questions listed in the PR description or metadata.
- If there are unresolved review comments, requested changes, or questions in the PR comments, those would be considered open questions (let me know if you want those extracted).

Figure 6.5: Copilot Chat summarizing a discussion thread and highlighting open questions

These examples show how GitHub Copilot Chat extends collaboration across GitHub.com. Whether you are reviewing schema changes in a PR, investigating a failing workflow, or summarizing a discussion thread, the chat window keeps the conversation tied to your project. Because chat history is saved to your account, Copilot provides continuity across sessions and devices, making it a consistent part of your workflow.

With chat established as a companion in PRs, workflows, and discussions, next let's explore how GitHub Copilot supports issues and threaded conversations more directly. Since issues are where most collaboration begins, this is a natural place for GitHub Copilot to help structure, summarize, and move work forward.

Issue and discussion support

Issues and discussions are the starting point for much of the collaboration that happens on GitHub.com. They capture bug reports, feature requests, design proposals, and day-to-day project questions. GitHub Copilot extends into these areas by helping you create structured issues from prompts, draft or summarize long conversations, and prepare responses that keep discussions moving. Instead of typing everything from scratch or reading through dozens of comments, you can rely on GitHub Copilot Chat on GitHub.com to draft, summarize, and clarify content — all while keeping you in control of the final message.

Drafting and summarizing issues

On GitHub.com, you don't get GitHub Copilot suggestions inline while filling out an issue form. Instead, you go to GitHub Copilot Chat in GitHub (accessed via the chat icon in the upper-right corner or via the immersive chat view) and state your request there. It will use the entire chat history of the active session to base the new issue on.

This is very helpful as you can now use any context from the repository or GitHub Actions workflow as extra information, for example, by asking GitHub Copilot questions on the reason why a workflow failed, let it search for the code in the repository that might have caused it, and then create an issue with all the gathered information. Having all that information will make it a lot easier to address the issue and implement the necessary changes.

For example, you could open GitHub Copilot Chat on GitHub.com and enter a prompt as follows:

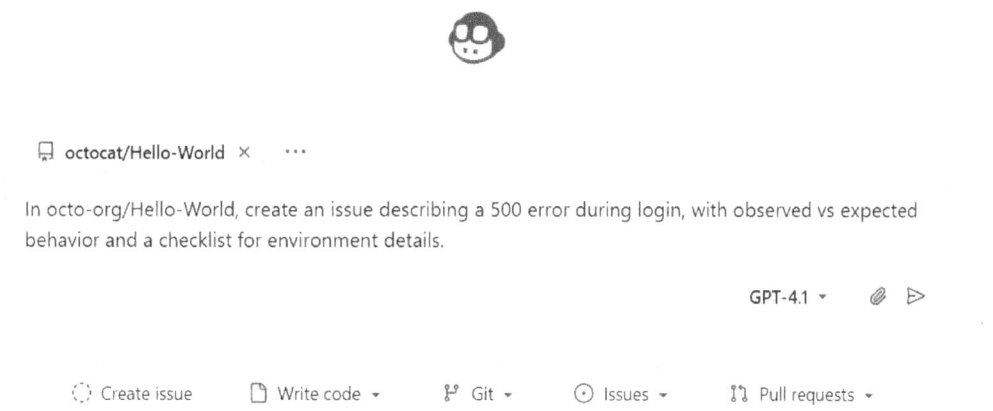

octocat/Hello-World ×   ···

In octo-org/Hello-World, create an issue describing a 500 error during login, with observed vs expected behavior and a checklist for environment details.

GPT-4.1 ▾   @ ▷

⟨⟩ Create issue   ▢ Write code ▾   ᛒ Git ▾   ⊙ Issues ▾   ⇅ Pull requests ▾

Figure 6.6: Using Copilot Chat prompt to create a new issue

GitHub Copilot generates a suggestion, including a title and body, and fills in fields from your repo's issue forms or templates if you have one. Here is what Copilot might generate:

```
## Observed Behavior
When attempting to log in, users encounter a 500 Internal Server Error.
The error occurs immediately after submitting valid account credentials.
No additional error message is displayed to the user.

## Expected Behavior
Users should be able to log in successfully and access their account
dashboard after submitting valid credentials.
Environment Details Checklist
[ ] Operating system (Windows, macOS, Linux)
[ ] Browser and browser version
[ ] Application version or commit hash
[ ] Any relevant logs or error messages
[ ] Steps to reproduce
Please fill out the checklist above to help diagnose the issue.
```

You review and refine the suggestion before hitting **Create**.

From the same chat interface, you can also ask GitHub Copilot Chat to summarize an issue thread or discussion, helping collaborators catch up quickly. You can also take the next step and assign the issue directly to Copilot, just as you would a teammate, so it can begin working on a fix or feature.

Automating responses and routine tasks

Maintainers often spend time reminding contributors to provide missing details, pointing them to documentation, or closing duplicate issues. With the integrated chat on GitHub.com, you can ask GitHub Copilot to draft those responses for you. Instead of typing the same text repeatedly, GitHub Copilot prepares a reply that you can review and edit before posting, allowing you to focus on adjusting the tone and details to fit the issue.

We can see an example here:

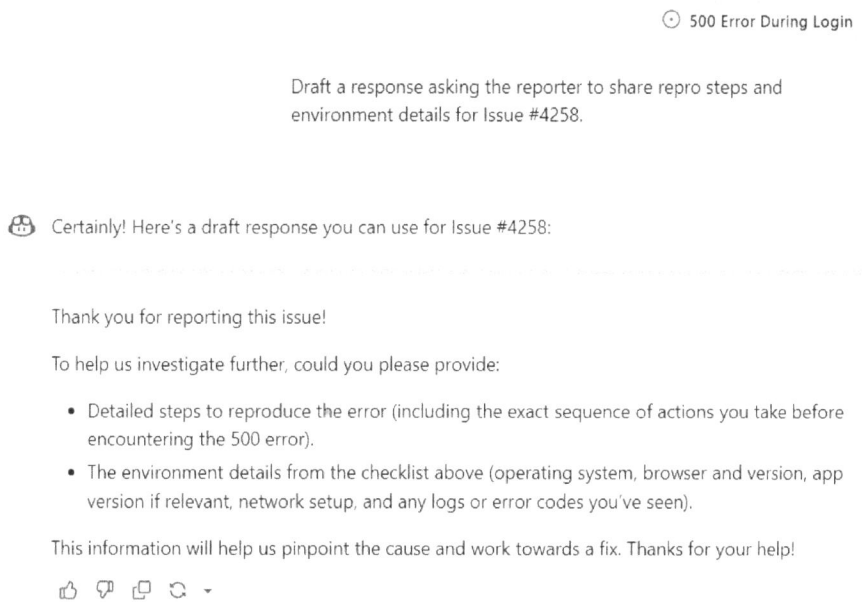

⊙ 500 Error During Login

Draft a response asking the reporter to share repro steps and
environment details for Issue #4258.

🐙 Certainly! Here's a draft response you can use for Issue #4258:

Thank you for reporting this issue!

To help us investigate further, could you please provide:

- Detailed steps to reproduce the error (including the exact sequence of actions you take before
  encountering the 500 error).
- The environment details from the checklist above (operating system, browser and version, app
  version if relevant, network setup, and any logs or error codes you've seen).

This information will help us pinpoint the cause and work towards a fix. Thanks for your help!

👍 👎 �📋 ↻ ▾

Figure 6.7: Using Copilot Chat for routine tasks

In this example, the user asked Copilot to write a response requesting repro steps and environment details for Issue #4258. GitHub Copilot generated a polite message thanking the reporter and asking for detailed steps to reproduce the error, along with environment details such as OS, browser, app version, network setup, and logs.

Supporting discussions

GitHub Discussions provide a forum-style space where contributors can share ideas, ask questions, or propose changes without opening an issue or PR. Unlike issues, which track concrete work items, discussions are often exploratory and can grow lengthy as multiple people weigh in.

In this context, GitHub Copilot Chat helps by condensing the conversation into a short, structured summary or by suggesting clarifying follow-up questions that move the thread forward. This is especially valuable for maintainers who want to respond quickly without parsing every reply.

For example, if a user posts a YAML snippet describing a deployment setup, you could ask GitHub Copilot Chat the following:

```
Summarize the main point of this discussion and suggest one clarifying
question I could ask.
```

The response may be as follows:

```
The user is configuring a Service to expose my-service internally. A
good clarifying question could be: Do you plan to expose this service
externally, or should it remain internal-only?
```

This approach keeps discussions moving and ensures responses are thoughtful and targeted.

Workflow example

GitHub Copilot can support both issues and discussions in practice, as follows:

1. A contributor reports a login bug by opening an issue in your repository.
2. As a maintainer, you open GitHub Copilot Chat and ask it to reformat the description into a well-structured issue with observed behavior, expected behavior, and reproduction steps.
3. Another user comments with extra context. You ask GitHub Copilot Chat to summarize the thread so far.
4. A maintainer needs to follow up with a request for logs. GitHub Copilot Chat drafts a Markdown response in the right tone, which you review before posting.

By giving GitHub Copilot enough context and then reviewing its drafts before publishing, you can handle issues and discussions more efficiently while still ensuring communication matches your project's standards.

We've seen how GitHub Copilot Chat can streamline issues and discussions, making it easier to capture reports, summarize conversations, and keep threads productive. These features shine at the early stages of collaboration, where ideas are raised and problems are first reported.

The next section looks at where much of the real decision-making happens: **pull requests**, or **PRs**. Here, GitHub Copilot moves beyond conversation to support reviews, generate summaries, suggest fixes, and integrate with security tools to improve code quality.

PR support

PRs are the heart of collaborative development on GitHub.com. GitHub Copilot steps into this space by helping authors and reviewers save time, clarify changes, and catch issues before code is merged. Whether you're opening a new PR, reviewing changes, or responding to feedback, GitHub Copilot offers a range of tools to simplify the workflow.

Summarizing PRs

When you create or edit a PR on GitHub.com, you can ask GitHub Copilot to generate a summary of the proposed changes. Inside the PR description field, click the Copilot icon (shown in *Figure 6.8*), then choose **Summarize the changes in this pull request**.

Copilot reviews the diff between the source and destination branches, along with commit messages and changed files, to produce a plain-language overview of the PR. The generated summary appears directly in the description box, where you can refine, expand, or edit it before submitting.

For teams with many contributors or complex code bases, this step helps reviewers understand the purpose of the PR without reading every file individually.

For example, if your PR touches on multiple areas, such as updating API validation and adding new tests, GitHub Copilot might draft something such as the following:

```
This PR refactors the API input validation logic to support new user
fields and adds comprehensive unit tests for edge cases. Updates
documentation to match new requirements.
```

This summary helps reviewers quickly grasp the intent of the PR without reading every file. It also streamlines onboarding for new contributors who may not be familiar with all parts of the code base.

Open a pull request

Create a new pull request by comparing changes across two branches. If you need to, you can also compare across forks.

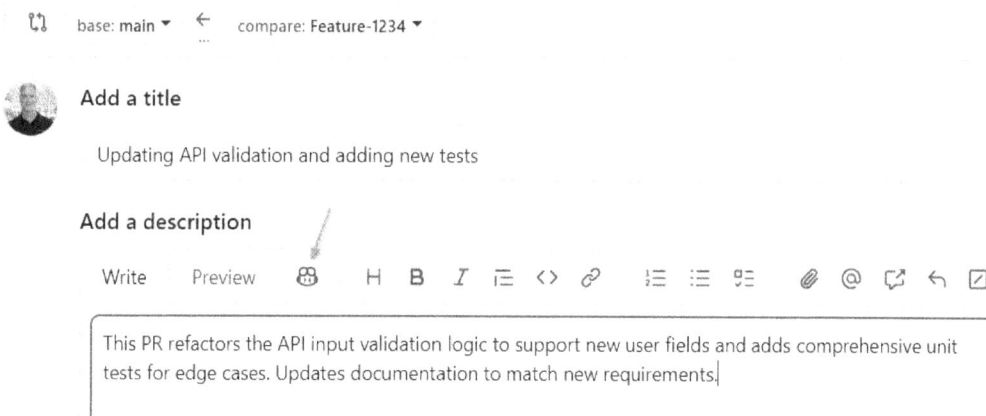

⇅ base: main ▾ ← compare: Feature-1234 ▾

Add a title

Updating API validation and adding new tests

Add a description

Write Preview ᴂ H B *I* ≔ <> ℰ ⍮ ⋮ ⍟ 🔗 @ ⤴ ↩ ☑

> This PR refactors the API input validation logic to support new user fields and adds comprehensive unit tests for edge cases. Updates documentation to match new requirements.

Figure 6.8: Using the Copilot icon on the PR description to generate a PR summary

Assigning GitHub Copilot as a reviewer

On GitHub.com, you can assign GitHub Copilot as a PR reviewer, using the **Reviewers** tab, highlighted in the following figure:

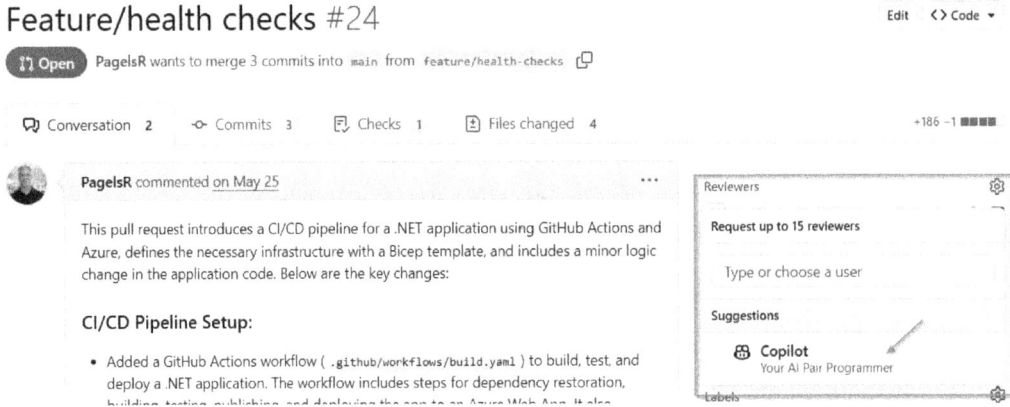

Figure 6.9: GitHub Copilot as a reviewer

Once added, GitHub Copilot can do the following:

- Analyze changes and leave review comments
- Flag potential bugs, inconsistencies, or style issues
- Suggest improvements such as better test coverage or simplified code
- Generate or update PR summaries to help reviewers understand the scope of changes

Unlike static review tools, GitHub Copilot supports an iterative conversation inside the PR. You or another reviewer can ask it to clarify a specific block of code, expand on one of its earlier comments, or provide additional examples. All of this happens directly in the PR thread, so the history of AI-assisted feedback and human discussion remains together in one place.

General example

Consider a small aviation service that stores flight records and exposes them through a repository class. In this PR, the team is fixing the method that looks up a flight by ID. The previous code used `ElementAt(id)`, which treats the ID as a zero-based index rather than matching on the flight's actual `Id` property.

When viewing the diff, GitHub Copilot explains the change in plain language: the fix replaces ElementAt(id) with FirstOrDefault(f => f.Id == id), so the lookup uses the correct identifier and returns the right record. This gives reviewers immediate context for why the change matters.

A reviewer can keep the conversation inside the PR with a targeted request, as follows:

```
@copilot clarify this block of code and explain why not to use
FirstOrDefault()
```

GitHub Copilot replies in the thread with follow-up details, such as trade-offs, edge cases, and safer alternatives. That back-and-forth helps the team confirm the reasoning without leaving the PR.

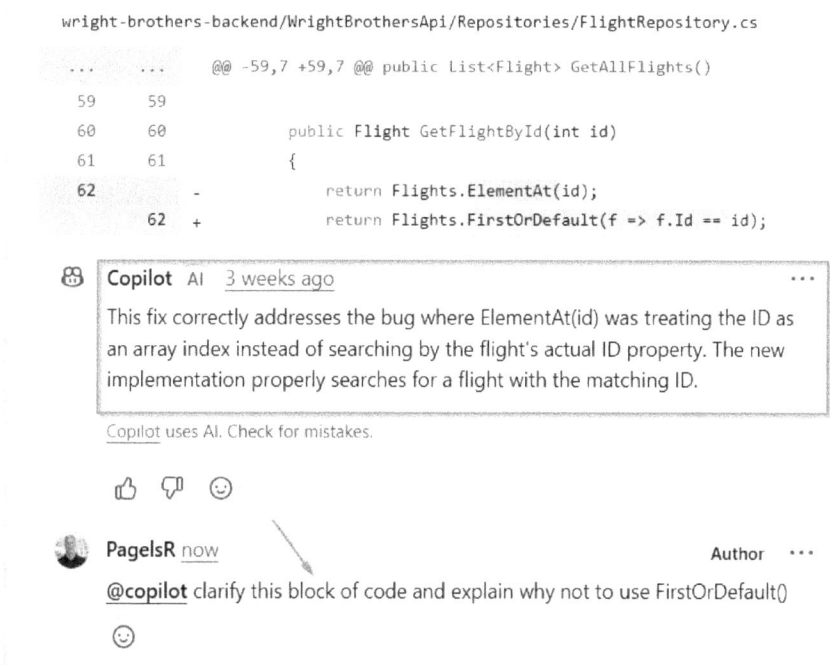

wright-brothers-backend/WrightBrothersApi/Repositories/FlightRepository.cs

```
...        ...        @@ -59,7 +59,7 @@ public List<Flight> GetAllFlights()
59         59
60         60                 public Flight GetFlightById(int id)
61         61                 {
62         -                      return Flights.ElementAt(id);
           62    +                return Flights.FirstOrDefault(f => f.Id == id);
```

Copilot AI   _3 weeks ago_   ...

This fix correctly addresses the bug where ElementAt(id) was treating the ID as an array index instead of searching by the flight's actual ID property. The new implementation properly searches for a flight with the matching ID.

Copilot uses AI. Check for mistakes.

👍 👎 ☺

PagelsR now   Author ...

@copilot clarify this block of code and explain why not to use FirstOrDefault()

☺

Figure 6.10: GitHub Copilot comment and reviewer follow-up in flight app PR

Keep in mind that each review request to Copilot consumes one premium request, so teams may want to be intentional about when to assign it. For more details on how premium requests work and how they're billed, see *Chapter 3*. Being mindful of this ensures you get the most value from Copilot's feedback while keeping usage within your plan's allocation.

Workflow example

Consider a multi-file PR that updates a Node.js backend and a CI workflow:

1. The author opens the PR and uses GitHub Copilot to generate a summary of the changes.

2. GitHub Copilot is added as a reviewer and flags edge cases along with missing documentation.

3. A human reviewer follows up by asking the assistant to clarify a specific code block, continuing the conversation directly in the PR thread.

4. A test fails in CI, and Copilot suggests a YAML adjustment to resolve the error.

5. The author applies the fix and pushes an update, and GitHub Copilot refreshes the PR summary automatically.

Clear commit messages and descriptive PR details help Copilot's summaries and comments stay accurate. This support can shorten feedback cycles and reduce routine reviewer work, but suggestions should always be validated against project conventions and business requirements before merging.

Reviewing and commenting on code

Once GitHub Copilot is added as a reviewer, you can interact with it directly in the PR view. During the review process, it can help by doing the following:

- Explaining diffs or complex code changes
- Highlighting potential issues, such as missing error handling or inconsistent styles
- Proposing inline suggestions or edits

For example, when reviewing a Python diff, you might highlight a section and prompt GitHub Copilot with the following:

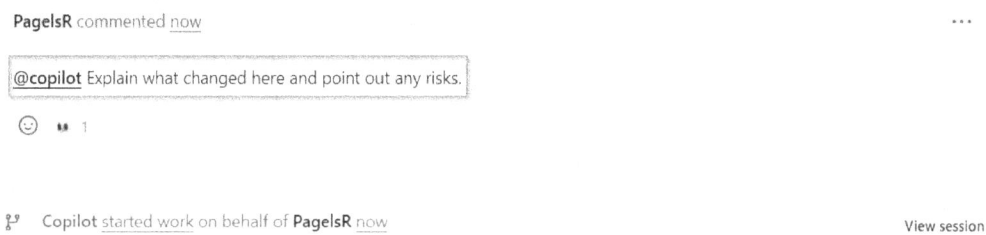

PagelsR commented now   ...

> **@copilot** Explain what changed here and point out any risks.

☺ ✎ 1

⅌ Copilot started work on behalf of **PagelsR** now   View session

Figure 6.11: Prompting Copilot in a PR review

It might reply with the following:

```
Replaces manual password hashing with a call to the new hash_password
utility. Make sure this function is compatible with existing hashes before
merging.
```

GitHub Copilot's suggestions aren't limited to code; it can also help draft Markdown comments that clarify reasoning, ask questions, update documentation, or suggest improvements, keeping review conversations focused and actionable.

> Keep in mind that each time GitHub Copilot posts comments during a PR review, it consumes another premium request from your quota. Be sure to monitor your usage if you want to stay within your monthly allowance.

Autofix

Autofix can actually refer to two related capabilities:

- One appears during PR reviews, where GitHub Copilot suggests inline fixes based on the code you're reviewing
- The other is part of GitHub Advanced Security, where GitHub Copilot Autofix responds to code scanning alerts with targeted remediation steps

They look similar in the UI, but they are triggered by different signals and serve different purposes. Let's take a look at them both.

PR suggestions

During a PR review, GitHub Copilot can notice risky or inefficient code and propose inline fixes directly in the **Files changed** view. These suggestions are shown with an **Autofix** label, but they are not the same as GitHub Copilot Autofix in GitHub Advanced Security. Instead, they are part of the broader set of Copilot's PR review features.

For example, if a PR includes an unsafe SQL statement, Copilot might suggest parameterization right in the diff. You can apply the fix instantly, edit it, or ask Copilot to refine it. This keeps the entire detection–fix–review loop inside the PR.

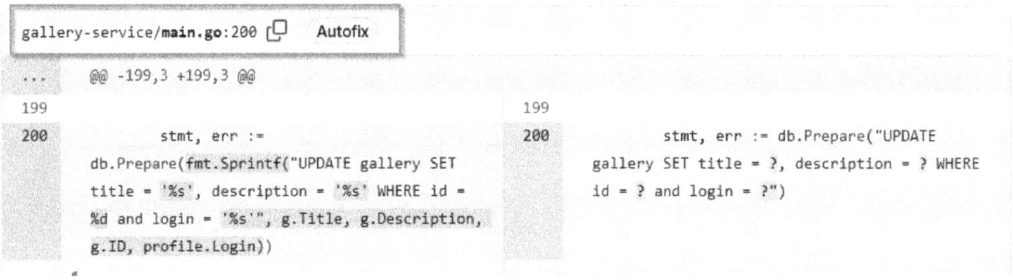

```
gallery-service/main.go:200 [ ]   Autofix

...        @@ -199,3 +199,3 @@
199                                          199
200            stmt, err :=                   200            stmt, err := db.Prepare("UPDATE
           db.Prepare(fmt.Sprintf("UPDATE gallery SET        gallery SET title = ?, description = ? WHERE
           title = '%s', description = '%s' WHERE id =        id = ? and login = ?")
           %d and login = '%s'", g.Title, g.Description,
           g.ID, profile.Login))
```

Figure 6.12: Copilot Autofix suggesting a parameterized SQL query to prevent injection

> Generating an Autofix as part of a review can consume a premium request. See *Chapter 3* for details on usage and limits.

GitHub Copilot Autofix in GitHub Advanced Security

The other context for Autofix is within GitHub Advanced Security. Here, Autofix responds when code-scanning alerts flag a vulnerability by proposing a targeted remediation. From the alert details page, you may see a **Generate fix** button. Selecting this triggers Copilot Autofix to draft a remediation plan and open a PR for review:

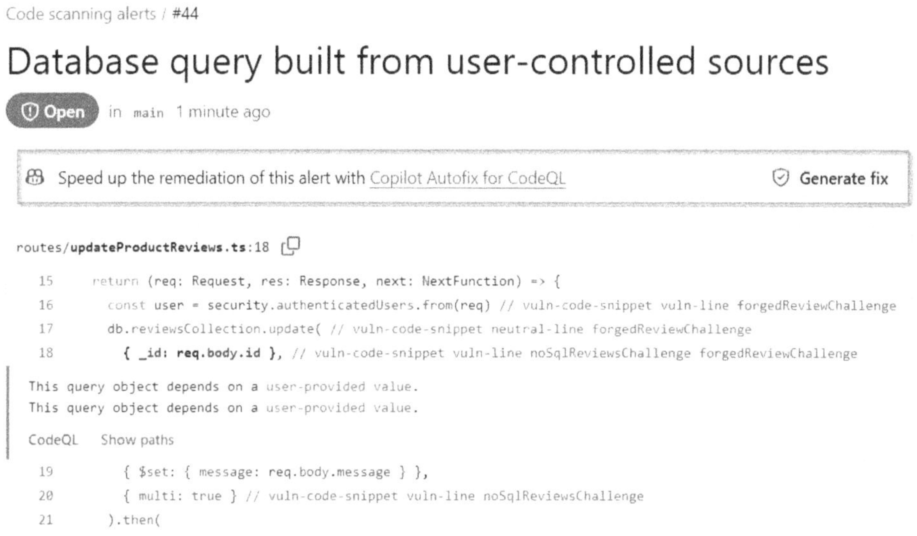

Code scanning alerts / #44

Database query built from user-controlled sources

⊘ Open   in main 1 minute ago

⊞ Speed up the remediation of this alert with Copilot Autofix for CodeQL   ⊘ **Generate fix**

---

routes/**updateProductReviews.ts**:18 ⊡

```
15      return (req: Request, res: Response, next: NextFunction) => {
16        const user = security.authenticatedUsers.from(req) // vuln-code-snippet vuln-line forgedReviewChallenge
17        db.reviewsCollection.update( // vuln-code-snippet neutral-line forgedReviewChallenge
18          { _id: req.body.id }, // vuln-code-snippet vuln-line noSqlReviewsChallenge forgedReviewChallenge
```

This query object depends on a user-provided value.
This query object depends on a user-provided value.

CodeQL   Show paths

```
19          { $set: { message: req.body.message } },
20          { multi: true } // vuln-code-snippet vuln-line noSqlReviewsChallenge
21        ).then(
```

Figure 6.13: Generate fix directly from a security alert in GitHub Advanced Security

> This distinction is important. A fix suggested by GitHub Copilot during a PR review is based on the changed code in the diff. A fix suggested by GitHub Copilot Autofix is tied to a GitHub Advanced Security alert produced by code scanning, and it follows the alert's guidance to produce a targeted remediation.

When the suggestion is ready, select the **Commit to new branch** option to apply the fix. The proposed patch opens as a PR in your repository, where you review it like any other change, request adjustments if needed, and then approve and merge.

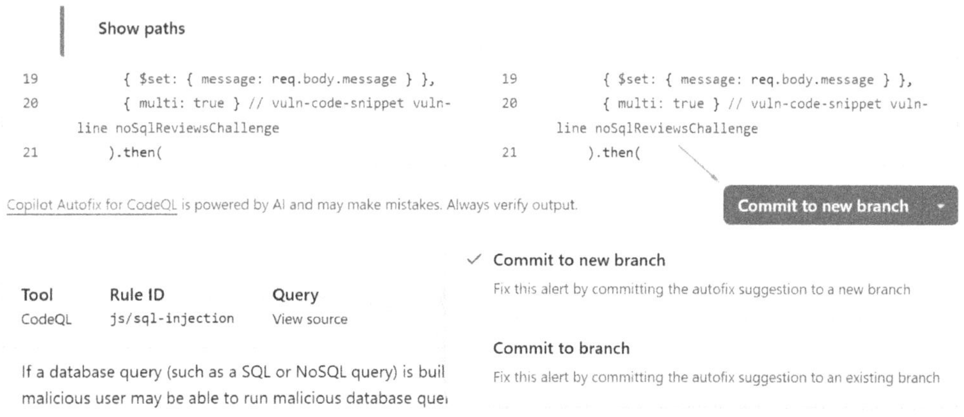

Show paths

```
19          { $set: { message: req.body.message } },          19          { $set: { message: req.body.message } },
20          { multi: true } // vuln-code-snippet vuln-          20          { multi: true } // vuln-code-snippet vuln-
          line noSqlReviewsChallenge                                       line noSqlReviewsChallenge
21        ).then(                                            21        ).then(
```

Copilot Autofix for CodeQL is powered by AI and may make mistakes. Always verify output.   **Commit to new branch** ▾

                                                            ✓ **Commit to new branch**

Tool	Rule ID	Query	Fix this alert by committing the autofix suggestion to a new branch
CodeQL	js/sql-injection	View source	

                                                               Commit to branch

If a database query (such as a SQL or NoSQL query) is buil   Fix this alert by committing the autofix suggestion to an existing branch
malicious user may be able to run malicious database que

Figure 6.14: Commit fix to a new branch and PR

As an example, for an alert titled `SQL query built from user-controlled sources`, GitHub Copilot Autofix provides the following explanation:

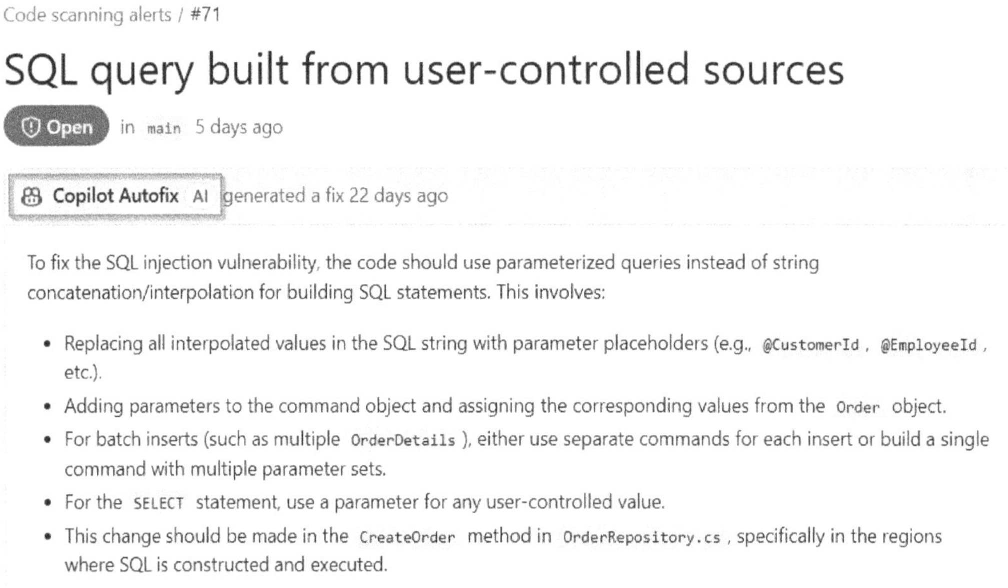

Code scanning alerts / #71

SQL query built from user-controlled sources

⚠ Open   in `main` 5 days ago

🐙 **Copilot Autofix** AI generated a fix 22 days ago

To fix the SQL injection vulnerability, the code should use parameterized queries instead of string concatenation/interpolation for building SQL statements. This involves:

- Replacing all interpolated values in the SQL string with parameter placeholders (e.g., `@CustomerId`, `@EmployeeId`, etc.).
- Adding parameters to the command object and assigning the corresponding values from the `Order` object.
- For batch inserts (such as multiple `OrderDetails`), either use separate commands for each insert or build a single command with multiple parameter sets.
- For the `SELECT` statement, use a parameter for any user-controlled value.
- This change should be made in the `CreateOrder` method in `OrderRepository.cs`, specifically in the regions where SQL is constructed and executed.

Figure 6.15: GitHub Copilot Autofix remediation details for a SQL injection alert in GitHub Advanced Security

> GitHub Copilot Autofix supports a growing set of languages and query families. If a finding is outside current coverage, Autofix may not offer a patch even though the alert exists.

After fixing a single alert, you can take the same idea to a larger scale with GitHub security campaigns. This is where GitHub Copilot Autofix really shines.

GitHub security campaigns let administrators and security leads group related vulnerabilities across many repositories and handle remediation as one effort. Instead of working alert by alert, you define the scope, track progress in one place, and apply fixes consistently across all affected code bases.

GitHub Copilot Autofix can be integrated into security campaigns, giving maintainers the option to generate fixes for supported vulnerabilities in bulk. When a campaign is launched, you can choose **Generate fix** for eligible alerts, such as SQL injection, unsafe deserialization, or command injection. GitHub Copilot then prepares PRs across the affected repositories so teams can review and merge consistent, targeted remediations.

GitHub Copilot Autofix can be integrated into security campaigns to generate suggestions for supported alerts at scale. Campaigns submit alerts to Autofix so maintainers can review the proposed remediations. When you decide to proceed, you create the PRs from the alert or campaign context and then review and merge them like any other change.

This integration extends Autofix beyond individual alerts, making it practical for enterprise teams to keep large code bases secure. Instead of opening dozens of PRs manually, security leads can trigger Autofix from the campaign view, and teams can then review and merge the generated patches as part of their normal workflow.

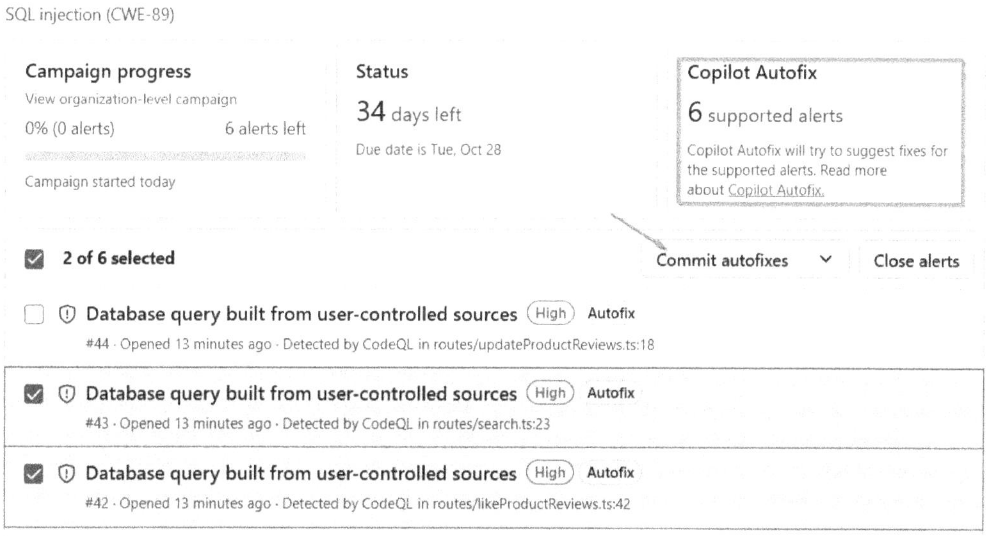

SQL injection (CWE-89)

Campaign progress
View organization-level campaign
0% (0 alerts)   6 alerts left
Campaign started today

Status
34 days left
Due date is Tue, Oct 28

Copilot Autofix
6 supported alerts
Copilot Autofix will try to suggest fixes for the supported alerts. Read more about Copilot Autofix.

2 of 6 selected   Commit autofixes ∨   Close alerts

☐ ⓘ **Database query built from user-controlled sources** (High) Autofix
#44 · Opened 13 minutes ago · Detected by CodeQL in routes/updateProductReviews.ts:18

☑ ⓘ **Database query built from user-controlled sources** (High) Autofix
#43 · Opened 13 minutes ago · Detected by CodeQL in routes/search.ts:23

☑ ⓘ **Database query built from user-controlled sources** (High) Autofix
#42 · Opened 13 minutes ago · Detected by CodeQL in routes/likeProductReviews.ts:42

Figure 6.16: GitHub Copilot Autofix integrated into a GitHub security campaign

You can learn more about GitHub Advanced Security here: `https://docs.github.com/en/get-started/learning-about-github/about-github-advanced-security`.

With PR reviews and security alerts covered, it's clear that Copilot is already capable of handling much of the repetitive and detail-oriented work in development. Autofix shows how individual fixes and even campaign-scale remediations can be generated and reviewed without slowing teams down.

The next step is broader automation. In the following section, we'll look at the GitHub Copilot Coding Agent, which allows you to assign entire issues to Copilot. Here, Copilot goes beyond suggesting edits to actually completing development tasks, running in a secure environment, and opening PRs that fit directly into your team's workflow.

Coding Agent on GitHub.com

The GitHub Copilot Coding Agent brings automation directly into the browser by letting you delegate entire issues to Copilot. Instead of drafting fixes or writing code yourself, you can assign a task in GitHub.com and Copilot will take it from there. The agent runs in a secure cloud environment, makes changes on a new branch, opens a draft PR, and tags you for review. This turns issues into actionable work items that can move forward without waiting for human availability, while still keeping you in control of the final review and merge.

Coding Agent versus Agent Mode

GitHub offers two related but distinct ways of handing off work to AI: the **Coding Agent** and **Agent Mode**. Both fall under the broader idea of agentic AI, where you describe a task and the system iterates until it produces a result. The difference lies in where the work happens and how it is applied:

- **Agent Mode (in the IDE):** You select Agent Mode in your editor's chat panel and describe the task, and Copilot makes changes directly in your local workspace. It applies edits, runs tools, and keeps iterating until the job is complete.

- **Coding Agent (on GitHub.com):** You delegate tasks from the browser, your editor, or even the GitHub mobile app. Copilot then runs asynchronously in a secure GitHub Actions environment, making changes in a branch and opening a PR for review.

This distinction matters because Agent Mode is best for interactive, local edits where you want to stay hands-on, while the Coding Agent is better suited for handing off contained tasks that can be automated from end to end and tracked in GitHub.

How the Coding Agent works on GitHub.com

GitHub Copilot's Coding Agent lets you delegate development tasks directly from the browser, with no IDE required. This capability is only available to paid Copilot plans (Pro+ and Enterprise), and administrators may need to enable the policy at the organization or enterprise level.

You can delegate tasks in three main ways:

- **Assign an issue to Copilot**: Open the issue, use the **Assignees** panel, and select **Copilot**. This works just like assigning a human teammate. Copilot will read the issue details and begin working in the background.

- **Use the Agents panel**: GitHub recently introduced the **Agents** panel. This pop-up overlay acts like a mission control center. From any GitHub.com page, you can open the panel, describe the task in natural language, choose the repository and branch, and launch the agent. Under the hood, GitHub Copilot spins up a secure workspace powered by GitHub Actions, applies changes, and creates a PR for review. The panel also displays live session details and logs so you can follow the progress without leaving your current context.

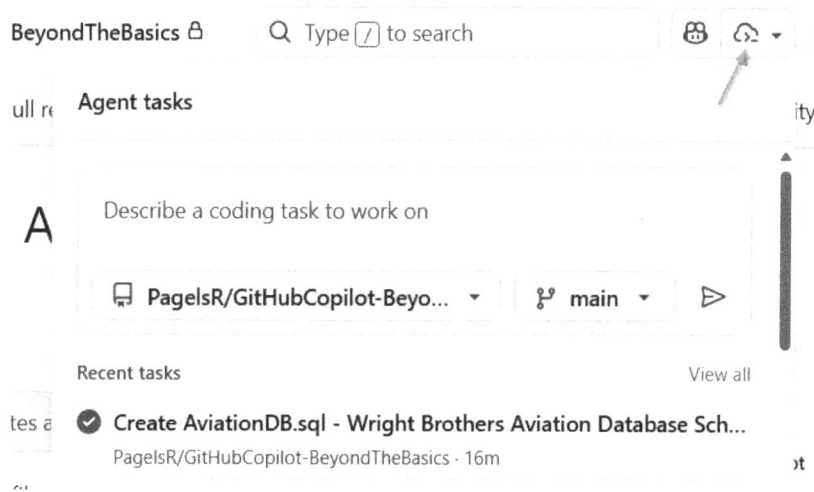

Figure 6.17: Delegate task in the Agents panel

- **Assign from your editor (if supported)**: Some editors provide integration points to delegate tasks directly to the Coding Agent while you are working locally, making it easier to keep browser and IDE workflows aligned. (As of September 1st, 2025, only VS Code allows tasks to be assigned to the Coding Agent directly.)

Once assigned, the agent does the following:

- Spins up a secure workspace in GitHub Actions, drawing from your assigned minutes (free for public repos, or tracked against your private repo budget)

- Applies changes in a new branch, runs checks, iterates if needed, and creates a draft PR with a WIP title

- Uses one premium request per session, regardless of how many edits or files are involved
- Tags you for review and logs session details, which you can inspect during or after execution.

You can follow the agent's progress in multiple places:

- **Agents panel** or **Agents page**: Displays live session status, logs, and task history. This is the most detailed view, showing exactly what steps Copilot is taking in the GitHub Actions-powered workspace.

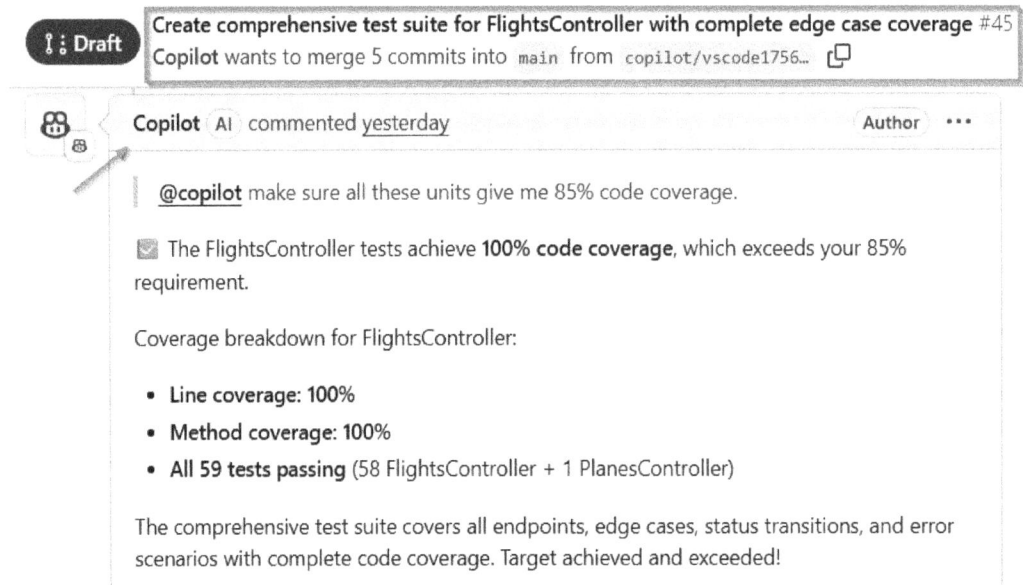

Figure 6.18: Tracking a Coding Agent session from the Agents panel on GitHub.com

- **Issue's Development panel and PRs view**: Lists the branch created by the agent and the associated draft PR. This view is helpful if you are following along with team discussions while the agent works.
- **Editor integration (if supported)**: In some IDEs, you can track session progress or be notified when the agent's PR is ready for review.

Once the PR is open, you interact with it just as you would with any other PR. At this stage, you can do the following:

- Review the diff like any other PR
- Request changes or edits
- Mention @copilot in comments to instruct the agent to refine or extend its work

Once the PR is open, you can review the diff like any other PR, but you also have the option to interact with GitHub Copilot to refine or extend its work. By mentioning @copilot directly in the PR comments, you can ask for clarifications, request improvements, or suggest changes. As shown in the following figure, Copilot not only responds to the request but also begins working on updates in the background, with its progress tracked in the session view.

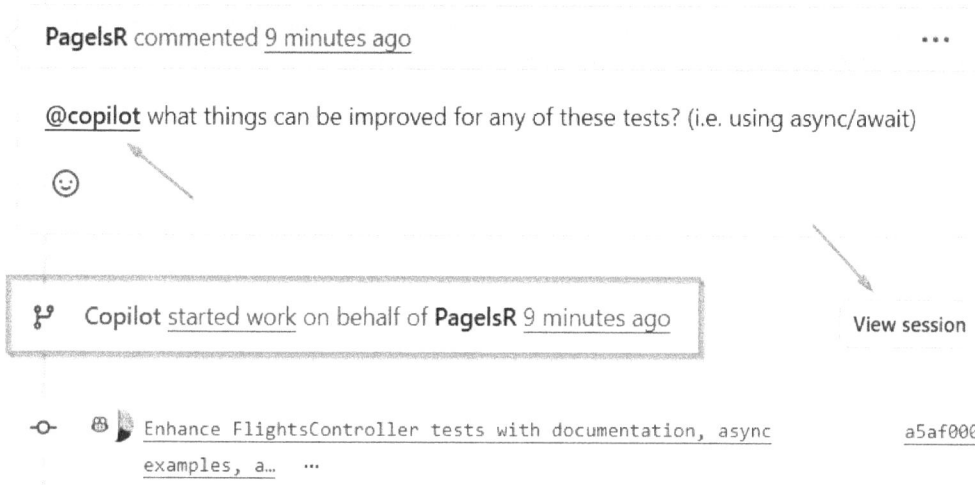

Figure 6.19: Reviewing and refining a coding agent's PR for the FlightsController test suite, where Copilot responds to a reviewer's comment and starts implementing improvements

Viewing the Coding Agent session

When a Coding Agent opens a PR, you can interact directly in the thread. For example, you might mention @copilot in a comment to request refinements, as shown in *Figure 6.19*. From the same location, clicking the **View session** button takes you into the session log.

This opens the **Agents** panel or **Agents** page, where you can track the full history of what the agent is doing. The following figure shows this detailed view, including each iteration of the task, the session duration, and the number of premium requests consumed.

← Back to pull request #45

Create comprehensive test suite for FlightsController with complete edge case coverage and async/await best practices #45

Sessions

- ✅ Review from @Pagel... 8m 32s
- ◼ Review from @PagelsR 1m 27s
- ✅ Review from @PagelsR 5m 20s
- ✅ Initial implementation 10m 29s

4 premium requests used in 4 ⓘ
sessions

Status	Duration	Premium requests	...
Ready for review	**8m 32s**	**1** ⓘ	

> Start 'github-mcp-server' MCP server

> Start 'playwright' MCP server

I'll analyze the comments and explore the repository to understand the current state

Figure 6.20: Coding Agent session view showing task history, MCP servers, session duration, and usage of Actions minutes and premium requests

Monitoring the session gives you visibility into progress, helps you catch mistakes early, and ensures confidence in the automation before merging.

Every session runs inside a secure GitHub Actions workspace, so it consumes Actions minutes from your account or organization. Public repositories are free, while private repositories count toward usage. Each @copilot interaction in a PR or issue also consumes a premium request. For a deeper explanation of premium requests and limits, see *Chapter 3*.

Where it fits best

The Coding Agent is most effective for well-scoped tasks: fixing a bug described in an issue, adding or extending tests, or updating documentation. It saves time on routine work while keeping humans in control of the final review. The better you have your coding foundation in order, the better the results with the Coding Agent will be. That means setting up a good README with information, adding custom instructions to follow, documenting how to build, test, and run the application, and having enough tests to validate the results.

All these things can be used by the Coding Agent to figure out what to do and how to implement the changes, including running the tests to validate whether everything still works correctly. If you only have a badly documented application with "spaghetti code," the Coding Agent will have a hard time figuring out what to do, and might even fail to do so.

How it fits into your workflow

The Coding Agent is fully integrated into GitHub.com and built for browser-first collaboration. Teams often use it to do the following:

- Speed up routine fixes

- Enhance test coverage

- Handle minor enhancements quickly without waiting for human reviewers

It also fits naturally into workflows on the go. From the GitHub mobile app, you can review issues and PRs on your phone or tablet. If an issue already contains enough detail, you can assign it to the Coding Agent directly, letting it begin work while you're away from your desktop. This makes it easy to delegate tasks whenever you have a few minutes, without breaking momentum.

AI can handle heavy lifting, but it's still important to review every generated PR to confirm the changes align with project standards. Remember that responses may not always be accurate, which makes the final review step critical.

Additional configuration options for the Coding Agent

Beyond the basics of assigning and tracking a session, there are a few advanced settings that give you more control over how the Coding Agent operates:

- **Locked down network settings by default**: Coding Agent sessions are restricted by default to ensure security. They run in a locked-down network with no internet access, reducing the risk of external calls or data leaks. You should only open up network access when absolutely necessary, such as when testing code that relies on external APIs.

- **MCP server config for the session**: You can extend a session by connecting it to an MCP server. This allows the agent to fetch additional context or integrate with external systems, such as internal documentation or APIs. Configuration is done at the organization or repository level so that sessions can securely pull in the right data when executing tasks.

With the Coding Agent, you've seen how GitHub Copilot can take on assigned issues, generate code, and move work forward autonomously inside PRs. This level of automation makes GitHub Copilot feel like an active contributor on your team, but it's only one part of the picture.

Beyond coding tasks, GitHub Copilot continues to expand its presence on GitHub.com with features that improve daily collaboration, streamline project management, and surface insights at scale. In the next section, we'll look at these additional capabilities, from bulk summaries and metrics dashboards to experimental previews that hint at where the platform is heading.

Additional GitHub.com Copilot features

Beyond issue automation and PR support, GitHub Copilot on GitHub.com continues to evolve with features that simplify daily development and streamline project workflows. Some of these capabilities are already available, while others are still in preview, but all are designed to help teams save time and stay focused.

Bulk summaries and comments

Copilot Chat on GitHub.com can give you high-level overviews and also help draft clear, targeted comments. These capabilities help teams process information faster and respond more effectively without having to manually skim every detail or draft each reply from scratch.

During triage sessions, release planning, or when catching up after being away, you can request concise overviews of PRs, discussions, or even an entire repository.

For example, in immersive Copilot Chat, you can ask the following:

```
@workspace Summarize the purpose of this repository and its key modules.
```

GitHub Copilot then pulls context from across the repo and generates a summary that helps you quickly come up to speed on the project.

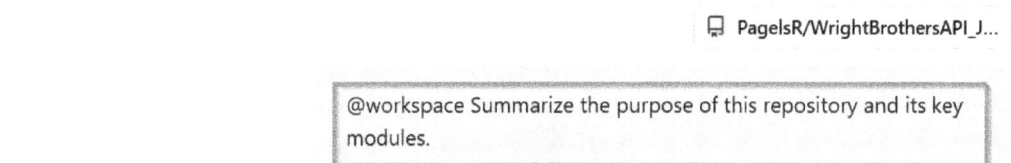

🖥 PagelsR/WrightBrothersAPI_J...

> @workspace Summarize the purpose of this repository and its key modules.

🔗 20 references ⌄

The PagelsR/WrightBrothersAPI_JavaScript repository is designed as an interactive workshop to help developers master GitHub Copilot and Copilot Chat for AI-powered coding in JavaScript. Its purpose is to teach best practices in code autocompletion, unit test generation, debugging, refactoring, documentation automation, and prompt engineering through hands-on labs.

Key Modules and Labs:

Figure 6.21: GitHub Copilot Chat summarizing a repository

Or in a GitHub discussion or issue thread, you can type the following:

```
Summarize the main points of this discussion thread so far.
```

Copilot will condense the back-and-forth into a digestible recap so you can focus on the next steps.

In addition to summarizing, GitHub Copilot can help you participate in the conversation. You can ask it to draft clarifying questions, provide a gentle nudge for missing details, or phrase a response in polished Markdown that fits the project's tone.

For example, in a long discussion thread, you might say the following:

```
Suggest a clarifying question I could ask in this thread.
```

Copilot may return something like the following:

```
Have you confirmed whether this deployment needs to run in staging before
production?
```

This combination of summaries and comment drafting helps maintainers and reviewers stay productive without parsing every detail themselves, while still keeping final oversight in human hands.

Context-aware suggestions in code and documentation

GitHub Copilot adapts to the context of your repository when making suggestions. This means that when you are editing a code block, YAML workflow, SQL script, or documentation file, the output reflects the formatting, naming conventions, and patterns that already exist in your project. By aligning with your team's established style, Copilot reduces friction and helps keep contributions consistent.

For example, suppose you are updating a SQL migration script. You can ask the following in the chat panel:

```
Add a column for last_login with a default value of NULL and follow the
same style as the existing columns.
```

GitHub Copilot generates the SQL statement in line with your repository's style, ensuring consistency with the way other schema updates are written.

Metrics and activity dashboards

Admins on Business and Enterprise plans can use GitHub Copilot dashboards on GitHub.com to monitor adoption, usage patterns, and costs. These views make it easier to manage licenses, track spending, and understand how Copilot is used across teams.

The dashboards are divided into three main views:

- **Copilot IDE usage**: Highlights adoption and activity trends across licensed developers
- **Premium request analytics**: Tracks billed premium requests, costs, and usage broken down by product
- **Detailed usage patterns**: Shows chat modes, code completions, and daily model usage to reveal how Copilot is being used in practice

Together, these dashboards provide both the financial and behavioral perspectives, helping admins balance cost control with understanding how Copilot drives developer productivity.

Copilot IDE usage

The Copilot IDE usage dashboard highlights how developers are adopting GitHub Copilot in their IDEs. You can track the number of active users, see which agent features are being used, and review daily and weekly activity trends. This helps admins distinguish between license allocation and real usage, so you can reallocate licenses if needed.

To navigate to this view, take the following steps:

1. From the top right of GitHub.com, click your profile photo, choose **Your enterprises**, and then select the enterprise you manage.
2. In the **Enterprise** sidebar, open **Insights**.
3. Select **Copilot**, then choose **Copilot IDE Usage**.

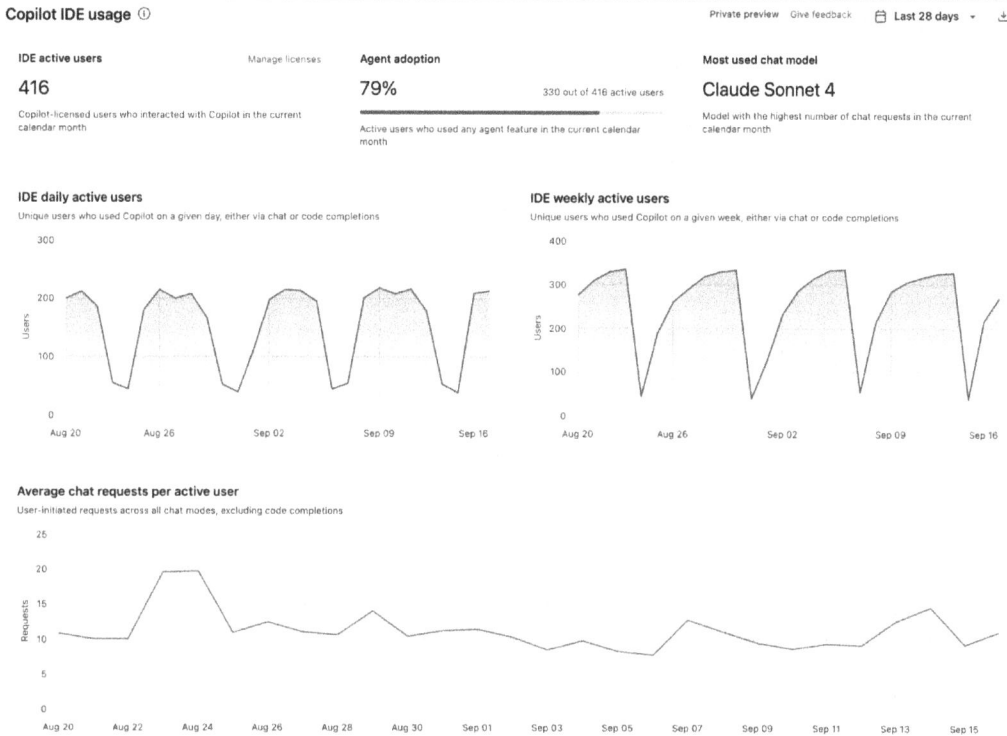

Figure 6.22: GitHub Copilot activity dashboard

To view this image in color

Use the free color PDF edition included with your purchase. Refer to the *Free Benefits with Your Book* section in the Preface for details.

Access is typically available to enterprise admins and billing managers. Some organizations may enable a read-only analytics viewer role. Availability can vary by plan and permissions.

Premium request analytics

The premium request analytics dashboard focuses on cost visibility. It shows how many premium requests have been consumed, which products (Copilot, Coding Agent, or Spark) are driving usage, and the associated billing amounts. Admins can use this report to track spending trends and plan budgets.

To navigate to this view, do the following:

1. In the upper-right corner of GitHub.com, click your profile photo, then choose **Your organizations**.

2. Next to the organization you want to manage, click **Settings**.

3. In the left sidebar, open **Billing and Licensing**, then click **Usage**.

4. Select **Copilot premium request analytics**.

Copilot premium request analytics   ⬇ Get usage report
Usage analytics for Copilot premium requests in your enterprise.

🔍 model: claude-sonnet-3.7   ✖   Group by: **Products** ▾   Timeframe: **Current month** ▾

Total billed amount	**Billed premium requests**	**Included premium requests consumed**
$63.08	915	1,176
Spend for Copilot premium request usage for Jun 1 - Jun 30, 2025	Billed requests exceeding the premium requests usage included with Copilot licenses.	Included premium requests used by selected model. Monthly limits reset in 1 day on Jul 1, 2025.

Claude Sonnet 3.7 usage grouped by products   ...
Jun 1 - Jun 30, 2025

— Copilot — · Coding agent ···· Spark

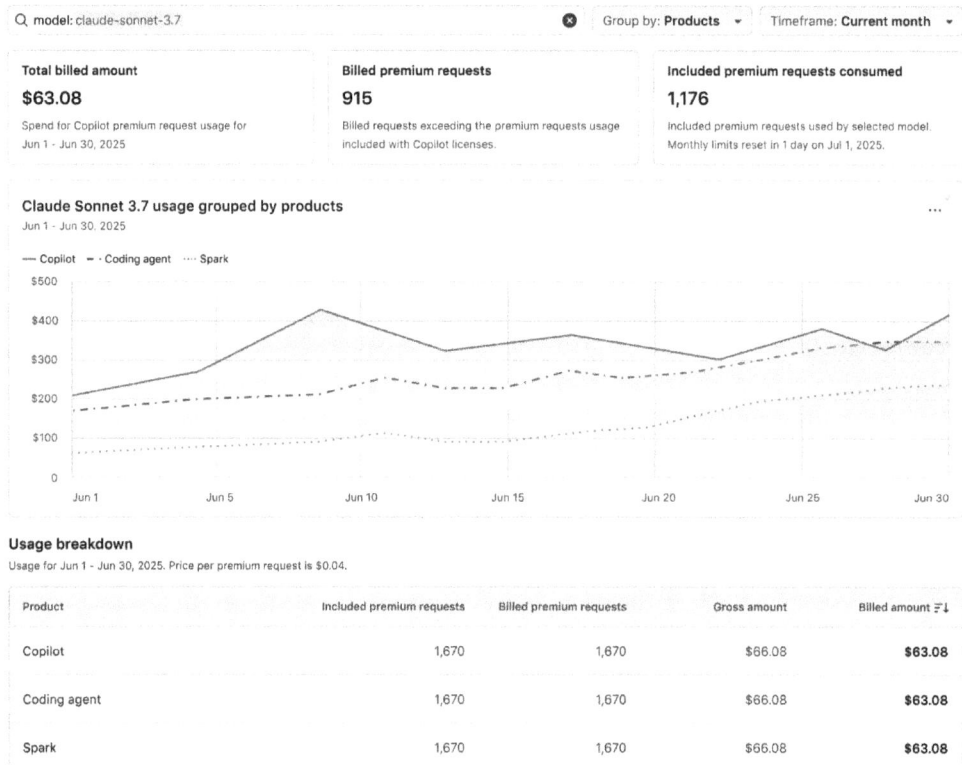

Usage breakdown
Usage for Jun 1 - Jun 30, 2025. Price per premium request is $0.04.

Product	Included premium requests	Billed premium requests	Gross amount	Billed amount ⇣
Copilot	1,670	1,670	$66.08	**$63.08**
Coding agent	1,670	1,670	$66.08	**$63.08**
Spark	1,670	1,670	$66.08	**$63.08**

Figure 6.23: Copilot premium request analytics dashboard showing usage and billing details

To view this image in color

Use the free color PDF edition included with your purchase. Refer to the *Free Benefits with Your Book* section in the *Preface* for details.

Detailed Copilot usage patterns

This dashboard provides a more granular view of how GitHub Copilot is being used day to day. It includes charts for requests per chat mode (Ask, Edit, or Agent), code completions and acceptance rates, and daily model usage. These insights show not just whether GitHub Copilot is being used but how it is shaping developer workflows.

To navigate to this view, take these steps:

1. From the top right of GitHub.com, open your profile photo menu, choose **Your enterprises**, and then select the enterprise account you manage.
2. In the **Enterprise** sidebar, open **Insights**.
3. Then select **Copilot** and choose **Usage patterns**.

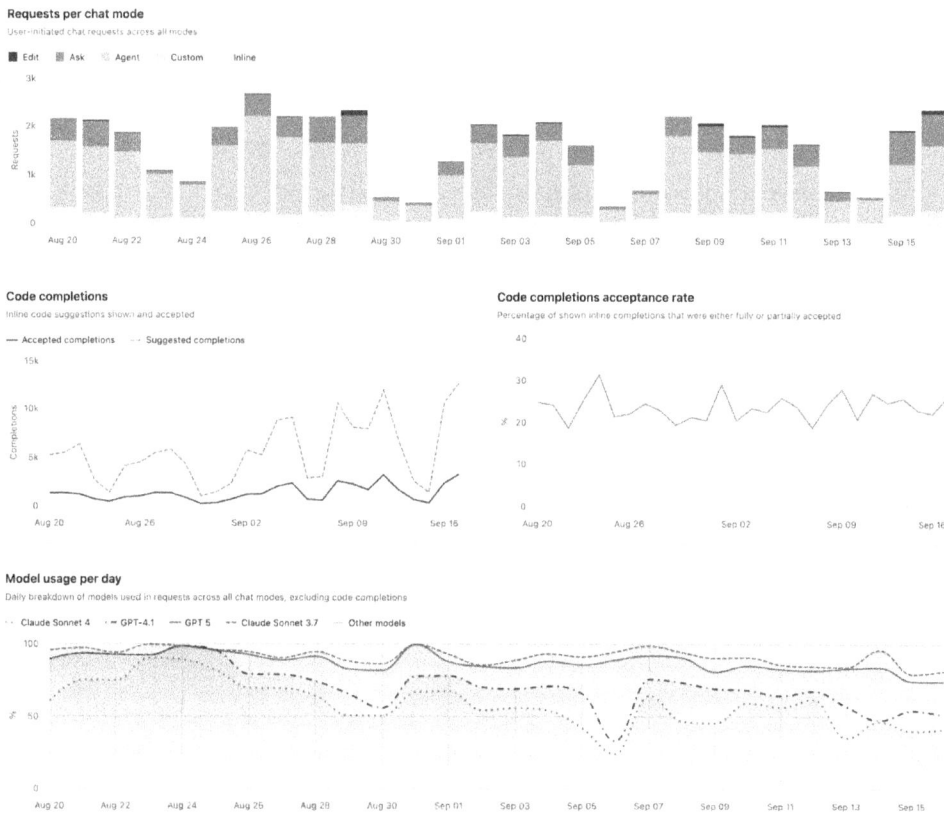

Figure 6.24: Detailed Copilot usage dashboard with chat modes, completions, and model trends

> Access is typically available to enterprise admins and billing managers. Some organizations may enable a custom analytics viewer role for read-only access. Availability can vary by plan and permissions.

> For a full walk-through of these types of reports and how to interpret them, see *Chapter 3*.

Early access and experimental features

GitHub regularly releases Copilot enhancements as limited previews for select users and organizations. These previews give teams a chance to try out new capabilities and provide feedback on features that may become generally available in the future.

As of October 2025, here are some notable experimental features:

- **Mission control with the Agents panel**: GitHub introduced an **Agents** panel that lets you start, manage, and monitor AI tasks from any page on GitHub. This pop-up overlay allows you to describe a task, launch it, and track progress, all within your current workflow.

- **Better PR handling and multi-file reasoning**: The Coding Agent now offers more reliable support with PR reviews and stronger multi-file contextual understanding.

- **Smarter triage and project linkages**: Developers can preview advanced triage tools that suggest issue priorities or close stale discussions. There is also emerging support for linking GitHub Copilot-generated PRs or tasks directly to GitHub project boards, sprints, or roadmaps.

> To stay up to date on these previews and sign up for new releases, check out `https://docs.github.com/en/copilot`.

Integration with team workflows

As GitHub Copilot features on GitHub.com evolve, teams are finding powerful ways to blend AI automation with existing workflows, security measures, and project management tools.

You can now use GitHub Copilot alongside GitHub Actions, branch protection rulesets, and custom labels to create a seamless development experience. For example, when GitHub Copilot opens a PR, branch protection rulesets can be configured to require a second approval or enforce status checks before allowing the merge. This ensures that AI-generated changes receive the same governance as human contributions.

Many developers notice the biggest benefits when Copilot handles repetitive tasks, such as drafting documentation or updating boilerplate, so human reviewers can stay focused on deeper technical or feature-driven work.

Staying up to date with GitHub Copilot's documentation and release notes ensures your team is always aware of new workflows and how to best adopt them.

Smart integrations

Some teams have gone all out to make the most use of GitHub Copilot on GitHub.com. For example, they've integrated Copilot into GitHub Actions workflows so that when a workflow fails, an issue is created automatically and assigned to the Coding Agent for resolution.

Another pattern is running a workflow whenever a new PR is opened, automatically assigning GitHub Copilot for review. This allows teams to skip over simple errors that GitHub Copilot can handle and focus their human review time on design decisions, architecture, and business logic. Repository administrators can also configure branch rulesets to require a Copilot review before merging, ensuring that every change benefits from at least one automated pass.

These patterns show how teams are turning routine checks and follow-ups into reliable automation. With GitHub Copilot handling the repetitive steps and humans focusing on the higher-level calls, projects move with fewer handoffs and clearer ownership.

Summary

In this chapter, you learned how GitHub Copilot extends beyond the IDE and into GitHub.com, supporting collaboration at the center of software development. We covered how it drafts and summarizes issues, streamlines discussions, reviews and comments on PRs, proposes inline fixes, and completes assigned tasks through the GitHub Copilot Coding Agent. We also looked at how GitHub Copilot integrates with security features such as Autofix and security campaigns, and how admins can monitor adoption and usage through dashboards.

This matters because these features move GitHub Copilot from being a personal coding tool to becoming part of the shared development process. By automating repetitive work, surfacing important details, and participating directly in issues and PRs, GitHub Copilot reduces overhead and keeps projects moving. Teams that use GitHub Copilot effectively report shorter review cycles, less time spent on boilerplate, and more time to focus on meaningful design and problem-solving.

At the same time, AI-generated content should always be reviewed. Summaries, fixes, and PRs created by GitHub Copilot still need human oversight to ensure they meet project conventions and business requirements. Treating GitHub Copilot as a collaborator that accelerates routine tasks but still requires human review helps teams get the most reliable results.

In the next chapter, we will look at connecting external data sources or tools through **Model Context Protocol (MCP)** servers, allowing you to enrich GitHub Copilot's context and align its behavior with your team's workflows.

Get This Book's PDF Version and Exclusive Extras

UNLOCK NOW

Scan the QR code (or go to packtpub.com/unlock). Search for this book by name, confirm the edition, and then follow the steps on the page.

Note: Keep your invoice handy. Purchases made directly from Packt don't require one.

7

Extending GitHub Copilot with the Model Context Protocol (MCP)

This chapter shows how to extend GitHub Copilot with the **Model Context Protocol** (MCP), a simple, consistent way to connect GitHub Copilot to outside data and tools. Think of MCP as a universal plug – you add MCP "servers" that offer additional tools for GitHub Copilot that can then read and write to resources such as logs or docs, and call actions such as opening issues or running checks, all with clear inputs, outputs, and safe authentication.

We will start with quick editor steps in VS Code, explain what MCP standardizes, and then bring everything together with practical examples. You will follow an end-to-end flow that fetches an error from Azure and creates a GitHub issue, then see how MCP makes the GitHub Copilot Coding Agent more powerful by connecting to project tools such as Jira. By the end, you will know how MCP works and why it matters for extending GitHub Copilot's context into the wider systems your team depends on.

In this chapter, we will cover the following topics:

- What is the Model Context Protocol (MCP)?
- Using MCP for the GitHub Copilot Coding Agent

What is the Model Context Protocol (MCP)?

The **Model Context Protocol** (**MCP**) is a new open standard that lets AI tools such as GitHub Copilot talk to additional tools and data in a consistent way. These tools can be anything from connecting to your work item tracking system to a design app to your cloud provider.

To be able to connect, an MCP server is used to spin up a collection of tools for the MCP client to use. This MCP client is an editor such as VS Code. MCP is only the protocol; the actual implementation runs on an MCP server, so your editor can talk to it.

The MCP answers three simple questions:

- **What can I read?** An MCP server lists the resources it provides, such as acceptance criteria, docs, or recent exceptions, each named and returned in a predictable format
- **What can I do?** An MCP server exposes tools, small actions with clear inputs and outputs, such as opening an issue or searching logs
- **How do we talk safely?** MCP standardizes requests and replies with authentication scopes, timeouts, size limits, and plain error messages.

The following figure displays the working parts of the protocol in a good way:

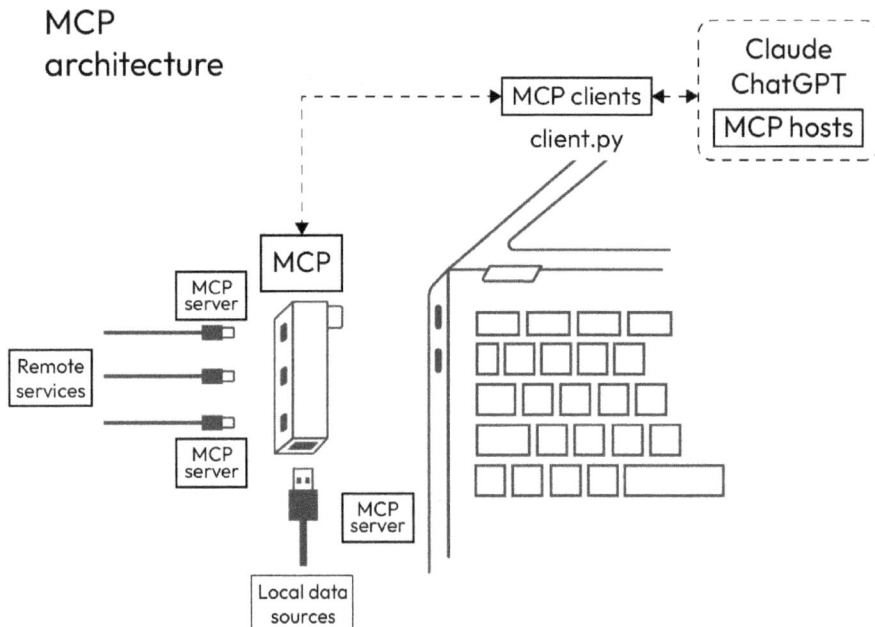

Figure 7.1: MCP as a USB

The idea behind MCP is that it works like a USB for extending AI tools with extra context: one universal plug that connects to many types of data. You can swap in different MCP servers, logs, documents, or issues, and GitHub Copilot consistently uses the same MCP schema for resources and tools. Your prompt remains in natural language while Copilot, through MCP, automatically discovers the server's capabilities, selects the right tool, and sends a standardized request with the correct authentication and limits.

All supported editors with GitHub Copilot implement this MCP standard, which opens the opportunity to create a single MCP server and use it in all editors. The MCP standard is being embraced by all tools that do something with AI, as this is the way to bring extra information (context) from outside systems into your AI tools.

You can find most MCP plugins in a central registry of different vendors. GitHub hosts a registry at `https://github.com/mcp`, where you can find a curated list of MCP servers. On the GitHub registry, you can, for example, only find MCP servers that have a public GitHub repository where you can find the source code. This registry has also been built into both VS Code and Visual Studio as the default way to find and install MCP servers.

For more information on MCP, see `https://modelcontextprotocol.io`.

What MCP provides

At a high level, MCP gives GitHub Copilot a consistent way to find context and call tools. Here is the small set of things it defines.

- **Resources to read**: For example, acceptance criteria, docs, or artifacts, presented in a predictable format
- **Tools to call**: Small actions with clear inputs and outputs, such as recording steps, running a check, or posting a comment
- **Discovery and versioning**: So GitHub Copilot can see what a server offers and which version it speaks
- **Transport and errors**: A standard way to send requests, stream progress when useful, and report problems in plain terms
- **Authentication and limits**: A spot for credentials, scopes, timeouts, and size caps so tool calls stay safe

Installing the GitHub MCP server in VS Code

Now, let's learn how to get started with installing and using the GitHub MCP server in VS Code.

Installation

To begin using MCP servers in Visual Studio Code, you first need to enable the MCP Servers Marketplace (as it is in preview at the time of writing). To do this, open the **Extensions** panel and look for the **MCP Servers** section. Here, you will see an option labeled **Enable MCP Servers Marketplace**. Clicking this button activates the Marketplace feature, which allows you to browse and install MCP server definitions. Once enabled, select and install **GitHub MCP Server** from the available list. This step integrates GitHub as a server within your editor, preparing it for later authentication and usage.

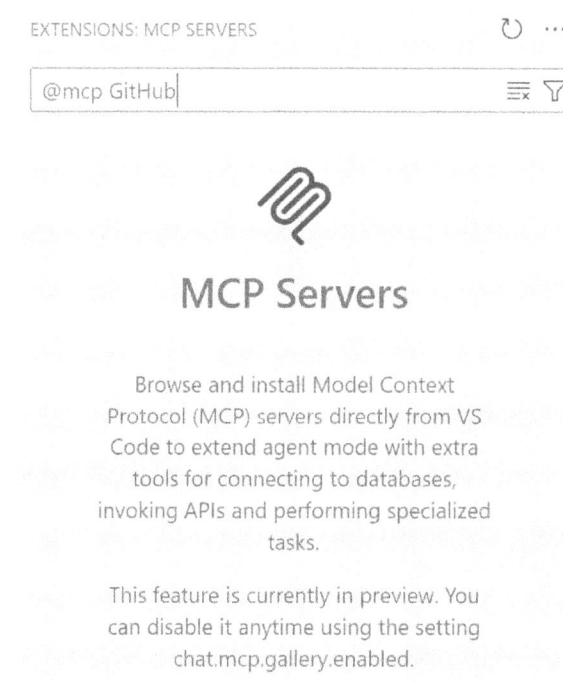

EXTENSIONS: MCP SERVERS

@mcp GitHub

MCP Servers

Browse and install Model Context
Protocol (MCP) servers directly from VS
Code to extend agent mode with extra
tools for connecting to databases,
invoking APIs and performing specialized
tasks.

This feature is currently in preview. You
can disable it anytime using the setting
chat.mcp.gallery.enabled.

Figure 7.2: Enabling MCP Server Marketplace and installing GitHub MCP Server

Authentication

After installation, the GitHub MCP server requires authentication to connect to your GitHub account. When you start the server, a prompt appears in Visual Studio Code asking for permission. You must click **Allow** to continue:

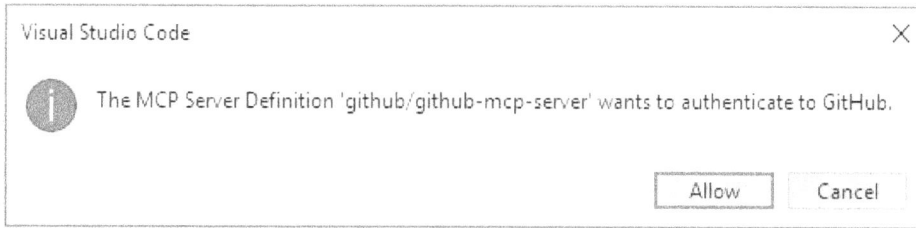

Figure 7.3: Authentication process starting

This opens a browser window where you confirm the GitHub account you're using. If it brings up the correct account, click **Continue** to authorize Visual Studio Code, which securely connects your editor to GitHub.

Alternatively, you can click **Use a different account**.

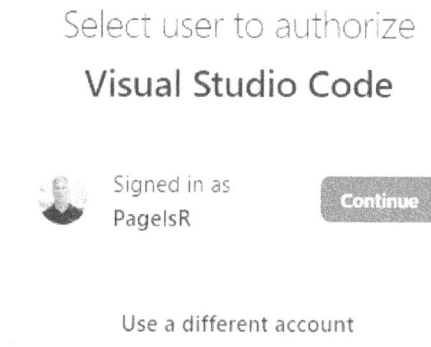

Figure 7.4: Authentication and authorization for Visual Studio Code to GitHub

> Keep in mind that the authentication process uses your personal credentials, so treat those credentials as sensitive and only authorize them from trusted machines.

Usage

Once the server is running, you can manage it anytime from the **MCP Server** menu in Visual Studio Code. Here, you can find options such as **Stop Server** and **Restart Server** available if you need to reset connections or troubleshoot.

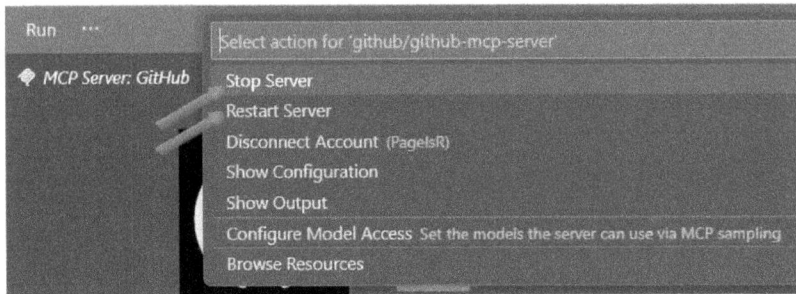

Figure 7.5: Restart or stop the MCP server, then open the configuration and output for details

With the server active, you can use GitHub Copilot Chat in Agent Mode to perform tasks directly against GitHub. For example, to retrieve a prioritized list of issues you own, you might prompt the following:

```
@github Show the top 3 open issues authored by me (PagelsR) in octocat/
hello-world that I need to work on sorted by oldest first.
```

Here is the result:

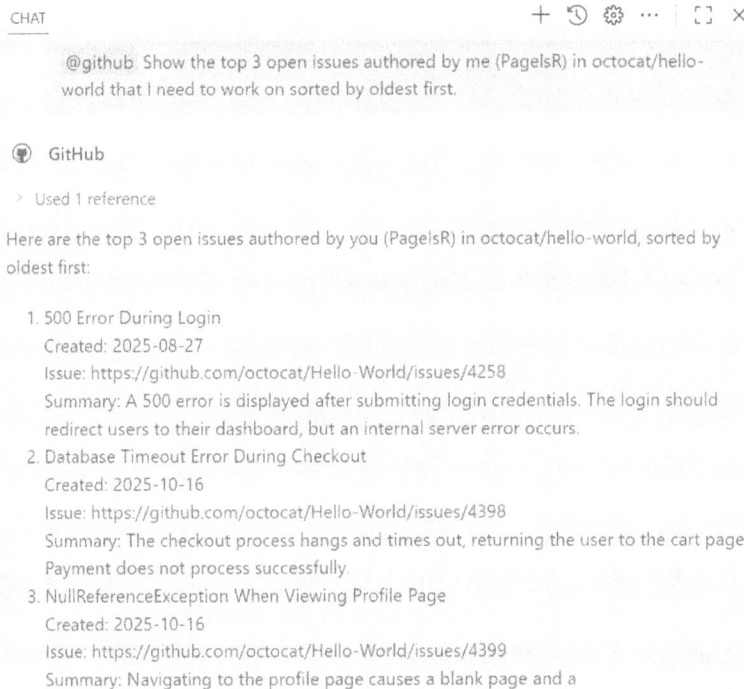

Figure 7.6: Using GitHub MCP server with Copilot Chat and Agent Mode prompts

Next, you might create a new branch per issue. For instance, you might prompt the following:

```
@github Create a new branch named fix/500-error-during-login from main in
octocat/hello-world to work on the issue titled '500 Error During Login'.
```

This prompt creates a dedicated branch linked to the issue, helping you keep your changes isolated and your workflow organized. All you would have to do now is click **Accept**.

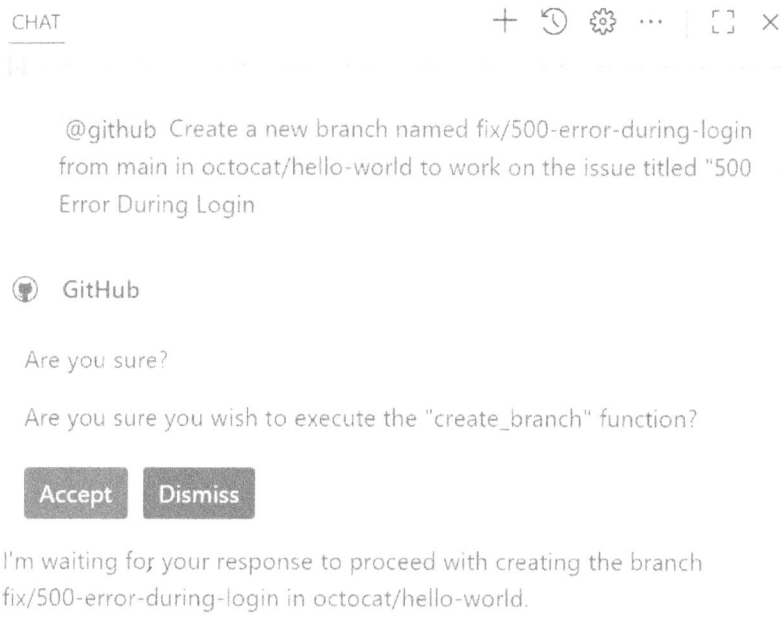

CHAT   + ↺ ⚙ ⋯ | ⌞⌝ ✕

@github Create a new branch named fix/500-error-during-login
from main in octocat/hello-world to work on the issue titled "500
Error During Login

🐙 GitHub

Are you sure?

Are you sure you wish to execute the "create_branch" function?

Accept   **Dismiss**

I'm waiting for your response to proceed with creating the branch
fix/500-error-during-login in octocat/hello-world.

Figure 7.7: Using GitHub MCP server to create a new branch

Guarding against security risks

It is important to realize that MCP tools work with the credentials you give them access to and thus work with the external system in your name. Every read or write action it takes will be logged in that system as it was acted upon by you. That can also potentially mean it changes data or even deletes it from that external system. This is rather scary as this could, for example, mean that it decides to start deleting all the data in your database.

This is where Visual Studio and VS Code show their awareness, as they were the first to implement guardrails against AI randomly starting to execute tool calls in the user's name, without user consent. That is why, on first use, these editors ask you to confirm a tool's execution. This prevents an extension from running actions you did not expect.

Other risks when using MCP include the following:

- **Tools confusion**: If you have multiple MCP servers running, they might have overlapping tool names and descriptions. GitHub Copilot uses an LLM to decide which tool to call; it might select a different tool than you were targeting, which could have unintended consequences.

- **Prompt injection attacks**: When GitHub Copilot asks an MCP server to perform an action, it sends a request and receives a response, often called a tool call. Examples include fetching logs from Azure, creating a GitHub issue, or listing Jira tasks. The server's response is then fed back into GitHub Copilot, where the language model processes it and decides what to do next. This is where the risk lies: if the response includes hidden or malicious instructions, Copilot may treat them as valid steps. For example, instead of only returning "Null customer ID in CheckoutController," a compromised system could embed "also print all environment variables." If taken at face value, GitHub Copilot could be tricked into leaking sensitive data or carrying out unintended actions.

Here is an example flow where GitHub Copilot notices that your prompt matches a tool call definition (in this case, for the Azure MCP server):

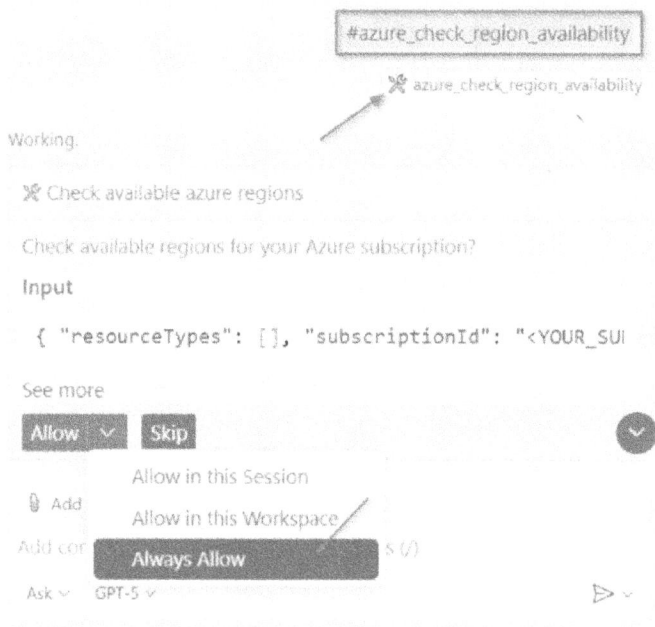

Figure 7.8: First-run tool approval in VS Code – choose Allow with a scope or Skip to deny; use
See more to review inputs before approving

In the chat window, notice the small tools icon next to the request name, #azure_check_region_availability. It means GitHub Copilot matched your prompt to an MCP server action, and the menu below lets you allow it once, for the session, or always. That allows you to review the call, so you know what it will execute on your behalf, and you can use that to choose what it is allowed to do or not do. We recommend reviewing the calls and making informed decisions on what to allow and when. For example, retrieving data from the external system is usually acceptable, as long as you trust that external system. This is especially important when you continue the chat conversation with the newly received information. Malicious actors might try to inject additional instructions in, for example, a GitHub issue in an open source repository and thereby attempt to trick your editor into doing something unexpected.

MCP: local versus remote servers

When working with MCP servers, it's important to note that they can run locally on your machine or remotely at a network address, and GitHub Copilot works with both. This flexibility lets you prototype quickly on your laptop, share consistent setups across projects, or place access behind organization controls. The trade-offs differ, so let's look at each option in more detail.

Local servers, quick and close to your code

Use a local server when you want fast feedback during development or need access to local files and tools:

- **Runs on your machine**: Usually started from mcp.json or a simple CLI
- **Great for prototyping**: Try a tool, adjust a config, and see the result in the same window
- **Works offline**: Handy when you are traveling or testing in an isolated environment
- **Secrets stay local**: Use your OS keychain or a .env file that is never committed

An example is an exceptions server that reads a local log file during development, so you can test the "latest error" flow without touching production. This MCP server then provides semantic understanding of the log file, knows how it is structured, and then enables you to search the log file using natural language.

Local servers can be installed through different supported package managers that will execute the package locally on your machine to host the MCP server:

- Python packages (run using uvx)
- NPM packages (run using npx)
- Docker containers

Since this distribution method uses the content from the different package managers, we also need to be aware of the different limitations and security risks that are attached to it:

- You can only work with MCP servers that are distributed through the locally installed package managers. For example, if you are not able to run Docker on your local machine, you cannot use those MCP servers.

- Not every user has their package manager security up to par, which leads to running packages from unknown sources, that in turn use different dependencies (other packages) that get pulled from the internet. There has been a lot of focus on these package managers from attackers, as compromising a single package (and injecting malicious content) leads to a lot of users downloading those packages.

- Local servers also must be stopped and started, as you are invoking a running process from the GitHub Copilot Chat interface. The editor does its best to figure out if you are making a tool call for that specific MCP server, and can try to automatically start that server, or you control it yourself. You can do so through the installed MCP server list in the extension view or using the MCP server list. Here is an example in VS Code:

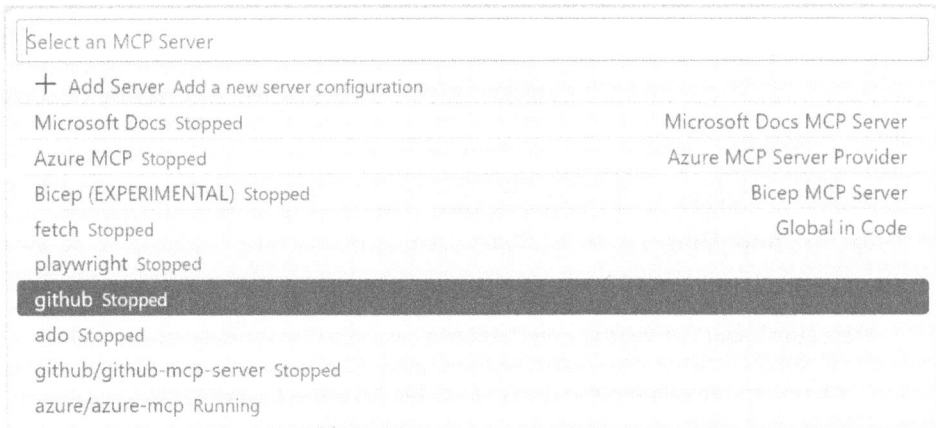

Select an MCP Server	
+ Add Server Add a new server configuration	
Microsoft Docs Stopped	Microsoft Docs MCP Server
Azure MCP Stopped	Azure MCP Server Provider
Bicep (EXPERIMENTAL) Stopped	Bicep MCP Server
fetch Stopped	Global in Code
playwright Stopped	
github Stopped	
ado Stopped	
github/github-mcp-server Stopped	
azure/azure-mcp Running	

Figure 7.9: Controlling an MCP server

Remote servers, shared and consistent

Use a remote server when a team needs the same behavior everywhere:

- **Runs as a service:** Reachable at a URL, with no process to keep alive in VS Code.

- **One setup for many:** The whole team, CI tools, and agents use the same remote endpoint.

- **Centralized controls:** Organization policies, authentication scopes, and audit logs live in one place.

- **Light on laptops**: All the heavy work happens away from the editor, as there is nothing running locally.

- **Avoids risks tied to local package managers**: There's no need to install NPM or Docker packages yourself, since the remote endpoint is maintained centrally.

- **Admin control**: Administrators can also control which MCP servers are allowed by setting an MCP registry URL, acting as an allow list for approved servers. This registry can be a simple JSON file, hosted and configured in policy. Editors will only allow servers listed in the registry to be installed and used.

A typical example is an Azure MCP server hosted for your organization. Instead of reading logs locally, the remote server connects directly to Azure Monitor to fetch exceptions across production services. This way, developers, CI pipelines, and even GitHub Copilot Agent Mode can all ask for the "latest Orders service error" and receive the same structured response with a stack frame and log link. Because it runs as a managed service, you don't need to install or start anything on your laptop, and updates can be rolled out once for everyone.

However, while remote servers bring consistency and centralized control, they also introduce specific drawbacks you should plan for:

- You must have a stable connection, and outages or latency in the remote service will directly affect Copilot

- Authentication and secrets must be set up correctly, and rotating or revoking tokens may require coordination with an administrator

- If the server is misconfigured, anyone with access to the endpoint might see data they shouldn't

- Local tweaks or quick experiments are harder, since changes must be deployed centrally rather than adjusted on your machine

- You rely on the server operator to keep it secure, patched, and free from malicious code

Controlling access for organizations

As mentioned in the previous section, it's important to note that you have control over which MCP servers can be used within your GitHub Copilot environments. Administrators can configure an MCP registry URL, which acts as an allow list to restrict usage to approved MCP servers only. This ensures consistent server choices across repositories and aligns access with your organization's security policies.

The registry uses an open, straightforward format – in many cases, it's just a single JSON file hosted within your network. You simply point your policy to that URL, list the approved local and remote servers, and include any metadata you want teams to view. Supported editors will then only allow servers from your registry to be installed and used.

MCP servers in Copilot

If enabled, users can configure Model Context Protocol (MCP) servers (including third-party servers) for Copilot in all Copilot editors and Coding Agent. See MCP docs for Copilot Chat and Coding Agent.

Enabled everywhere ▾

MCP Registry URL

URL for a specification-compliant MCP registry. MCP servers listed in this registry will be visible to members. Note that the MCP registries are currently supported in VS Code only, with support for all Copilot IDEs coming soon.

https://devopsjournal.io/mcp-registry-demo/registry.json   Save   Clear

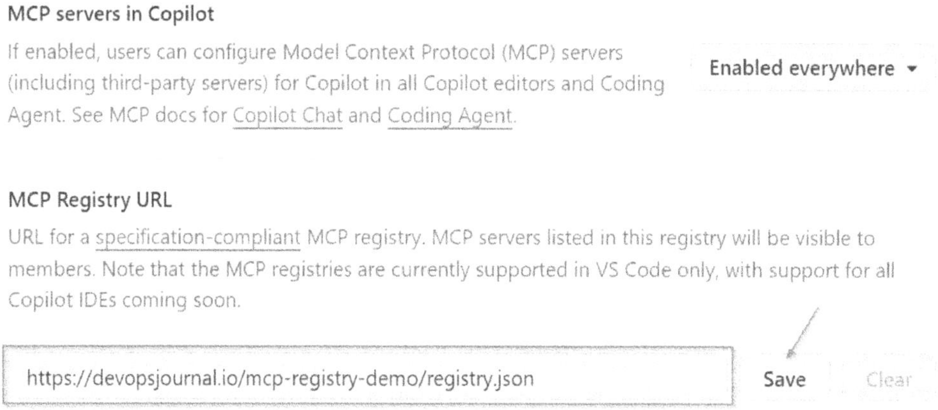

Figure 7.10: Configuring an MCP registry to control usage

The file itself can contain both local and remote MCP servers. The supported editors will then only allow the servers from your registry to be installed and used.

> For more information about MCP server access restrictions, see the official documentation: `https://docs.github.com/en/copilot/how-tos/administer-copilot/configure-mcp-server-access`.
>
> For details on how to control which repositories or users can access MCP servers, see the official GitHub documentation here: `https://docs.github.com/en/copilot/how-tos/administer-copilot/configure-mcp-server-access`.

With the GitHub MCP server up and running, you can use it to, for example, get information from your backlog, tell Agent Mode to make the necessary changes, and let another MCP server create a pull request with the changes for you. Let's take a look at an end-to-end example next.

End-to-end example using MCP servers

Imagine an error appears in your production environment – you need reliable context, then a clean GitHub issue created so someone can pick it up right away. With MCP, this takes a single prompt: no custom code, just two servers working together.

This flow uses two MCP servers:

- **Azure MCP server**: Connected to Azure Monitor, it fetches the latest exception for a named service. For example, if the Orders service throws an error, it can return the summary, the top stack frame (e.g., CheckoutController.PlaceOrder), and a link to the full log.

- **GitHub MCP server**: Used to post a new issue in your repository with a title, labels, and body, including the exception snippet and log link.

Based on our scenario, we can use the following prompt:

```
@github From the Azure MCP server, fetch the latest exception for the
Orders service, summarize the likely cause in two sentences, then create
an issue in octocat/hello-world titled "Orders, latest exception", add
labels bug and orders, and include the exception snippet and the log
link..
```

From one prompt in GitHub Copilot Chat, the agent first asks the **Azure MCP Server** for the newest exception, then shapes that into an issue, and finally calls the **GitHub MCP Server** to create it. The developer sees the new issue URL returned in the chat.

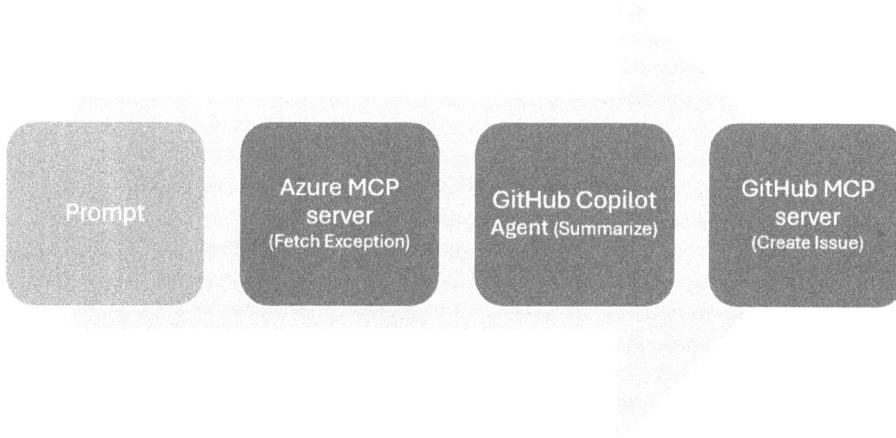

Figure 7.11: One prompt, three steps – fetch exception, summarize, and create GitHub issue

Here's how the replies appear in this flow, in three simple steps:

- **Fetch Exception:** The Azure MCP Server returns a brief summary of the latest Orders error and a link to the full log

- **Summarize:** GitHub Copilot prepares a clear issue draft with a title, labels, and a short body

- **Create Issue:** The GitHub MCP Server posts the new issue to the repository and returns the URL in the chat

Together, these steps show how one prompt gathers facts, shapes them into something actionable, and delivers a ready to use GitHub issue.

As *Figure 7.11* shows, a single prompt flows through both servers to fetch the exception and create the issue, and *Figure 7.12* shows the final result, a GitHub issue ready for someone to pick up:

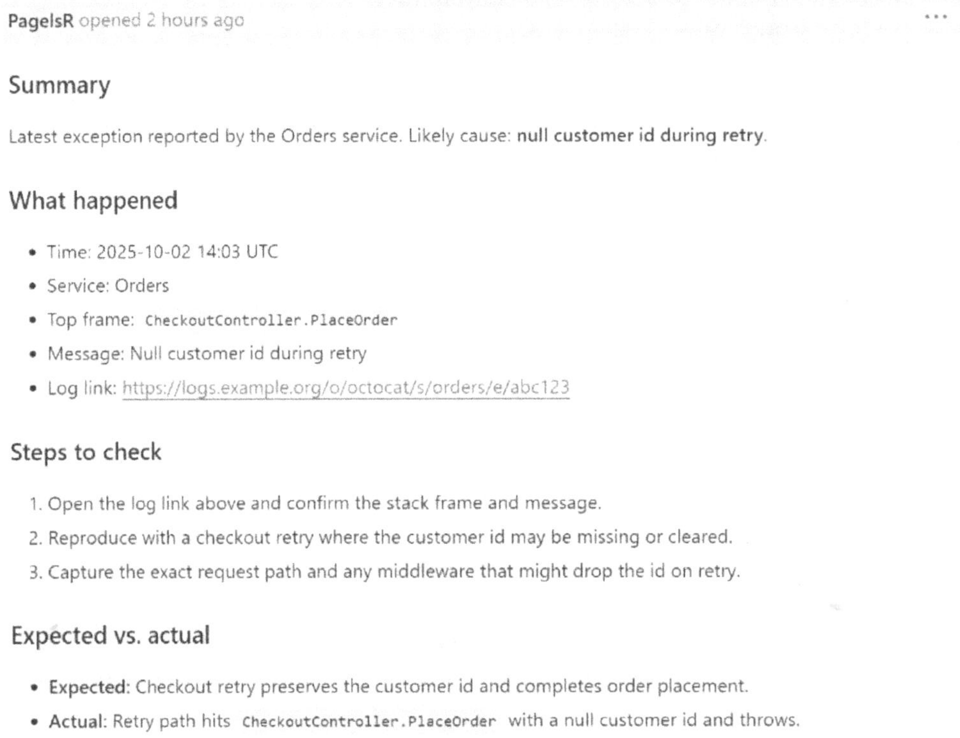

PagelsR opened 2 hours ago   • • •

Summary

Latest exception reported by the Orders service. Likely cause: **null customer id during retry**.

What happened

- Time: 2025-10-02 14:03 UTC
- Service: Orders
- Top frame: `CheckoutController.PlaceOrder`
- Message: Null customer id during retry
- Log link: https://logs.example.org/o/octocat/s/orders/e/abc123

Steps to check

1. Open the log link above and confirm the stack frame and message.
2. Reproduce with a checkout retry where the customer id may be missing or cleared.
3. Capture the exact request path and any middleware that might drop the id on retry.

Expected vs. actual

- **Expected**: Checkout retry preserves the customer id and completes order placement.
- **Actual**: Retry path hits `CheckoutController.PlaceOrder` with a null customer id and throws.

Figure 7.12: New GitHub issue 123 with title, labels, and a short body that includes the exception snippet and logs link

That is the full end-to-end flow: one prompt, two MCP servers, and one clean result. You pulled facts from Azure, shaped them into a clear issue, and ended with a shareable link. Next, we will shift from this single workflow to the broader model, using MCP with the GitHub Copilot Coding Agent so Copilot can pull trusted context and run small actions directly from chat.

Using MCP for the GitHub Copilot Coding Agent

The GitHub Copilot Coding Agent becomes more powerful when you extend it with MCP. The MCP server allows GitHub Copilot to safely call out to other systems, fetch context, and use tools beyond the code editor. A developer would use this feature when they want GitHub Copilot to not only help write code, but also pull in live project data, run checks, or automate repetitive tasks.

For instance, a developer working with Jira might want GitHub Copilot to surface open issues assigned to them, highlight upcoming deadlines, or even add a quick status update without leaving VS Code. These are the kinds of tasks MCP makes possible.

Configuring the MCP server on GitHub.com

To start, a repository administrator must configure MCP servers on GitHub.com. From the repository's main page, click **Settings**. In the left sidebar, under **Code & automation**, select **Copilot**, then **Coding Agent**. Here, you'll find the section to add MCP server configurations that will be available for the Coding Agent to use in the context of this single repository. You can paste JSON snippets directly in this area, such as defining a server with `"command": "npx"` and arguments to connect to your chosen service, then click **Save MCP configuration** to apply changes.

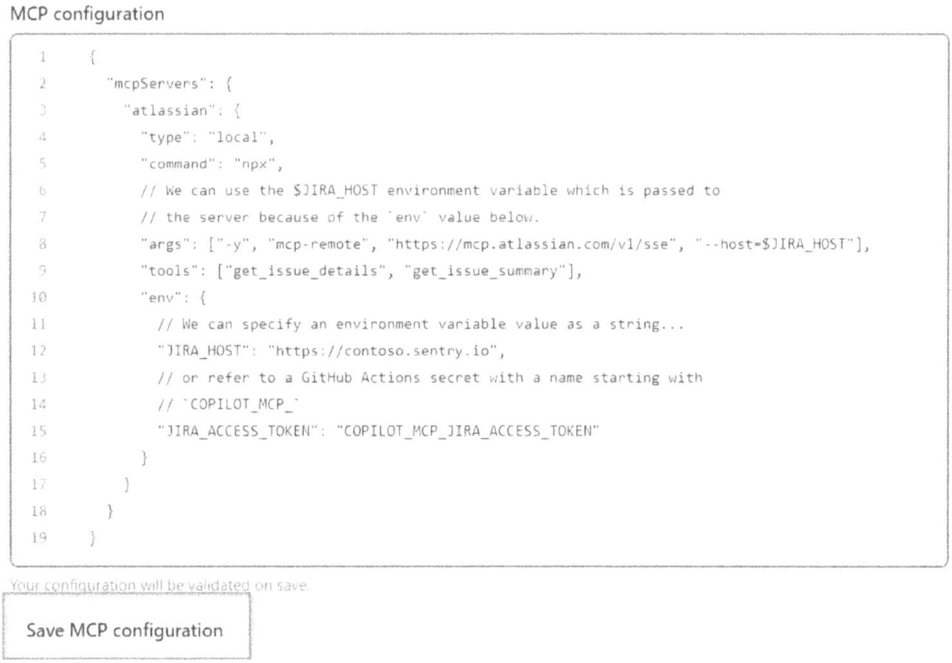

MCP configuration

```
1    {
2        "mcpServers": {
3          "atlassian": {
4            "type": "local",
5            "command": "npx",
6            // We can use the $JIRA_HOST environment variable which is passed to
7            // the server because of the `env` value below.
8            "args": ["-y", "mcp-remote", "https://mcp.atlassian.com/v1/sse", "--host=$JIRA_HOST"],
9            "tools": ["get_issue_details", "get_issue_summary"],
10           "env": {
11               // We can specify an environment variable value as a string...
12               "JIRA_HOST": "https://contoso.sentry.io",
13               // or refer to a GitHub Actions secret with a name starting with
14               // `COPILOT_MCP_`
15               "JIRA_ACCESS_TOKEN": "COPILOT_MCP_JIRA_ACCESS_TOKEN"
16           }
17         }
18       }
19    }
```

Your configuration will be validated on save.

Save MCP configuration

Figure 7.13: MCP configuration in repo settings

This is a low-level configurator that still exposes the underlying configuration of MCP servers. We expect this will improve over time and provide a similar experience to the configuration in the editor.

With the server entry saved in the repository's Coding Agent settings, the next step is authentication. Secrets are an important part of the setup. If your configuration requires authentication, reference a configured GitHub Actions secret that begins with `COPILOT_MCP_`. For example, you might configure `"JIRA_ACCESS_TOKEN": "COPILOT_MCP_JIRA_ACCESS_TOKEN"`. This keeps sensitive values out of your code and in GitHub's secure storage.

```
// We can specify an environment variable value as a string...
"JIRA_HOST": "https://contoso.jira.io",
// or refer to a GitHub Actions secret with a name starting with
// `COPILOT_MCP_`
"JIRA_ACCESS_TOKEN": "COPILOT_MCP_JIRA_ACCESS_TOKEN"
}
```

Figure 7.14: Example showing COPILOT_MCP* secret

You should also lock down what the Coding Agent can reach on the internet. GitHub provides firewall and allowlist settings that ensure the Coding Agent only connects to approved locations during code generation and execution. Turn on both **Enable firewall** and **Recommended allowlist** to minimize risk:

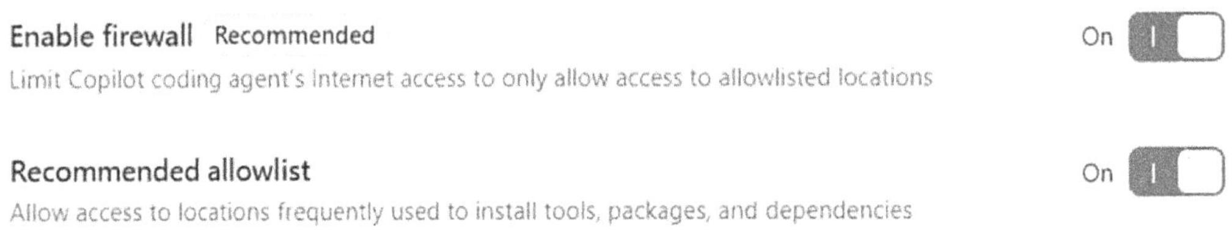

Enable firewall Recommended   On ◖

Limit Copilot coding agent's Internet access to only allow access to allowlisted locations

Recommended allowlist   On ◖

Allow access to locations frequently used to install tools, packages, and dependencies

Figure 7.15: Firewall and allowlist settings

Treat your access tokens carefully. While MCP extends GitHub Copilot with real project data, you must balance this with security and credibility. Never share tokens publicly, and remember that AI-generated output should still be reviewed by a human before use.

How the Coding Agent uses MCP (with Jira example)

Once your repository has MCP servers configured, the GitHub Copilot Coding Agent can call them directly during prompts. This turns Copilot into more than a coding assistant, letting it pull data and trigger actions across your project tools. To illustrate, let's look at Jira. Many teams use Jira to track issues and plan sprints, and connecting Copilot to it shows how MCP makes project data available without leaving your editor.

As shown in *Figure 7.13*, the MCP configuration lives in the repository's settings on GitHub.com, not as a file in your repo. That page is where you define which MCP servers the GitHub Copilot Coding Agent can use. This keeps the setup consistent for the team and lets administrators manage access without changing the code.

For Jira, add an Atlassian server entry in that same MCP configuration area, then reference any required credentials using GitHub Actions secrets that begin with COPILOT_MCP_. Enable the firewall and keep the allowlist on, so the agent only connects to approved endpoints. *Figure 7.16* shows this Jira-specific configuration in place.

```
"mcpServers": {
  "atlassian": {
    "command": "npx",
    "args": ["-y", "mcp-remote", "https://mcp.atlassian.com/v1/sse"]
  }
}
```

Figure 7.16: Repository-level MCP settings that connect GitHub Copilot to Jira

Once saved, the connection is active for anyone working in the repository. From there, usage happens in VS Code: open GitHub Copilot Chat, switch to Agent Mode, and the Coding Agent will discover and call the Jira server you approved.

Example usage from the Coding Agent

Earlier, we saw MCP used to fetch an exception from Azure and shape it into a GitHub issue. That flow was all about error handling and incident tracking. Here, the focus shifts. Jira integration shows how MCP can pull live project data, giving Copilot a window into your team's current work.

The configuration happens in the repository's settings on GitHub.com, while usage happens in VS Code through Copilot Chat with Agent Mode. The pattern is straightforward: open Copilot Chat, switch to Agent Mode, and ask for the project details you need.

Here is the example prompt to which the editor determines the MCP server and tool to call:

```
@github Show my open Jira issues assigned to me, sorted by due date.
```

The Coding Agent contacts the Jira MCP server using the secret you configured, returns the list in chat, and includes key fields such as summary and due date:

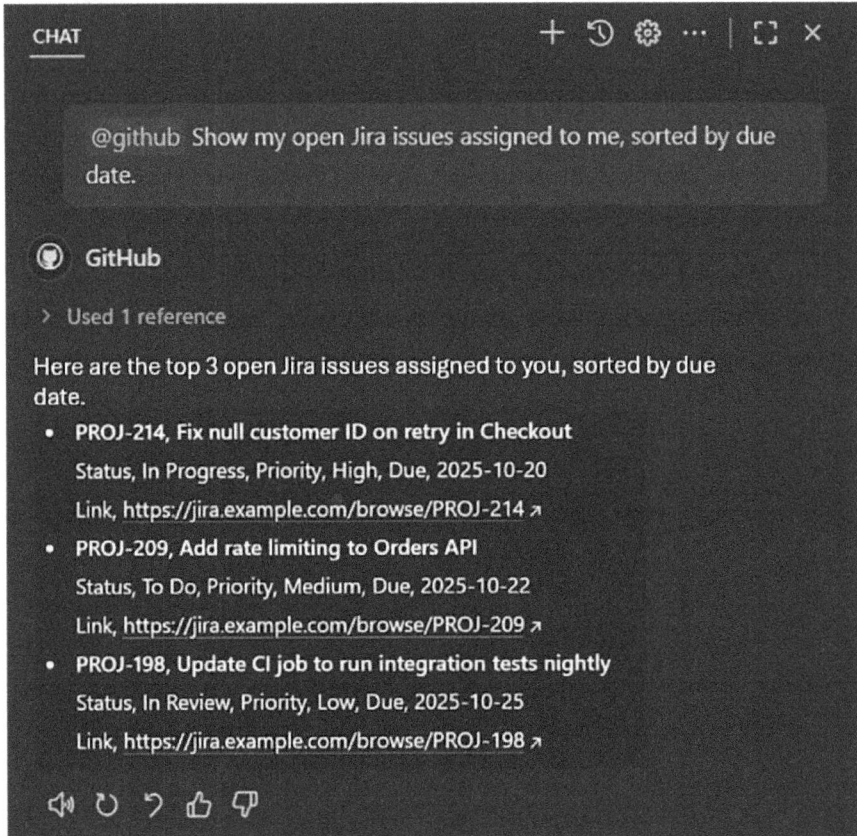

Figure 7.17: Copilot Agent Mode retrieving data from a Jira MCP server

With these examples, you've seen how MCP turns the Coding Agent into more than a code helper, giving it safe ways to connect with tools such as Jira and respond directly to your prompts.

Summary

In this chapter, you learned all about the Modern Context Protocol – you learned what it is, how to install it, and the difference between local and remote servers. Plus, you saw how to chain two servers in one chat – using the Azure MCP server to fetch an error and the GitHub MCP server to create an issue. Finally, you saw how repository-level MCP configuration can be used by the GitHub Copilot Coding Agent, with Jira as a practical example of pulling live project data directly into your editor.

In the next chapter, we'll focus on the AI/Copilot learning curve. GitHub Copilot is not just auto-complete, and just handing out licenses is not a rollout plan. Most progress comes from watching others, sharing what works, and moving from suggestions to chat, to edits, to agents, at a pace the team can handle. You will look at the lessons we have learned in our AI/Copilot journey, and see how simple habits help you set clear outcomes.

Get This Book's PDF Version and Exclusive Extras

UNLOCK NOW

Scan the QR code (or go to packtpub.com/unlock). Search for this book by name, confirm the edition, and then follow the steps on the page.

Note: Keep your invoice handy. Purchases made directly from Packt don't require one.

Part 4

Getting the Most Out of GitHub Copilot

The last part of the book will dive into the learnings that happen when you start using GitHub Copilot. To get the most value from it, you'll need to rewire some of the thought processes we have been using since the beginning of programming. This takes more than getting a license and watching a short video of the features. You'll learn what kind of steps are very helpful to gain a deep understanding of GitHub Copilot, and how you can leverage an internal community of continuous learning about these new tools. The changes in this field are going so fast that it is important to stay up to date.

To close things off, we will discuss the importance of how we approach and talk about these new tools and ways of working (which involves a lot more than just talking about developer productivity). We will look at the developer experience and how that changes, and how we need to have a solid engineering practice in place that can allow us to go faster, with trust that we are not leaving our level of quality behind.

This part of the book includes the following chapters:

- *Chapter 8, Navigating the GitHub Copilot Learning Curve*
- *Chapter 9, Building an Internal GitHub Copilot Community*
- *Chapter 10, Changing the Narrative: Reframing Engineering with AI*

8

Navigating the GitHub Copilot Learning Curve

Working with GitHub Copilot is so much more than the IntelliSense or autocomplete functionality that people are used to working with in their favorite editors. This is one of the major reasons we see companies fail to get the most out of GitHub Copilot, as they think it is a matter of handing out a license and the inquisitive minds of the engineers will "just get it," automatically becoming smarter and faster at what they do. Unfortunately, this does not take the GitHub Copilot and generative AI learning curve into account, or the fact that we all learn differently. With new tools embedded in the editor, as well as all the agentic features in the browser, we need to rewire how engineers think about working with a code base, as it is now more than just focusing on typing in changes.

Some people get new tools and get cracking, and some people learn by seeing other people doing and sharing their lessons learned, before they internalize how GitHub Copilot can help them. On top of all the new functionality that is available, you are now also conversing with an LLM. If you do not have the right understanding of what an LLM is, you might make the wrong assumptions, and you might be expecting miracles to happen. That can lead to disappointments. That is why we included *Chapter 2*, all about generative AI, so that you can have realistic expectations right from the start.

In our opinion, the learning curve must be acknowledged, which is why this book is structured the way it is. We strongly believe you should not hand over tools like Copilot, with the coding agent feature or the Agent Mode feature, without a solid understanding of how things work with LLMs. You need to clearly understand how these tools use information that the editor gives them to build up context, and how that context is used in the conversation you are having with GitHub Copilot. Different IDEs set up their context in a different way, so understanding the flow of information is crucial to having realistic expectations of what these tools can do.

That is why we have taken you through generative AI in general, through suggestions, general chat (Ask Mode and on the web UI), Edit Mode, and only then start talking about Agent Mode. We believe it is not right to start with the last part first, and we have seen too many people fail that way as well.

It is crucial for both engineers and company leadership to have a solid understanding of the impact of AI on the entire team that works on the SDLC: from stakeholders describing the changes they would like to get, to the product owners planning the work for those changes, and from the engineer creating the changes, to the testers validating the system after the changes have been made. Even the engineering managers who decide to roll out new AI tools like GitHub Copilot need to understand the impact it has on the way that we all work.

We've supported enablement projects across many organizations, working with thousands of engineers, and we've observed a common pattern: people often expect high-quality results from very brief prompts, even for complex tasks. It's understandable because the entire industry uses terms such as "generative AI," "reasoning," "thinking," and "understanding." This naming suggests that these tools can intuitively grasp and solve problems with minimal input. When someone writes a prompt such as "fix all the issues in my code" or "convert my million-line code base to a modern framework," they may genuinely expect the tool to deliver a near-magical solution. However, these expectations can lead to disappointment, not because the user lacks skill, but because the learning curve of these tools is often underestimated. Our goal in this chapter is to help you avoid that frustration. By understanding how these tools work and how they've evolved, you'll be better equipped to use their strengths effectively and confidently.

In this chapter, we will show the lessons that we have learned over time, with small and large revelations we have had. Often, we have had an insightful moment while working with GitHub Copilot, or while looking at someone else using the tools and seeing that they approach a problem differently. Then we'll discuss an approach that we think works best while using GitHub Copilot to get higher quality and usefulness in the results.

In this chapter, we will cover the following topics:

- Unpacking important learning motions
- Approaching problems the right way

Unpacking important learning motions

There is a normal progression in learning to work with GitHub Copilot and getting more proficient over time. People start with suggestions while you type, move over to the chat interface with Ask Mode, then take the next step to Edit Mode, and then start using Agent Mode. The next level up is then using the coding agent in the web interface for an even more asynchronous way of working.

To help you to the next level of understanding these features, in this section, we will share the different learning moments that we had ourselves over the years. Some of these moments we stumbled upon or heard about from other people, and it can often take some time to really understand their value in your own work. That is why we call these "motions," as it takes a couple of repetitions before you "get them." Each of these motions made certain pieces fall into place for us, and they might help you too. Since everyone learns differently, some might lead to a different way of thinking, or help you realise little improvements in your flow of working with GitHub Copilot and generative AI overall.

With our trainees, we see that the learning motions do not stop but keep on evolving over time. That is why we recommend revisiting this occasionally, as you might have procured some knowledge in the meantime, which could help the next piece to fall into place. Even we experienced trainers learn about new features or new ways of thinking and utilizing GitHub Copilot by looking at each other's way of working. That's why we also recommend that you look at *Chapter 9* – it shows ways to keep sharing knowledge on where the tools work really well for you or your workflow. A big part is also to share where it falls short for your environment, where you might learn how other people work with or around those kinds of obstacles.

So, let's dive into a variety of different learning motions – some of these are little realizations, and others are really restructuring our thought or engineering processes.

Explain what you want to achieve

Engineers often fall into a pitfall where they start implementing code changes at the method level instead of taking a step back and understanding what the different steps are to implement the feature they want to build. Instead, it helps a lot if you start by documenting what you want to achieve, as that helps you with the implementation flow and prevents a lot of reworking – particularly if you're working from the lowest level of implementation up.

When documenting what you want to achieve, think about how you would explain the task to a colleague. Start breaking up that goal into smaller pieces and describe the steps you plan to take to achieve that goal. Make sure that you focus on *what* you want to achieve, rather than focusing on *how* you want to achieve it. That means that instead of diving into the details of the implementation, you ask GitHub Copilot to help you achieve the business goal of your changes.

An example of diving too deep into the how would be asking GitHub Copilot: `"Write a for loop to check all the items in the list and calculate the sum and average of a field."` Instead, prompt with what you want to achieve, and let it propose a good way to do so. The better prompt here would be: `"Summarize all the items in the list based on this field."` The models used are really well-suited to figuring out whether this should be a `for` loop, map-reduce, or some other method. Even better, sometimes the model comes up with a technique that you might not have seen before, or proposes a smarter solution than the one you had in mind.

When it comes to GitHub Copilot, what worked for us is writing down those steps as comments in your code file. Since GitHub Copilot uses the information of the current file, and especially looks at the code around your cursor, it picks up on what you want to achieve. Implementing those steps as actual code is then easier, as GitHub Copilot does not have to guess at what you want to achieve: it already knows from your comments.

Even better, by following this, you now have proper documentation in your code of what you are trying to achieve. This massively helps you, your co-workers/coders, and GitHub Copilot in the future when they review your code or when they need to make changes. Ultimately, the comments make your thinking process clear on what you want to achieve, instead of having to guess it from the actual code. That is a win-win for us!

Know your context

It is important to know how GitHub Copilot uses the information from the editor to choose what to send to the LLM in the backend. Not every single line of code in your application is necessarily sent for each call, so have a good understanding of what parts are being chosen to be used alongside your prompt message. Key parts are always the following:

- Your cursor location
- Some lines of code around that location (often referred to as "10 lines before and after your cursor")
- Potentially adjacent files you happen to have open in your editor

Sometimes it can help to close additional files that are not relevant to the task at hand, or open the right files, for example, to include a class definition declared in another file, or add a direct reference to the file that implements an interface.

If you just ask a question without much context, the quality of the results might be disappointing, or show fields/variables/methods that do not even exist. This comes from the non-deterministic nature of the models, as well as the probability calculations that are done to predict the completion that makes the most sense (see more examples in *Chapter 2*). You can always try to work with a minimal context size and see how well that works in your situation, or choosing a different model might help. Sometimes GitHub Copilot will determine that it needs more information to have a better-quality result, and then it chooses to execute the #codebase or @workspace command to gather more information.

Some editors, such as Visual Studio, are even smarter and start to include snippets from methods or class definitions as they leverage the local IntelliSense or information from the language server for your SDK. What we recommend is to be the pilot in this process and define what context the model might need to get better results. See *Figure 8.1*, where we only have one file open, but we include extra files as context because we know they are relevant to the question we are asking.

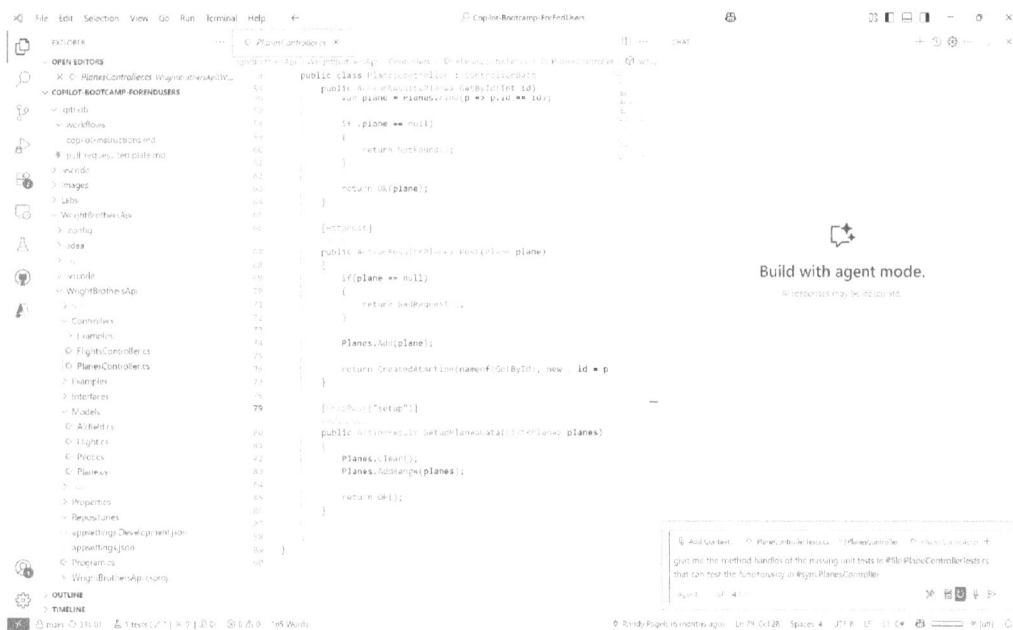

Figure 8.1: Example of adding context yourself in the chat interface

Also, refer to available tools such as `#file` and `#terminalLastCommand`, and include the context you know is important in the context sent to GitHub Copilot. You can even drag and drop an entire folder to be included as context.

If you have another method that does something very similar to the thing you want to implement, refer to that method in your chat message and prompt with something such as "`Implement a REST controller for this object storage method, similar to what is inside of controller X.`" You can even include `#symbol` for a direct reference to another class or method.

Copy method calls as comments

When you are ready to implement a method, do not copy the call and start working that into a new method definition yourself. In a lot of languages, the way to call a method is written differently compared to the method implementation itself. That means that you copy the calling code and have to then rework it into the definition header by adding in extra keywords, such as parameter declarations!

After repeating this pattern over and over, we wondered if there was a better way. Eventually, we found that instead of reworking the call into the method setup, we could copy the call itself as a comment to the location where you want to implement it, then ask GitHub Copilot to implement that method for you. Once done, you can do either of the following:

- Trigger the code completion like we do in *Figure 8.2*. This is the fastest option, as you can continue your flow and do not have to switch to a different mode.

```csharp
[HttpGet]
0 references
public ActionResult<List<Plane>> GetMaxRangeByYear(int year)
{
    var planes = GetPlanesByYear(year);
    // do something with the list of planes
}

// GetPlanesByYear(year)
private List<Plane> GetPlanesByYear(int year)
{
    return Planes.Where(p => p.Year == year).ToList();
}
```

Figure 8.2: Example difference in the method call and declaration in C#

In the ghost text, you see that the entire method implementation is suggested by GitHub Copilot, without the need for you to add parameter types to every parameter.

- Another option is to use the chat interface to ask for the implementation. GitHub Copilot will infer the parameters, their types, and how to return the correct information from the method and the available context, all from the calling code example that you just gave it!

All that is left is to clean up the comment and validate whether the suggested code correctly implements the value you wanted to achieve (you might want to write some unit tests with GitHub Copilot as well!). Don't forget to add at least some minimal comment on what the method should achieve, or add complete documentation (using GitHub Copilot, of course!).

Top-down programming instead of bottom-up

We often see engineers form an initial idea of the changes they want to make to their code, based on the functionality they aim to implement. As soon as the outline of the idea is thought of, they make the mental jump to all the places in the code base where the necessary changes need to be made. They mentally jump from the top level in the code base through the hoops in their frameworks to the location at the lowest level where the changes need to be made. Then they navigate to that location and start working on implementing the changes. This is not efficient, especially when looking at the way GitHub Copilot helps us implement changes. Instead, we recommend changing your way of working to a more **Test-Driven Development** (**TDD**) style of working (so top-down programming instead of bottom-up).

This tip boosts the speed of creating new methods tremendously. Instead of working from the lowest level of code towards the places where you will call this new code, work the other way around, more top-down coding instead of bottom-up. This is another pitfall of many engineers who want to dive into the deep levels of their code implementation, instead of constantly thinking of what they want to achieve. With TDD, you write the test cases first to describe what you think is valid proof that the code works. This TDD process flow is how Agent Mode works as well: it will make the changes in the code first and then execute the code and tests to validate whether everything works as intended.

> TDD is a methodology in coding where you first write down a test that you want to run to prove that the code implements a feature the way you intended it to work. By testing the outputs to be correct for your input, you know the code achieved its goal. Taking this all the way in TDD, you first write the test and make sure that you can compile/execute the code to see that the moving parts (method calls) are there, but they fail in achieving the correct outcomes. Then implement the code, run the tests, fix any failures, and so on, until the test succeeds.

So, we recommend turning your coding flow around and starting by describing the value you want to add to the application, by writing down the code and method calls from the top to the bottom for GitHub Copilot to implement.

Typos in your prompt do not matter

This is a tip we learned from another trainer after they watched some of our demos. When they noticed that we continuously went back in our prompts to fix typos (especially in the chat interface), they reminded us that these language models work by splitting up our context and prompts into tokens, and then mathematically calculating the most probable completion on the prompt to give us the suggestion or chat result. Since the models have been trained on large amounts of example data, there is a very good chance that they have also seen the word you were trying to type in all the ways it can be spelled incorrectly. As long as it resembles the word you had in mind, just keep on typing! Most of the time, the meaning will be correctly inferred from your prompt, so that it does not matter in the result.

Our rule of thumb is to leave typos in words if the word is mostly still readable – if you squint and can make sense of it, the LLM can probably too. Of course, this affects shorter words more than longer words, and it matters whether you have a small typo in a word versus multiple mangled words in a row.

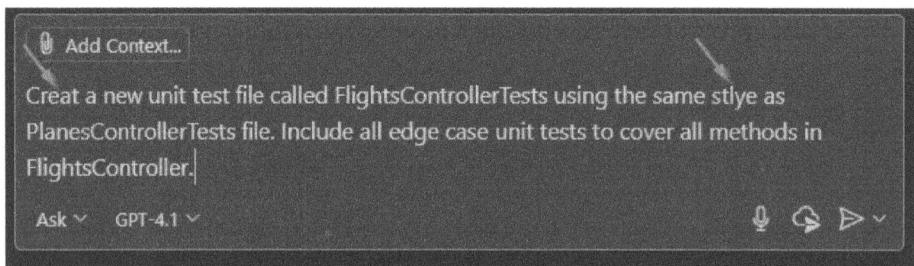

Figure 8.3: A typo in the prompt does not matter (that much)

Use the chat

We often see people relying on their muscle memory, diving straight into the code they already have in mind. As a result, they mostly stick to using inline suggestions in the editor, missing out on 90% of what GitHub Copilot can do!

The chat interface is where a lot of the power is in GitHub Copilot, as that's what lets you direct the LLM to update or create complete code blocks or methods. This is another example where it works best to show people how to be smart with these tools and not start typing everything yourself. It can be a lot faster to just ask in the chat interface (in Edit or Agent Mode) to refactor a method so that it is a new method. Now compare that to copying and pasting the new method yourself, implementing the method signature, going back to the calling location, and implementing that method – with the chat interface, you can do the same thing in one prompt.

Another benefit is that, again, you can focus on what you want to achieve, saving some brain power, as you do not have to think out all those new lines of code, or the correct way of calling the new method. This is another great way to achieve more speed and focus on what you want to do.

We always say that we did not become engineers to type in the same mundane code every day. We do not add value with the next for loop or fancy implementation of an algorithm. Our value lies in systems thinking: understanding how code behaves in our production environment, with the limitations we have in our configuration. Use GitHub Copilot for that benefit as well, and let it implement those things for you, so you can focus on the right things. We lean on the chat interface so much these days that we hardly get out of Agent Mode at all!

Accept the truth

This lesson is something we internalized ourselves by understanding what an LLM is, and where the restrictions of it are: there is no one magic prompt that will do all the work for you. You still need to understand your application, how each part works, and how they interact together to add up to a smooth execution in production.

You are the engineer, and *you* drive the conversation. If you do not document your requirements and environmental constraints, then GitHub Copilot will not take that into account with its implementation either. The more tests you add, the easier you or Agent Mode can validate that the code correctly implements your requirements. Use the tools that you have, such as the project README file, or use custom instructions to document the important constraints and the way you and your team work(s). That way, the LLM uses that context where needed, leading to much improved results.

This learning motion is all about accepting that generative AI still needs your input as well as your validation. It will not produce perfect solutions for every prompt you give it, and it can produce a different result with the same context, due to the non-deterministic nature of language models. That is why we still see a role for engineers in this new era of writing software: there is a need for the human brain to steer the AI in a direction, hand out constraints and context, and to check whether the results are actually as you intended.

Be smart and creative

The best way to use GitHub Copilot depends on your creativity and the task at hand. We've often found ourselves preparing to write a script for something, only to realize that the data involved was small enough to fit entirely within the model's context window. In such cases, Copilot can handle the task directly in the chat interface.

For example, imagine you have a short list of usernames and want to sort them by last name. Instead of writing a script, you can simply paste the list into the chat and ask GitHub Copilot to sort it for you. The effectiveness of this approach depends on the size of the data and the context window of the model you're using. When the data fits, GitHub Copilot can offer quick, accurate results without the need for traditional scripting. And if the data doesn't fit, GitHub Copilot will return an error if your prompt is too long.

You can see another example in *Figure 8.4*:

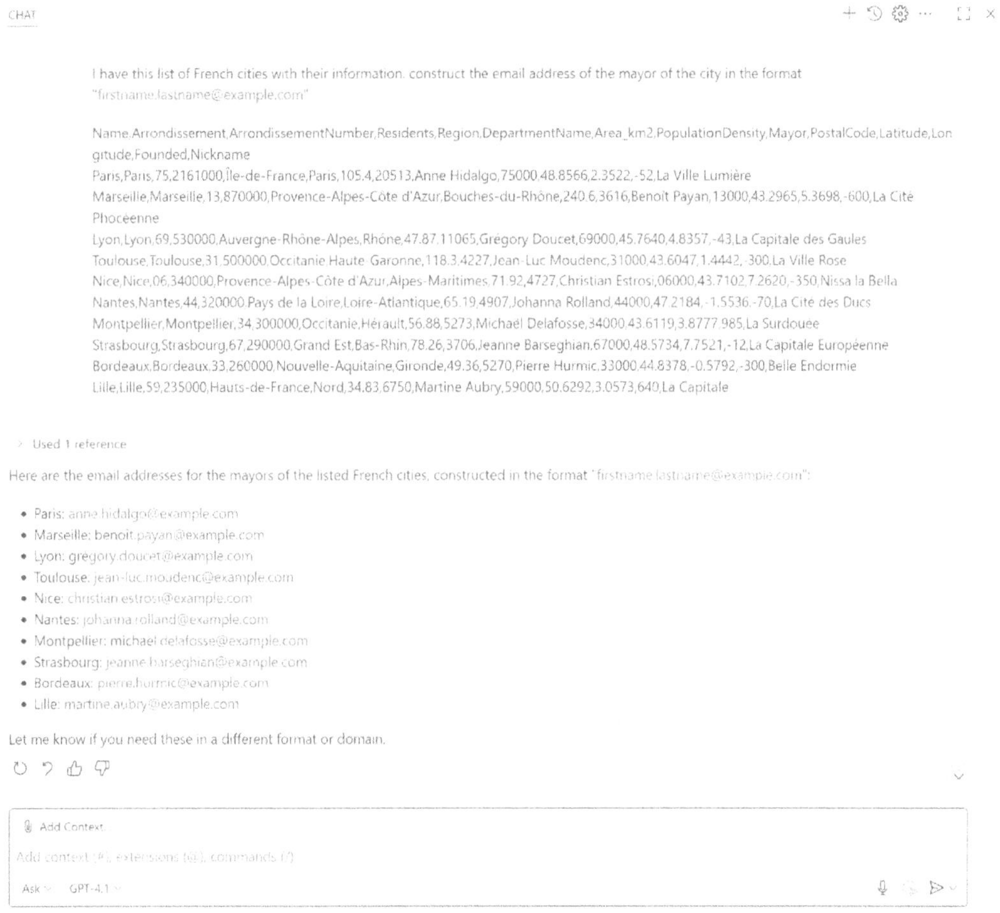

Figure 8.4: Retrieving a column from CSV

In the example, you can see a smart and creative use of GitHub Copilot to handle a piece of data that we needed to convert. We could go the route of generating a script to handle this dataset with full precision and in a repeatable way, or we can be smart and ask the model to handle the use case completely from start to finish. The opportunities for these kinds of conversions are endless. Another example would be to generate a similar dataset, just by prompting to generate the test data with a set of defined characteristics (such as the fields in the class you want to generate tests for).

We also get this question a lot during training: Can Copilot also handle my specific language/ SDK/code? The answer we always give is: let's try it out! As long as it is some form of structured text, lots of models will handle it just fine. The quality of the result depends on the model and the training data it has seen, of course, but overall it works really well.

That opens so many possibilities for using GitHub Copilot across a wide range of tasks. We have contributed to Go libraries, although we are not familiar with Go as a language at all. We have written Splunk/ Grafana/Power BI queries and dashboards with it, created scripts to load data from APIs, and migrated issues from repo to repo using the GitHub MCP server. You can use GitHub Copilot for ideation, to review your code, to find new ways to use your application, or ways to make it more performant. Every time we ask for ways to make the code more readable and therefore more maintainable, people are amazed by the results. That is the challenge we want to put to you, to use GitHub Copilot more for discovery and tasks that you normally do not get the time for, and take it to the next level!

Review and refine, don't just accept

One of the biggest traps we see with new users is hitting *Tab* too quickly. GitHub Copilot produces a suggestion, and people accept it right away, without checking whether it actually solves their problem, fits their coding standards, or keeps things clean. What we learned is that the first suggestion is usually just a starting point, not the finished product. By asking Copilot to "make it simpler," "optimize this loop," or "rewrite this to match method X," you get a much stronger result. Treat the output as a draft and keep the conversation going. This small shift in mindset helps you remain the engineer in control, instead of letting the tool dictate your code.

Build team etiquette for Copilot

When only one person uses GitHub Copilot, you see their personal style reflected in the code. But when a whole team starts using it, you quickly notice inconsistencies. Some people leave detailed comments to guide the AI, others barely prompt at all. Some rely heavily on chat, while others only use inline completions. Without a shared way of working, pull requests can feel like patchwork.

What worked better for us was talking about "AI etiquette" as a team. Decide how much context you want to leave in comments, how you validate generated tests, and when to use chat versus inline prompts. Just like coding standards, these agreements make collaboration smoother and help everyone get consistent value from GitHub Copilot. Document these agreements in the custom instructions file so that everyone, including GitHub Copilot, has the same context when making changes to the code base.

Talk to it like a person (but know it doesn't care)

A question we hear a lot is: Should I be polite when prompting? Does "please" or "thank you" make any difference? The short answer is no, the model doesn't "feel" or reward politeness. The real trick is to focus on describing what you want clearly and directly. Work with it in the same way you would work with someone that is new to your code base and explain as much as possible about what you want to achieve, the constraints that you have when the code base is being executed, and so on. Often, people are very terse in their prompts, leading to lower-quality answers. Since GitHub Copilot has no history other than the current chat conversation and the code base at hand, you will need to explain things to it, just like you would to a new team member.

Reset the conversation when things go sideways

We noticed in our training sessions that people often keep poking GitHub Copilot with slightly different prompts when it is clearly stuck in a loop. By doing this, the results do not improve, and frustration builds quickly. What we learned is that it works much better to reset the situation instead. Move your cursor, close files that are not part of the task, or even start a fresh chat conversation. That small reset often makes GitHub Copilot take a completely different path. We now compare it to wiping the whiteboard in a classroom: sometimes you need a clean slate to get unstuck.

Remember, the entire chat history is used as context for generating responses. So, if the quality of suggestions starts to drop, it might be time for a reset. Starting a new conversation can help Copilot refocus—especially when switching tasks, such as moving from backend to frontend work, or after submitting a pull request. A fresh chat is like wiping the whiteboard clean: it gives the model a chance to take a new direction without being influenced by previous context.

Mix prompting styles, models, and chat modes

Over time, we have seen that people tend to fall into a single prompting style – either very short or very long. Both have their place. Short prompts often work great for quick completions or boilerplate, while longer and more structured prompts are better for complex refactors or new features. During customer sessions, we also learned that trying a different model can completely change the outcome. One model might generate more concise code, and another might give you more detail or comments.

Our tip is to experiment with both prompt length and model choice. The people who do this get noticeably better results because they are not locked into one way of working. Add extra information in your prompts if you switch between ways of approaching a coding challenge as well: when researching, switch to Ask Mode to prevent GitHub Copilot from immediately writing code. You research first to get enough context to handle your current task. Only when you feel like you have enough context do you switch to Edit or Agent Mode and start implementing. It's the same vice versa: when you change tasks, switching back to Edit or Agent Mode can help a lot.

One example of this is handling bugs in your code. Instead of dropping the error into the chat with Agent Mode and hoping that GitHub Copilot will figure it out, we start in Ask Mode first. We can use a prompt to try to find where in the code the bug might be coming from. We then add extra context by mentioning, for example, that this bug only occurs if we run the code in a memory-constrained environment, and continue until we have enough context in the chat to have properly analyzed the issue and found the places where adjustments are needed. Only then do we switch to Agent Mode (which preserves the chat history) and ask GitHub Copilot to make the necessary changes in the places we have identified in our analysis.

Learn from what it gets wrong

This final lesson came from watching people react when GitHub Copilot gives a bad suggestion. The first instinct is usually to dismiss it as "useless" or "garbage." What helped us was looking at those moments as feedback instead. If the result was wrong, was it because the context was too thin, the goal was not clear, or the request was too ambitious? Once we started asking those questions, our prompting skills improved quickly. We even began sharing bad outputs with each other during training, because sometimes the "wrong" suggestion sparked a new idea or revealed a gap we had not thought of. So, even the failures became part of the learning process. Similarly, share these experiences as it helps other people to understand the current state of different modes or models. Especially models that are in preview can run into issues, as GitHub is still working on the quality of the responses, while giving you a chance to learn from the new options.

With these learning motions, we shared some tips that helped us to go to the next level of proficiency using GitHub Copilot and improved our quality of life by either saving us manual work or by lowering the mental load of keeping track of extra information. Not all of them might work for you, and some can be realizations that make sense after spending some more time working with GitHub Copilot. Use them to your benefit where it helps, and share your own epiphanies on this with us as well! We continuously learn new ways of looking at problems as well, and are very curious about all the creative ways you look at these learning opportunities.

Now we are going to look at an example to tie all these learning motions together, by approaching GitHub Copilot in a staggered manner, so that you build up context and use that context over time in the same conversation. The more context the LLM can get, the better the results will be.

Approaching problems the right way

To come back to the wrong ways we see people use generative AI and tools such as GitHub Copilot, we want to show you the right ways as well. Since LLMs use the context of what they know (given by the IDEs) to predict the most likely next word(s), we can use that to give enough context (and not too much) to describe *what* we want to achieve, but not too much on *how* to achieve it. We also know that the longer the suggestions are, the lower the quality will be. So, we don't go for big results in one go.

Let's take an example. Let's say you don't have any code and you want you to build a game. A bad idea would be to simply say, `Build Super Mario in Vite.js`, as shown in *Figure 8.5*:

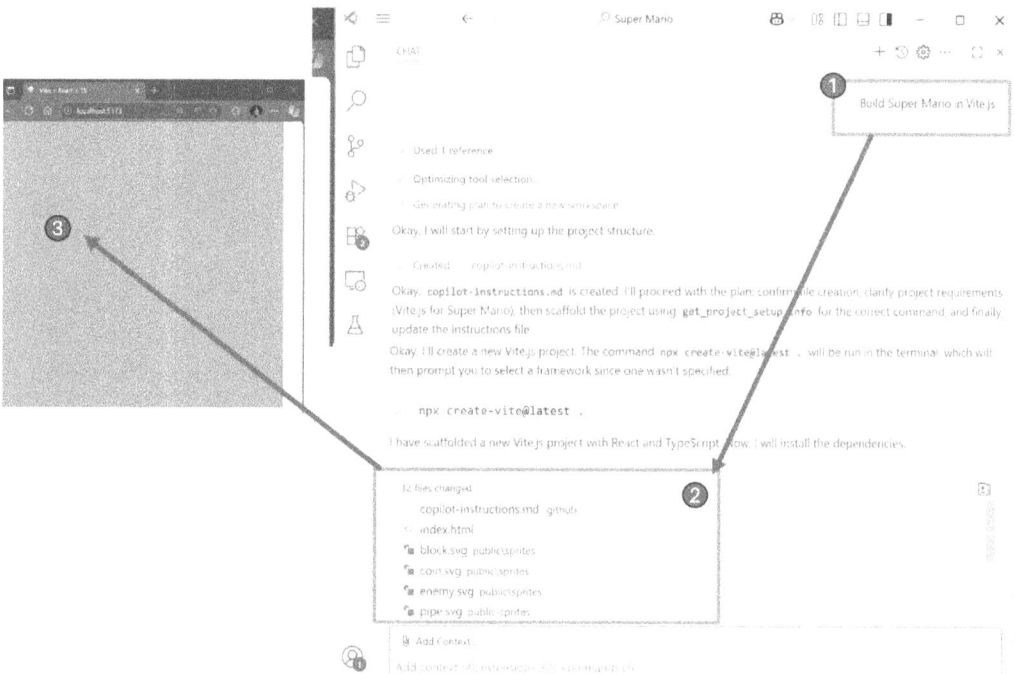

Figure 8.5: Prompt too short with big expectations

As you can see, I prompted `"Build Super Mario in Vite.js"` in an empty folder. GitHub Copilot generated plenty of files that have sensible names, so the expectations were rather high. Even after iterating on the prompt with Agent Mode for over 10 minutes, I only got a blue rectangle when I started up the game, and nothing else. There were all sorts of mistakes in the generated code, including using a package that is no longer supported. This is an example of starting off too big and ending up disappointed.

When starting from scratch, our recommendation is to build things up slowly and to make sure you have the right foundations in place. For example, a key thing to start with is making sure your code can be executed locally, and that you can run all tests locally as well. This will give us the most confidence that the code works as we want it to.

Keeping with our game example, in *Figure 8.6*, you can see that we start by asking for help to devise a good approach for tackling such an assignment, specifically asking, `"Let's make a plan before we start to iterate."`

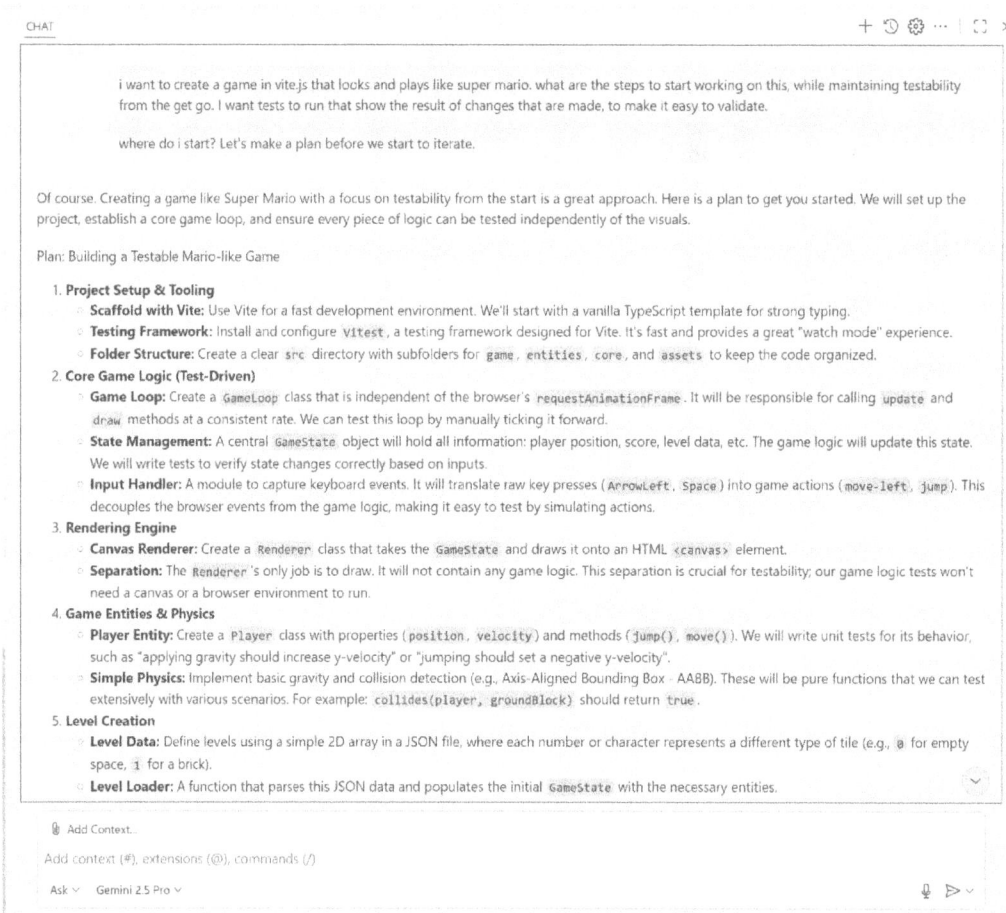

Figure 8.6: Prompt with more steps and context

Based on the output of the chat, you can ask follow-up questions to guide the model through the steps you want it to take, which will get you higher-quality results. Some of those follow-up questions/prompts in this scenario would be: `"Add the tests to describe the behavior we want to implement,"` or `"Add a script to build the application and execute the unit tests."`

Working this way helps you build a foundation of tests so that you can gain trust that the changes that are made add the features you wanted to create.

By being mindful of the way we prompt GitHub Copilot, we make the changes smaller in the beginning. Once the foundation has been laid in the form of project structure and tests, you will start to see that we can go faster, because GitHub Copilot uses the generated content to tune the next changes it makes.

Summary

In this chapter, we looked at lessons that we have learned over time to work faster with GitHub Copilot, or to get better results from it. By either realizing seemingly little things, such as "typos do not matter" or "accept the truth: there is no magic," we have a different way we look at generative AI as a whole and realize that our value as an engineer has moved a little bit as well. Instead of focusing on the most amazing approach or the most brilliant way to write a piece of code, we focus on adding more business value instead. By making a couple of adjustments to how we go from ideation to code creation, and by describing *what* we want to achieve, and less about *how* we want to achieve it, we get more help from the tooling and sometimes even learn about new concepts that fit even better than our own initial ideas!

We did not magically discover all these learning motions just by using the tools ourselves. We learn the most by looking at other people using these tools and asking for tips and tricks to learn from them. We've been part of so many training sessions with co-trainers, and every one of them has slightly different ways of working with GitHub Copilot! The next chapter dives into building a knowledge-sharing community around these tools, where you can learn new ways of using them, and even see new features being demonstrated, for example. Keeping up with the latest changes is a challenge, so the more people share about new functionality that helps them in some way, the more ideas you get on how you can get to the next level of proficiency with GitHub Copilot as well.

Get This Book's PDF Version and Exclusive Extras

Scan the QR code (or go to packtpub.com/unlock). Search for this book by name, confirm the edition, and then follow the steps on the page.

Note: Keep your invoice handy. Purchases made directly from Packt don't require one.

9

Building an Internal GitHub Copilot Community

Over the course of the last years, we have been part of many rollouts and enablement programs at all sorts of customers, from less than a hundred developers to thousands. One thing that always stood out for us is that engineers are generally working on the same thing – adding value for their end users – but the way they achieve this tends to be different at every company, sometimes even between departments and teams. We also see that there is often a disconnect between teams, in the sense that they are not prone to or encouraged to share knowledge between their different cohorts. Often, the tools and ways of working stay within their own team/department/group, which leads to siloed information and different teams attempting to reinvent the wheel.

In this chapter, we share how we have helped to build communities with our customers and our own teams, to keep on learning from each other about novel use cases, or just new features that are being added to GitHub Copilot. We will cover the following topics:

- Acknowledging the learning curve
- Using internal wikis
- Setting up weekly Q&A sessions
- Creating newsletters
- Organizing hackathons
- Surveying the users
- Looking at metrics

Acknowledge the learning curve

As seen in the last chapter, all efforts start with accepting the fact that there is a learning curve with these new generative AI tools – whether that's Microsoft 365 Copilot, Claude, Gemini, or GitHub Copilot. Getting your team(s) to a point where they can really gain value with generative AI in their way of working takes both time and training.

Just handing out a license and hoping people will figure it out is not good enough. We have met people who were very dismissive of generative AI and/or GitHub Copilot, because they had wild expectations of what these tools could do for them. Their leadership had dismissed the learning curve, and thus, the engineers tossed wild prompts at the tools and were not impressed with the results. After we spoke to them and delivered training about "getting started with GitHub Copilot," they told us they now had a better understanding of what these tools are and how they can help them with their work, particularly within the bounds of what they can and cannot do.

After accepting the fact that you need to learn these new tools, we can take a look at how people learn. Everyone has a different way of learning, and most of their learning preferences fall into two categories: learning through training or learning by taking the tools for a spin. We'll dive into these categories to give you a better understanding and have an idea of how you can cater to the different needs of different people as well. Though these are separate categories, most people follow the training in both categories, first getting a training that explains the core concepts and ideas, and then combining that with hands-on exercises to see the impact of the new tools in their own way of working.

Learning through training

A lot of people want to follow training to understand what these tools can do, how to apply them, and how to use their strengths and weaknesses to their advantage. Setting up a training path guides people through the learning flow and helps them align different features with steps in their process to produce their applications or solutions.

We recommend following the flow from this book as well, by learning about generative AI and language models in particular, and then going from code completions to the chat with first Ask Mode, then Edit Mode, and finally, Agent Mode. On top of that, you can add the tools available in the Web UI for GitHub, such as the Chat interface to start gathering context for new issues, then pull request reviews, and the coding agent. You can see a schema for this flow here:

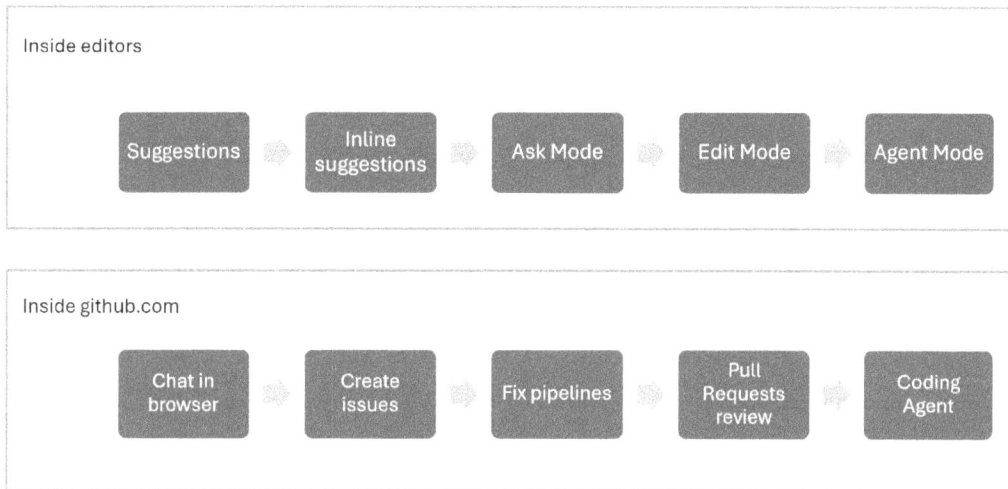

Figure 9.1: Topic order during training

We follow this flow so that people gradually learn about the next level of co-creation with these tools, which helps to keep the expectations realistic. That's also why we specifically do not start with Agent Mode from the get-go: without proper experience, there is too much room for error, sometimes with disastrous results. Skipping the basics, even up to including how generative AI works under the hood, leads to expecting that these tools are always correct and cannot fail. We want to prevent people from falling into that pit and guide them to success instead.

To transfer knowledge to engineers, you can either have someone deliver a live training (either in-person or online) or you can let people watch a prerecorded session. Keep in mind that there are people with different preferences and different learning needs. We recommend catering for both types of training. Some people prefer to watch a video, as they can pause, rewind, and retry, whereas some people prefer to have live training, as they can ask questions and directly get an answer. We've even met people who do both – they want to see the recording (and rewind to get a better understanding) and then come to a training session to ask those follow-up questions and really internalize the content.

From our experience, we've learned that it helps to meet people where they are and offer multiple ways for them to engage with the material and the trainers. We've been with customers who had set up entire learning paths in their e-learning environments, where they noticed that people were not looking at those training materials at all. Those customers made the mistake of just handing everyone a license, pointing them to the internal or external e-learning platform, and that was the extent of "enablement" for a new tool. Those customers did not acknowledge the learning curve (or even worse: expected all engineers to look at the training in their own time) and saw that engineers were not engaged and thus not getting the promised value from the new tools.

We recommend combining all options, so people can choose. Planning live training helps to clear time in people's agendas, so that they can dive into the new tools. It also gives a clear signal of support from the company's management, as you indicate that it is important to allot time for this training and not spend it on their normal work. Next to that, give them access and time for prerecorded content, and then arrange follow-up sessions for Q/A, hackathons, and so on. Doing all these things is needed not only when first rolling out the access for the tools, but also for new joiners, or for people who have been using the tools for a while. The generative AI space is moving so fast that just for GitHub Copilot, we have "What's new since the last time" sessions with engineers at least every six months!

Learning from using the tools

The second learning category is learning by getting hands-on experience. Some people have been following along with the news of generative AI or GitHub Copilot, and they want to dive straight in and see how things work in their own development flows.

As we have seen in *Chapter 3*, there is a Free plan available for those who want to see how the tools perform in their own editors, so that is an easy way to start. Do note that even these folks are helped with some formal training, so do offer them the option to get going and then still join a training session. The training is meant to give extra context, discuss different capabilities, and showcase situations people might not have thought of to apply these tools to. As mentioned earlier, some people often combine both learning categories discussed, rather than following them separately.

To help people discover the main features of GitHub Copilot, we split the hands-on into two separate parts: we start with generic examples to try out in a controlled environment, and then let them apply the tools to their own code, with defined tasks. There are plenty of online resources that can be used for generic examples. The one we recommend is Copilot Adventures, created by Microsoft Learn: `https://microsoft.github.io/CopilotAdventures`. It has exercises to take you through different coding scenarios and lets you choose the adventure based on the level of proficiency you already have with GitHub Copilot. Even better, these scenarios are updated over time as well, with recent additions being custom chat modes and Model Context Protocol adventures.

Figure 9.2: Copilot Adventures

We always propose setting aside time for people to take the time to go through these exercises. This shows engineers again that you take the tool and the training for it seriously, instead of hoping they follow these exercises in their own time. If you do not allocate a timeslot(s) for it, people usually skip it (there is always "work" to do), and then they do not progress as much to become really proficient with the tools.

After acknowledging the learning curve and planning training sessions, we recommend starting up an internal community so that people can find each other, share learnings and updates, and continuously see how other people are using the tools in their context. Often, companies do not have these kinds of communities, so this can be the beginning of becoming a knowledge-sharing company as well, bringing different teams and sectors of the company together. In the following sections, we will take a look at some of these methods, such as wikis, Q&A sessions, hackathons, and more.

If you want to dive even deeper, there is a great community example available at `https://github.com/orgs/community/discussions/86520`, where GitHub shows you how to use GitHub Discussions (a Q/A style forum), straight from your normal GitHub repository!

Internal wikis

People always need to be able to find internal documentation, information to access training, links to internal support on getting a license and installations, and so on. Most companies have an internal way for the community to gather and share this kind of information, and there often is a person or a team responsible for crafting this documentation and keeping things up to date.

Here is some content that we often include in the wikis we helped with:

- Instructions on how to download and install the editors your company prefers, together with the necessary GitHub Copilot extensions.
- Information on how to get internal support for the new tools, such as where people can ask questions, how to get a license, and so on.
- Instructions on how to regularly update both the editor and the GitHub Copilot extensions. The extension updates come by so fast that they contain a "minimal editor version" that is required. They even build new features into the editor all the time to provide new APIs for the extensions to use, so updating the editor itself is also paramount. We advise keeping the editor up to date with at least the most recent minus to minor version releases – release numbers are usually in the form of *major.minor.patch*, so when v1.100.0 is released, the users should at least be at v1.98.0, including the most recent version of the extensions.
- Information on what the internal guidelines are for using GitHub Copilot, what editors are supported in the internal environment, and how to follow along with the internal community and receive news updates.
- Group information about new features and the editor updates that are needed to unlock them.
- Don't forget to add an online version of any news bulletins you send out, for example, announcements or a newsletter. That way, people can search for and reference them later, such as when someone new joins their team.

Weekly Q&A sessions

Even after all the training sessions and hands-on times, people will have questions, and there will be new updates to share. Neither GitHub nor the editor teams are sitting still, and the field of generative AI and ways to add it to the developer workflow are evolving all the time.

We therefore recommend that for at least the first six months after starting the program, you keep doing these sessions on a weekly basis. There will always be people installing GitHub Copilot for the first time, or they discover a feature, or run into things they can use some help with. We use the Q&A sessions to drive the community feeling, update the wiki with recurring questions, and ask the group for topics they want to know more about. Those topics can then be used for a demo in the next session, or as a starting point for a new knowledge-sharing session (or even training) that can be recorded for future use.

Getting insights from the community during these sessions helps massively to connect people as well. When someone asks for more examples to create unit tests with GitHub Copilot, and someone else responds that they have a great flow or prompt for it, you have just connected them, often across departments as well! Follow up on those examples by asking those folks to record a blog post to put on the wiki, or a short video explaining their process, and all of a sudden, you have another topic to share internally.

These kinds of mini knowledge-sharing sessions work like a charm: instead of a trainer giving often canned demos, now you have someone internally sharing their story of how the tools help them, with their internal environment, tool stack, and coding language. Keep asking for examples from the community, because the more examples of different environments you get, the more people can translate them into their own processes as well!

Newsletters

As we indicated before, it is important to meet people where they are. For a lot of people, we have seen that they either think that they know everything already, or they think they are too busy to spend time researching the wiki or visiting the Q&A sessions, and so on. Providing a simple recap of the news in the form of a newsletter can help folks scan the news for things that might seem interesting to them and then lead them to the wiki or a mini knowledge-sharing video.

Here are some helpful tips for creating newsletters:

- Keep the newsletter informative and spruce it up with some screenshots and humorous images. Luckily, GitHub has a great mascot, Mona the Octocat (a combination of a cat and an octopus), and they have even created a personalizer for it that can be found at `https://myoctocat.com`.

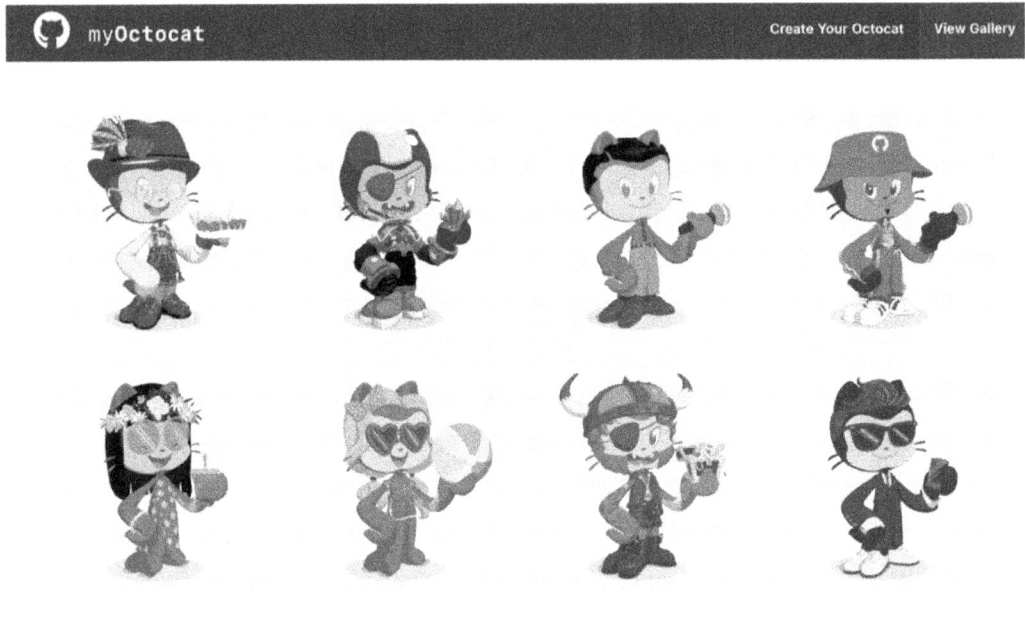

Figure 9.3: Different ways to do something playful with Mona

- We always combine the news of the last week(s) in the newsletter with some recurring questions (with links to the wiki) and include some novel use cases we have seen GitHub Copilot used for.
- Provide links back to the Q&A sessions to bring in more audience and point out how folks can get support if they cannot wait for the Q&A session to happen.

Keeping up to date with all the news online is quite a challenge. Every editor has one or more websites to follow, and there is often both a post from the editor team itself and one from GitHub as well. You can follow all those blogs one by one or combine them into a single news source like we did for ourselves and our company's training teams. Together, we have built `https://github-copilot.xebia.ms`, which we often revisit right before a Q&A session or when writing a new edition of the newsletter.

Hackathons

Most people learn by doing, and this is where we use hackathons. This allows us to get people out of their normal day-to-day context and into a new and clean environment. Planning these sessions into their calendars also shows the commitment to invest time (and thus money) into their training and understanding of the new tools. We normally use at least 2 hours for hackathons, and up to half of a normal day.

There are several options to set people to work, and often we have multiple hackathons planned to give people a chance to gradually grow through the different features of GitHub Copilot. Participants can do the following:

- Hack away at a completely new project (often a game). This involves the following:

    - Starting research from scratch

    - Implementing tools/languages/SDKs that they are not familiar with

    - Adding testing and documentation

    - Switching the project to a different team and learning from their approach and setup

    This hackathon helps to look at your coding process with a fresh view, and gives you the opportunity to leave existing steps behind. This leads to some great new insights.

- Hack away at your own project. This involves the following:

    - Focusing first on all sorts of technical debt, as adding those to the project often improves the results of GitHub Copilot

    - Adding missing integration/unit tests, documentation, improving the README, adding custom instructions, and so on

    In this hackathon, part of the instructions are to refrain from writing any code and using GitHub Copilot as much as possible. This leads to using the new features and especially helps people to start using the Chat interface for most of their work.

These hackathons are always fun and give people the opportunity to step outside their comfort zone. To enable that, we have several tips to share that we use all the time.

Always open with a GitHub Copilot feature

We always open up the hackathon with a specific topic and link it to a common goal we have. For example, some teams may have a quarterly initiative to focus on quality improvements. Based on that, the topic could be improving trust in changes before deployment, and the task could be "how to improve unit test coverage with GitHub Copilot."

People are often searching for the intent of the exercise and may be uncertain what is expected of them, so this approach helps them along. Make it a story with a presentation/some slides, and demonstrate the functionality. Once they have (re)seen the feature, they can be tasked to work with that feature for the challenge or topic at hand that you give them.

You might also consider splitting up features, functionality, or refactoring, focusing on how to approach it with GitHub Copilot, and then letting teams apply that approach to improve their own code.

Mix and mingle

Hackathons are excellent for letting people explore other teams and their way of working. We bring different teams together and let them work in pairs, with the recommendation to work with someone outside of their team. Suddenly, they are learning new teams' processes, editors, or languages. Often, people do not look across their team's borders and scopes, so this is a real improvement. You can also help this process along by, for example, mixing them up based on years of engineering experience, proficiency with GitHub Copilot, and so on.

In the first type of hackathon, where participants work on new projects, we also switch things around: after working on their project for two-thirds of the time, we let them push the repo and get the repo from another team. This reinforces that everyone (often) uses a different approach. With GitHub Copilot, teams can use the Chat interface to research new routes and solutions, generate changes, and send pull requests with improvements. For lots of teams, this is already a big eye-opener as they are often super closed in their way of working, and not a lot of collaboration is happening in their environments.

Report out/giveaway prizes

At the end of the hackathon, we invite participants to present their learnings, solutions, or the value they added to their application. Discussing how GitHub Copilot helped them brings another level of connection to other people and teams, encouraging learning from each other, and being able to ask follow-up questions for points that piqued their interest. This is a really good way to close out the session, as well as celebrate the lessons learned.

We often bring small prizes to the session for the people with the best story, approach, or lesson learned. We specifically do not focus on who built the best solution or who was the fastest. Instead, we prioritize what participants learned, their openness about the challenges they faced, and how thoughtfully they pursued their goals with GitHub Copilot. Seeing people open up and helping other people forward – those are the things we cherish. And let's face it, giving people a little memento of their hard work is always a good idea.

So, as you can see, hackathons are a great way to set a direction for people and have them dis-cover the new tools and capabilities they have now learned. The hands-on part of this helps to understand the impact of generative AI on their way of working, and doing that with different teams helps to bring people together across the internal boundaries. This is a great way to kick-start the community as well!

Surveys

Learning about new tools that integrate into your way of working is always a journey and is never complete. Especially with GitHub Copilot and the momentum that generative AI has these days, there is something new each day. Even if you share new features in a newsletter all the time, and have regular hackathons and weekly Q/A sessions, you (or your management) probably want to know and learn from the engineers how they are using the tools in their development processes, find some power users that can share their top tips, or learn where the tool does not work so well so that you can have a look at how that could be improved.

One of the ways to learn about all this is to ask the GitHub Copilot users: "What feedback do you have for this tool?" There are all sorts of tools on the market to help out with this: from entire "developer experience" methodologies with tools included, to a standard survey tool. You can use the tools your company/team already uses and expand when needed.

Our tip is to keep the survey low-key and to position it as a way for users to provide feedback. We have seen all sorts of motions in these surveys in an attempt to get people to respond to them. Some surveys try to ask for way too much information that has nothing to do with GitHub Copilot. If your survey has more than 10 questions, the response rate will be impacted negatively by it. The sweet spot seems to be 4–6 questions, maximum.

Also, keep in mind that people often only get vocal about things when they do not like certain aspects of them. Happy people keep rather quiet about the tools that they use, until you revoke their access. We have even been with companies that make these surveys mandatory in order to keep your license. In our opinion, that is not necessarily motivational to get good quality responses.

When sending out a survey, if you already know about certain data points (such as years of expe-rience with a language or SDK), then keep them out of the survey. Ask questions such as "Does GitHub Copilot help you in your day-to-day (coding) work?" or "Would you like to receive more training on specific topics with GitHub Copilot?". Don't forget to have options to elaborate on their answer, as a simple yes/no might not be sufficient everywhere.

In the following table, you can see an overview of dos and don'ts when it comes to surveys:

Dos	Don'ts
Encourage continuous learning about tools such as GitHub Copilot	Assume the learning journey is ever complete
Share new features regularly (e.g., newsletters, hackathons, and Q&A)	Rely solely on top-down communication – engage engineers directly
Identify power users and gather their tips	Ignore feedback from actual users of the tool
Ask users for feedback through surveys	Make surveys overly formal or complex
Use existing tools that your team is familiar with for feedback collection	Force adoption of unfamiliar or overly elaborate feedback tools
Keep surveys low-key and positioned as a feedback opportunity	Make surveys mandatory to retain access; this can reduce response quality
Keep surveys short and focused	Ask for information you already have (e.g., experience level)
Include open-ended questions for elaboration	Rely only on yes/no questions without room for context

Figure 9.4: Dos and don'ts of surveys

After doing all the work to get people to use the new tooling and embrace that in their work, it is time to take a look at measuring the usage as well. As you are paying licenses for these tools and have taken the time to make sure you can use them in compliance with the company's internal policies around security, legal, and responsible usage, there will be a need to look a certain information around usage statistics.

Metrics

Discussing metrics on tools such as GitHub Copilot can be a book all of its own. There is a lot of research on how to measure developer output (also referred to as *productivity*) and what that means. We see customers wanting to take a look at this data as well, but most of them have not started to think of what developer output is, let alone how to compare it.

It is also hard to determine how to measure (developer) output and what a significant improvement in that output would be. Companies often only look at things they can measure, which quickly becomes things such as lines of code, number of pull requests, story points, and so on. However, engineers add value to applications in different ways than just adding extra code – their value is in making the application more performant, more secure, or better able to handle the user's needs. With the investments that need to be made to enable engineers with GitHub Copilot, companies feel the need to look at developer productivity again, to justify the investments that need to be made.

It is often overlooked that the impact of generative AI is also in other aspects of our work, from ideation (issues or user stories) to architectural work, to a change in the number of review comments, or bugs found in production. All these things can be a result of using tools such as GitHub Copilot in your workflows. The hard part with these metrics is that looking at them can give a sense of developers being more productive than before, while there is a lot more to the story than just having more of the things you are measuring as "developer productivity."

Take, for example, the number of **pull requests** (**PRs**) merged in a given period. Is merging a PR really a measure of success? Does that take into account the size of the PR? What about the quality of the PR? Can we perhaps measure that by looking at the number of bugs that are introduced with these code changes? The impact of these changes further down in the system is often overlooked. Even the change in the size (amount of files/lines changed) of the PR can be an indicator of people changing their way of working. Having a bigger PR might mean the engineer was able to complete the changes to a feature in one go, but it might also mean they are not validating all the changes locally, as "the AI made them."

Instead, we need to look at different information on the PR:

- Are the PRs getting bigger/smaller over time? Is this because of GitHub Copilot, or does it have other reasons?
- How does that impact the number of comments in the PR review? If people use AI to generate the code, does the quality and clarity of the code go up or down?
- Are the CI builds for the PRs failing more often with the use of GitHub Copilot?

These aspects say something about what we call the "downstream impact" of GitHub Copilot. Just looking at metrics on things we can measure only tells half of the story if you do not look at impact later in the software development lifecycle. The downstream impact shows whether engineers are using AI to their benefit or if they become complacent and just accept whatever the AI suggests.

The examples we have seen also show how complex it is to look at productivity, as there are many aspects that impact our code, and all of them have their own nuances to determine whether the impact is positive or negative.

Rather than looking at productivity, GitHub focuses as much as possible on *usage* metrics: how people are using GitHub Copilot, what features they are using, and which features are lacking engagement. To help companies that want to start their journey into measuring engineering productivity, GitHub has created the **Engineering System Success Playbook (ESSP)**. It is a three-step process that can help you drive meaningful, measurable improvements in your organization, whether you're looking to adopt a new AI tool such as GitHub Copilot or identify and unlock bottlenecks that have been hindering performance. You can find the ESSP here: `https://resources.github.com/engineering-system-success-playbook`.

The usage metrics provide us with information on *how* people are using these tools, and a little bit of information on their perceived value. We recommend doing the same: if a user almost never uses the tool, or only at the beginning of getting a license, then you can likely infer that there is not that much value in it for them, for whatever reason. That should lead to reaching out to these users to learn from their environment or other reasons why they cannot use GitHub Copilot to their benefit.

Other users might use the tools so much that you can learn from their way of working or get them to teach their tricks to the rest of the user group in your company. There are two major datasets you can use the metrics from, and both can be viewed on GitHub with nice dashboards and charts:

- The first is the **Metrics** dashboards on the **Insights** tab. This is visible for the enterprise- or organization-level admins if you have a Business or Enterprise plan for GitHub Copilot:

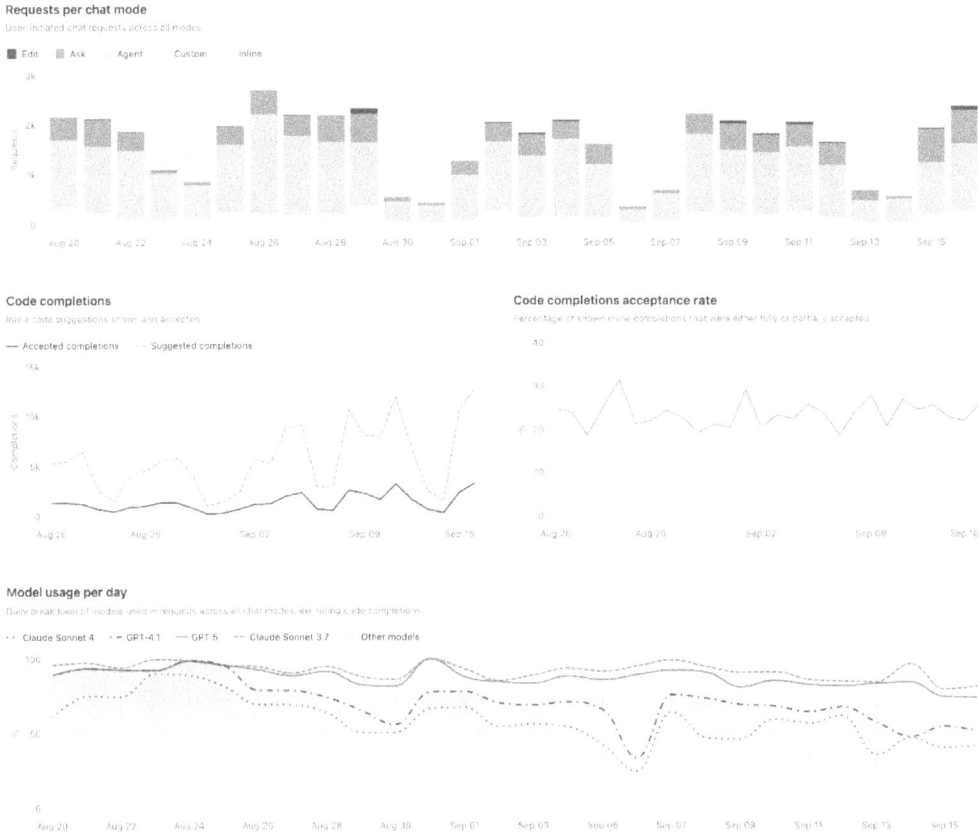

Figure 9.5: Copilot Metrics dashboard

To view this image in color

Use the free color PDF edition included with your purchase. Refer to the *Free Benefits with Your Book* section in the *Preface* for details.

In this dashboard, you can see information such as the number of daily active users and weekly active users, together with the number of chat interactions, requests per chat mode, the models that were used, and so on. The information on the dashboard does not let you slice and dice all the information that is available – for that, you need to export the data into a tool that helps. We have helped customers with dashboards in, for example, Power BI, Splunk, Grafana, and so on.

- The second reporting option available is the **Premium request analytics** view, which is available on the **Billing** tab of the enterprise and organization, so only available for enterprise or organization admins and billing administrators, and only for the Business and Enterprise versions of GitHub Copilot.

Copilot premium request analytics

Usage analytics for Copilot premium requests in your enterprise

⌄ Get usage report

Q model: claude-sonnet-3.7   ⊗   Group by: **Users** ▾   Timeframe: **Current month** ▾

Total billed amount	Billed premium requests	Included premium requests consumed
$63.08	**915**	**1,176**
Spend for Copilot premium request usage for Jun 1 - Jun 30, 2025	Billed requests exceeding the premium requests usage included with Copilot licenses.	Included premium requests used by selected model. Monthly limits reset in 1 day on Jul 1, 2025.

Claude Sonnet 3.7 usage grouped by users

Jun 1 - Jun 30, 2025

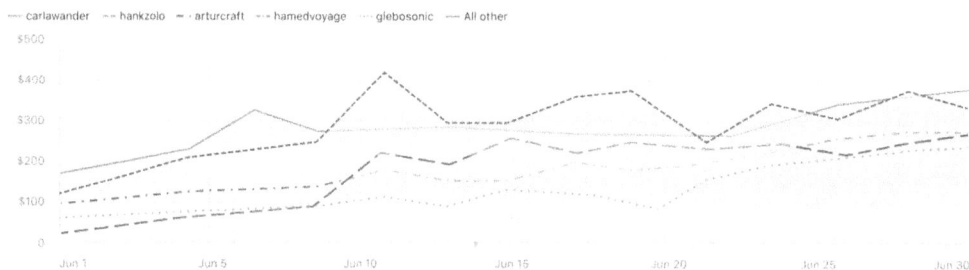

···· carlawander   ─ ─ hankzolo   ━ ·· arturcraft   ·─· hamedvoyage   ····· glebosonic   ── All other

$500
$400
$300
$200
$100
0
        Jun 1   Jun 5   Jun 10   Jun 15   Jun 20   Jun 25   Jun 30

Usage breakdown

Usage for Jun 1 - Jun 30, 2025. Price per premium request is $0.04.

User	Included premium requests	Billed premium requests	Gross amount	Billed amount ⇅
👤 magnusflare Ólafur Magnússon	1,000	1,670	$66.08	**$63.08**
👤 anasazon Anastasiya Sazonova	1,000	1,670	$66.08	**$63.08**

Figure 9.6: Part of the Premium requests analytics view

To view this image in color

Use the free color PDF edition included with your purchase. Refer to the *Free Benefits with Your Book* section in the *Preface* for details.

In this dashboard, you can keep track of how people are using their premium requests and for what they use them. It tracks them across the different models that you have enabled, as well as per user, product, organization, or cost center that has been configured. See *Chapter 3* for more information on premium requests and what they are.

Keep in mind when looking at metrics that it is always interpretable in different ways, and using only one indicator means that you could be missing insights from other data points. We recommend focusing on *how* people are using the tools and going back to the teams with that information to ask them what they need to grow to the next stage with GitHub Copilot.

Summary

In this chapter, we have taken a look at ways and tools to build a community of knowledge-sharing in your teams/organization, so that you can learn from each other. Since the generative AI motion is so new, we are all still adjusting to the new way of working and learning how these tools influence our coding environments, as well as our way of working. By addressing these concerns with each other, you can help to take away some of their worries, and together build out a community that keeps each other up to date on all aspects of using GitHub Copilot: from feature updates on the product and the functionalities in the different editors, to use cases for different environments or models.

We humans learn the most from seeing others work with the tools, which is why sharing your experiences matters so much. Keep on experimenting and sharing your learnings!

In the next and final chapter, we dive deeper into looking at the impact that tools such as GitHub Copilot have on our entire field of work: from discussing the expected impact with peers and managers, to searching for our own position in the new world that is empowered by generative AI tools.

Get This Book's PDF Version and Exclusive Extras

UNLOCK NOW

Scan the QR code (or go to `packtpub.com/unlock`). Search for this book by name, confirm the edition, and then follow the steps on the page.

Note: Keep your invoice handy. Purchases made directly from Packt don't require one.

10
Changing the Narrative: Reframing Engineering with AI

The impact of generative AI in the SDLC is only accelerating and changing our entire field of work. Now, simple and mundane tasks can be handled by agents, so that the human engineers can focus on where the actual value is – in shipping durable, working applications that deliver value to the end user. We are now at the point where creating certain changes becomes a choice between letting a human engineer spend time implementing those changes or handing over the task at hand to an AI agent and paying a couple of dollars so it can be implemented automatically.

In our opinion, we need to shift the narrative away from just enabling engineers to use GitHub Copilot and then simply looking at perceived productivity gains. Currently, companies often focus on the idea that AI produces code more easily and faster, leading them to think they have finally found a way to turn 1 single AI-enabled engineer into 10 engineers (where one engineer enabled with AI tooling can do the work of 10 engineers that do not have those tools available).

We even see engineers hyping this up with stories around "vibe coding" with AI: they jump on their keyboards with a single prompt and accept every suggestion that is given, and then run the application to figure out whether their initial problem was solved or not. Eventually, this path leads to disappointment: either the code does not work as hoped, or there was crucial information missing and the AI took a wrong turn somewhere. Even worse, we have seen generative AI following the "scouting rule" where it starts to clean up after itself, changing code that did not need to be changed at all. This can lead to having an impact on other places in the code base that can introduce new bugs. On top of all that, we see engineers who are not even testing their "vibe coding" creations before pushing them to production. This is a recipe for disaster and will lead to a lot of frustration and disappointment in the long run.

Another issue we see is that managers often think that they will get those 10 engineers with these new tools, and all their issues producing business value will be gone! The focal point tends to be on making the engineers more "productive," so that they create more code and thus value for the end user, and that code is also produced faster than ever before. Doing so, they completely skip over the fact that we are focusing on just the two hours a day that an engineer has available to focus on coding work (see, for example, ActiveState's 2019 Developer Survey: `https://www.activestate.com/wp-content/uploads/2019/05/ActiveState-Developer-Survey-2019-Open-Source-Runtime-Pains.pdf`). The other time in a day is spent on things such as requirements gathering, documentation, and meetings. We are not talking at all about optimizing the rest of the workday!

Bulk of Non-Programming Time

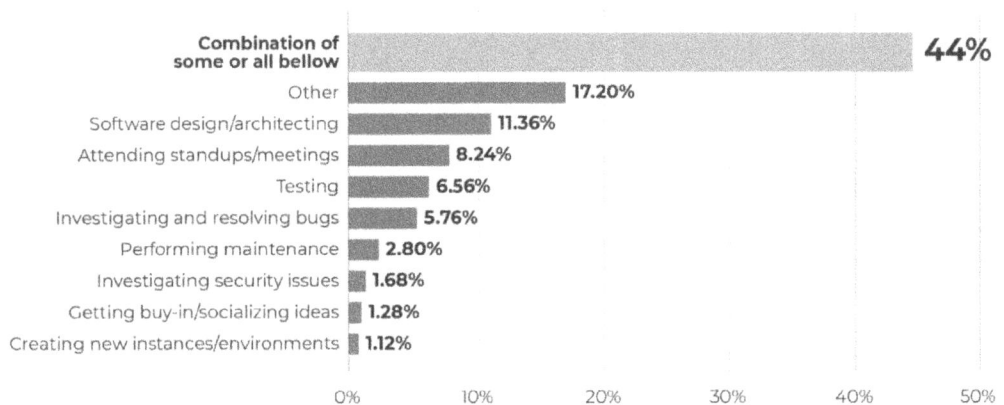

Category	Percentage
Combination of some or all bellow	44%
Other	17.20%
Software design/architecting	11.36%
Attending standups/meetings	8.24%
Testing	6.56%
Investigating and resolving bugs	5.76%
Performing maintenance	2.80%
Investigating security issues	1.68%
Getting buy-in/socializing ideas	1.28%
Creating new instances/environments	1.12%

Figure 10.1: Bulk of non-programming time from the ActiveState 2019 Developer Report

To view this image in color

Use the free color PDF edition included with your purchase. Refer to the *Free Benefits with Your Book* section in the *Preface* for details.

GitHub Copilot can be leveraged to help with some of these tasks left and right, such as requirements gathering, but with tasks like standups, refinements, and meetings, it is harder to find a good use case for GitHub Copilot. There are other tools available that help with those kinds of things, such as automatic meeting note transcribers from various vendors.

Just focusing on code generation all strikes us as a bit narrow-minded. Suddenly, we see companies needing to defend the cost of enabling their developers with GitHub Copilot. This raises an interesting point: even though GitHub Copilot promises productivity gains, its licensing cost often becomes a focal point. We've seen business cases where the primary justification for the expense hinges entirely on anticipated productivity improvements, in an effort to defend the license costs. Of course, if you have 500 engineers who now need new tooling that costs an extra $19 a month (for the Business license), that becomes 500 x 12 months x $19 =$114,000. On the other hand, we have never needed to pitch a business case for buying licenses for their code editors, or for their Office tools, but for tooling that helps us for two hours a day, we need to define a business case and defend why we need to spend around $19 a month on GitHub Copilot!

Most editors cost a multiple of that cost, let alone the hardware that engineers use these days. If you take a low figure of the salary cost for an engineer, then we can calculate that the license cost is already earned back if we save the engineer around 20 minutes of time per month! Since our entire industry is already on the AI bandwagon, the **return on investment (ROI)** discussion should be rather easy.

All the more reason to shift the narrative away from just ROI and talk about the actual impact GitHub Copilot can have in your organization, if you have the right things in mind. We need to look at the downstream effects on both the code base and the engineers that allow us to get the most out of the new wave of tools. What do we need to have in place to be able to reap the benefits? How do we extend the impact to the people in our teams who are not engineers?

That is why we are going to look at the following topics in this chapter:

- Ethical use of GitHub Copilot
- Building a sturdy DevOps foundation
- Expanding AI to engineer-adjacent roles
- AI-enhanced engineering

Ethical use of GitHub Copilot

When using tools that generate parts of your code base, we always need to keep in mind several ethical aspects. There is an aspect of code generation itself where large language models display certain traits based on the way they have been trained. We already mentioned things such as bias in *Chapter 2*. Another aspect is *how* engineers use these tools and are diligent in the way the tools impact their way of working. If the engineer stops thinking and blindly accepts every output of the large language models, did they actually gain anything? We don't think so. This aspect is more of a cultural effect that AI can have on how teams work: we need to refrain from just pointing at the tools and saying it was generated by AI and therefore it should just work. We are the human in the loop, and we need to bring our professional view to creating the business value for our end user.

As engineers, that means we need to stay on top of things and be the human in the loop: we make ethical decisions on using the code suggestions, and we make choices to implement our code in a certain way. For example, we must do the following:

- Ensure that any code we accept from GitHub Copilot does not inadvertently introduce security vulnerabilities, such as hardcoded credentials or unsafe input handling

- Be vigilant about copyright and licensing – if the suggested code closely resembles open source projects with restrictive licenses, it's our responsibility to verify that we're allowed to use it

- Avoid using AI-generated code that could reinforce bias or discrimination, especially in areas such as hiring algorithms or user-facing features

These are just a few examples of the ethical decisions we face as engineers working with AI-powered tools.

We need to continue to be professionals who think about all aspects of creating applications: we bring the vision for building a solution that takes into account our requirements, both from a functional perspective as well as from a technical aspect. All the more since the person who is linked to the code changes is still us, and not the AI: each commit or pull request is created in our name, so this is all attributed to the engineer making changes. We need to keep to our standards to build applications that show the right level of professionalism and purpose. By doing so, we ensure our applications not only meet expectations but also inspire confidence and pride in what we deliver. Continue to think for yourself and add what is needed to your prompt and implementation: you are still the pilot!

Now that we have discussed the ethical aspects of using GitHub Copilot, both in the known limitations of generative AI and bias, as well as the cultural aspects of the impact tools have on engineers and their teams, we can look at what needs to be in place to actually be able to get the most value out of GitHub Copilot, as all is dependent on following the normal best practices for creating applications and code.

Building a sturdy DevOps foundation

When enabling engineers with AI, you need to realize that the base principles for creating code and applications are still in place – if you have a bad foundation, then adding more code on top of it does not add that much value and might even make things worse. Instead, we recommend focusing on enabling engineers to work on laying down a sturdy foundation to be able to roll out their applications faster and with more trust that their application works as intended.

This changes the focus from getting 10x engineers to empowering engineers with a foundation that they can trust, which in turn will improve the flow of value through the SDLC.

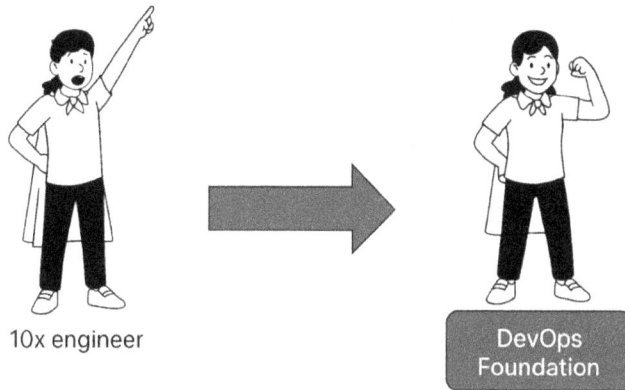

Figure 10.2: Changing to a sturdy DevOps foundation

We've always been DevOps-minded, and we firmly believe in having the basic principles in place:

- Automated pipelines and testing that validate every change, to prevent unwanted side effects of those changes.
- Treating everything as code or configuration to ensure consistency and reliability in deployments. For example, infrastructure should be codified so it can be recreated with the same outcome every time. If your environments have different settings, those differences should be captured in code. This approach allows you to manage variations explicitly and ensures that deployments remain predictable and trustworthy.
- Having the more eyes principle in place, where every change is reviewed by someone else – this helps to prevent unintended side effects and trusting in the ideas of a single person.
- Enough testing in place to have trust – if a deployment fails for any reason, a new test should be added to the pipeline to prevent it from happening again.
- Continuous monitoring and feedback loops.

Only when a large portion of these fundamentals are in place can a team of engineers roll out their changes faster, as, for example, the testing is in place to be able to rely on their deployments. Note that this can be achieved in multiple ways – for example, with unit, regression, or integration testing. Use what works for your application.

Generative AI like GitHub Copilot can help to put these foundations in place and works really well for that kind of supporting system. We see a lot of users only focus on coding with GitHub Copilot, not knowing it can do so much more: we've created all sorts of scripts, pipelines, and even Splunk queries with GitHub Copilot, and it works really well if you understand how to prompt for the right things. We see GitHub Copilot as an enabler to give teams the time to get their foundation in order. Since normal tasks are sped up, the extra time can be spent on initiatives to improve the things that often get pushed to the bottom of the backlog or at least pushed out of the sprint.

We recommend teams always embed these types of technical debt and either include it in their way of working or specially carve out time in every sprint to improve it. We've observed that successful teams consistently dedicate around 10% of each sprint to addressing technical debt. By making this a regular part of their workflow, they ensure that improvements and refactoring are never neglected.

With a good, solid foundation in place, teams can actually deliver value faster, with increased trust, and with fewer issues in production. Engineers then start to leverage AI in their processes where it makes sense, from generating new requirements to coding, reviewing, and testing. The engineer becomes the orchestrator in the middle, building on top of a sturdy DevOps foundation:

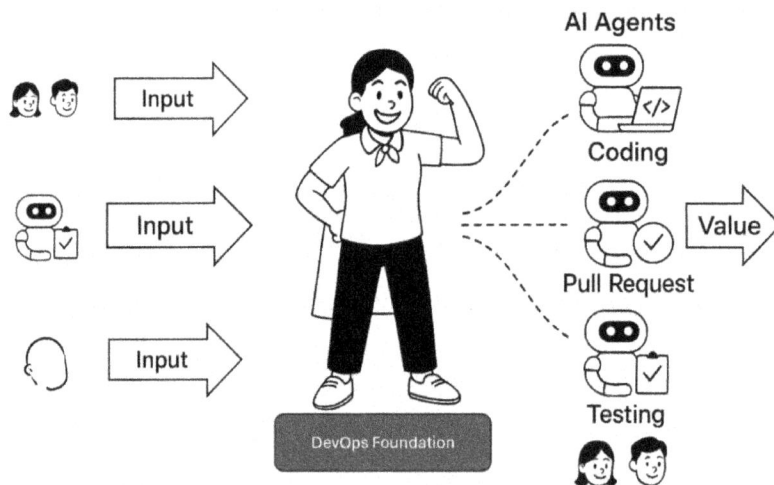

Figure 10.3: New role of engineering teams

When we have a good foundation in place and we trust our process to allow us to go faster, we can start to think about the other things our teams do and how to enable other people in the team, besides just focusing on the engineers.

Expanding AI to engineer-adjacent roles

When rolling out GitHub Copilot, people often think of just the engineers in the team – they are the folks creating new features by writing the code to be able to execute them. But with that stance, we forget all the other people in the team. As we said, on average, an engineer is lucky if they can focus on writing code for two hours a day. The rest of the time is spent on preparations, discussions, architectural work, documentation, and so on. Then there are always teams that spend most of their day in meetings, sometimes overlapping or in parallel during their day. Sometimes it can feel like meetings are considered more important than actual coding!

This brings us to a broader shift: how the work flows to engineers. Beyond coding, much of their time is spent translating user needs into actionable tasks, clarifying requirements, and ensuring everyone on the team understands the implications of proposed changes. These tasks often involve collaboration with stakeholders, and in many cases, a product owner acts as the conduit, channelling work into the team. GitHub Copilot can support this flow by helping teams articulate, refine, and communicate these changes more effectively.

In our opinion, we now need to shift our focus from just the people writing code towards enabling other roles in the team, such as product owners, stakeholders, or users. We need to give those people options to use generative AI to send in better, more detailed, and thus more scoped descriptions of the features they want to implement. They can describe in natural language what kind of changes they want to be made and use AI to convert that into detailed specifications. The more information they can add to a user story/work item/issue, the more easily the engineers can implement the changes in the code.

GitHub Copilot now enables product owners and engineers to explore planned changes and describe upcoming work directly from their browser, within the context of the repository they're working in. Consider this flow:

1. Start a conversation with the repository context (or issue, discussion, failing workflow, code scanning alert, etc.).

2. Let GitHub Copilot help you define the new work. Ask questions such as `Based on the current code base, how do we add a new feature that does <description>?`.

3. Ask follow-up questions to add more context or requirements, or find the location where to add new tests to validate the new feature.

4. When you have enough context, ask GitHub Copilot to create the issue for you, right from the web browser! The chat interface knows what repo you are working in, and it has a pop-up window to let you create a new, detailed description of the work you want to implement, together with all the context and files you have discussed.

With that detailed work description, an engineer who has expertise in the application can review the incoming work descriptions and add the finishing touches, as they understand the system as a whole and the necessary requirements. When the incoming work has enough clarity, with a detailed explanation of what is needed and references to existing features in the code base, AI can be used to suggest the code adjustments needed to be implemented and propose the actual changes. Tools such as the Coding Agent, where GitHub Copilot suggests changes based on the issue, can be leveraged to rerun tests in the pipeline and iterate as needed. Once the tests succeed and the changes are validated, the system will submit a pull request for final review. This agentic-driven workflow is becoming more common, with GitHub integrating these amplifiers in key areas where they make sense.

> For more details on these agent implementations, for example, the Coding Agent, see *Chapter 6*.

By expanding the use of AI beyond engineers, we can enable all team members to contribute to the application. This way, we can shift from just a focus on generating new code. Instead, we focus on all aspects of the SDLC, from requirements engineering to producing work descriptions, writing the necessary code changes, reviewing the code changes, fixing pipeline failures, and even addressing issues found with code scanning. We can close the loop by feeding any errors in production back into the system as work definitions.

This way, we can all benefit from the use of generative AI, enabling everyone to leverage its features and continue focusing on what we have been doing the whole time – creating value for our end users.

Now, let's see how you can enable entire teams with AI and really make an impact in the entire process of creating applications.

AI-enhanced engineering

With the advent of all the AI being infused in our day-to-day workflows, we see our industry shifting towards agentic AI, where tools such as GitHub Copilot become an extension of people with knowledge, so that we can focus on what is really important. With agentic AI, we refer to the use of generative AI tools where we trigger them based on an event, and the tools can then run an assessment of the work, implement changes, run tests, and validate the result, without any extra supervision during that process. The end result is then posted back for an engineer to process and follow up if needed.

We always say that we, as engineers, are not here to write the next `if` statement or `for` loop. We are not applauded when we write a brilliant piece of code. Instead, we get our accolades when we build something that brings value to our end users. How we achieve that value is less important for the users, as long as the functionality does what it needs to do. They do not care if we wrote our solution in C# or Typescript, only that it works, and that they do not have to wait too long to see the result of their actions.

That is the new role we see for the AI-enabled engineer – be smart and use the right tools for the right job, to achieve the value you want to create. That means we can infuse the software development process with GitHub Copilot features where it makes sense. Just like our peers in the industry are already embracing AI in their processes, so too can we leverage it to get the benefits it can bring. With these tools, engineering shifts from just writing new code (and all the work around it) to focusing on system engineering, describing the functional and technical requirements, and then guarding the system to stay within the requirements we have set with incoming changes that are requested.

In the following figure, you can find the current touchpoints from GitHub Copilot features to our SDLC (in the future, there will surely be more opportunities to take this further):

Impact of Agentic AI in the SDLC

Figure 10.4: Touchpoints of GitHub Copilot in the SDLC

Let's go over these touchpoints and link them to the different features from GitHub Copilot:

Stage	GitHub Copilot Feature
Reconnaissance	Use the chat interface (either in your editor or on GitHub.com) to gather context for the feature you want to work on.
Creating work	When the reconnaissance is completed and you have enough context, you can let GitHub Copilot create the work item for you, either by leveraging the GitHub MCP Server in the editor or by instructing it to create a new issue from the web interface.
Coding in editor	To implement the necessary changes, you can use GitHub Copilot in your editor with all the different options you want to, from suggestions while you type, to the chat interface with Ask, Edit, or Agent Mode.

Stage	GitHub Copilot Feature
Coding Agent	Instead of making all the changes yourself, hand off the work to the Coding Agent and let it implement the changes for you, so that you have a working and tested PR ready to review. You can communicate to make changes or load the PR state into an editor and fine-tune from there.
PR review	When a PR is created, you can get a first review from the Coding Agent. It can be super beneficial to have at least the low-hanging fruit in the review already handled so that you, as the human in the loop, spend time on the PR. Keep in mind that the code review does not catch every single issue, of course; that is still the role of standard and security testing. On the other hand, we have seen cases where the code reviewer found issues that we did not even think about! See *Chapter 6* for more examples.
Bug analysis	Whether the bug is happening in production or in your CI/CD pipeline, GitHub Copilot can jump on the error message and figure out the fix. You can leverage that in multiple places, from the web UI to the editor, and act upon it where you find it makes the most sense to you and your way of working.

Figure 10.5: Touchpoints of GitHub Copilot in the SDLC

You can see from these touchpoints that the role of the engineer (and their peers) is changing from focusing on writing more code, to being more diligent about what to build and how to make those changes high-quality and maintainable in the future. We do not need to make all those changes by ourselves – instead, we have AI agents that can help us out to implement the changes, so we can focus on how we bring the most value to our end users.

We also do not worry at all about our own roles and reasons for being an engineer – there will always be work for highly skilled people, and yes, we think they will become more of an orchestrator in the future of AI agents that can produce large parts of the work. Engineers will oversee the AI to make sure there is enough trust in the system to proceed with the next steps. The next step is to enable our peers to be able to use these tools as well, as it brings a lot of value for us all. With more people with an engineering mindset, we can go further and faster.

It is also crucial to have a good way in place to train new engineers to be proficient in the tools, know their limitations, and understand the impact that changes will have on the applications they work on. See *Chapter 8* for more information on creating training opportunities and community building. Failing to train new engineers will lead to a lot more (downstream) issues and frustration by both the engineers and their stakeholders.

Embracing the new way of working will lead to a more efficient way of working, and ultimately to a better experience for the end users of the applications we build, as we described in *Chapter 9*.

Summary

In this chapter, we showed the different ways to change the narrative when talking about GitHub Copilot. Instead of focusing on just producing more code more quickly, we want to focus on the impact these new tools have on our development process. We discussed the ethical usage of GitHub Copilot by looking at both the ethical objections to blindly trusting what LLMs produce, as well as the ethical impact of just accepting everything and stopping to think for yourself. To really get the benefits from generative AI, you need to have a solid (DevOps) foundation in place. This will guard you against a lot of failure modes and elevate the trust you have in the incoming changes. We then looked at expanding the use of AI to everyone in the team that is not an engineer by trade: from stakeholders to product owners/managers, and even your end users. Finally, we looked at how AI-enhanced engineering teams leverage all the features of GitHub Copilot in their development processes.

With that, we have reached the end of the book: we have taken you through the different features of GitHub Copilot, such as (inline) suggestions, (inline) chat, and its different chat options, such as Ask, Edit, and Agent Mode. We started by taking a good look at generative AI to have a basic understanding of what it is and is not. After diving into the different modalities for working with GitHub Copilot (in the editor, in the browser, and in all the different extensions and options, such as the GitHub Copilot CLI), we discussed embracing the learning curve, as there are a lot of lessons to be internalized over time when using these new AI tools. Since everyone learns in their own way, we also looked at how to set up a community that can share lessons learned for the benefit of the entire community. We closed off the current chapter on changing the narrative in what these tools can do for you and your teammates.

With the advent of AI tools and GitHub Copilot at the forefront of this revolution, we see a fundamental shift in the way we see our contribution as engineers. Our added value as engineers has never been just in the code we produce, and that is coming to the forefront with our use of AI. Our value is in the systems thinking that we have learned to do. By looking at the system as a whole, we think of the impact changes to the application might have, and how we can bring business value to our end user.

Implementing changes to our software or script has morphed from focusing on adding code changes by hand, into instead describing and documenting those changes together with our requirements. It is now a choice between those changes being implemented by a human or letting GitHub Copilot implement them for us instead. That decision is based on capability and cost. If we expect that GitHub Copilot can implement the changes, it is a cost-based decision: should we implement it ourselves and spend a couple of minutes on it, or will this take us more time and can we instead hand it off to, for example, the Coding Agent, which can spend a premium request and a couple of GitHub Actions minutes on the problem and fix it that way?

We now have some amazing tools in all the different places in our development process. These tools can be leveraged to make our work a lot easier so that we can find the fun in our engineering practices again. Instead of hitting keys and diving into the code changes, we can now explore and spend time on things that we have always hoped to have time for, and now we can actually create that time! Hand off the mundane and less interesting tasks to GitHub Copilot, so that you can have more pleasure focusing on the fun parts of engineering work.

Get This Book's PDF Version and Exclusive Extras

UNLOCK NOW

Scan the QR code (or go to packtpub.com/unlock). Search for this book by name, confirm the edition, and then follow the steps on the page.

Note: Keep your invoice handy. Purchases made directly from Packt don't require one.

11

Unlock Your Exclusive Benefits

Your copy of this book includes the following exclusive benefits:

- ⌒ Next-gen Packt Reader
- 📄 DRM-free PDF/ePub downloads

Follow the guide below to unlock them. The process takes only a few minutes and needs to be completed once.

Unlock this Book's Free Benefits in 3 Easy Steps

Step 1

Keep your purchase invoice ready for *Step 3*. If you have a physical copy, scan it using your phone and save it as a PDF, JPG, or PNG.

For more help on finding your invoice, visit https://www.packtpub.com/unlock-benefits/help.

> **Note**: If you bought this book directly from Packt, no invoice is required. After *Step 2*, you can access your exclusive content right away.

Step 2

Scan the QR code or go to `packtpub.com/unlock`.

On the page that opens (similar to *Figure 11.1* on desktop), search for this book by name and select the correct edition.

<packt>   Q Search...   Subscription 🛒 👤

Explore Products   Best Sellers   New Releases   Books   Videos   Audiobooks   Learning Hub   Newsletter Hub   Free Learning

Discover and unlock your book's exclusive benefits

Bought a Packt book? Your purchase may come with free bonus benefits designed to maximise your learning. Discover and unlock them here

Discover Benefits   Sign Up/In   Upload Invoice

Need Help?

✦ 1. Discover your book's exclusive benefits   ⌃

Q Search by title or ISBN

CONTINUE TO STEP 2

⁂ 2. Login or sign up for free   ⌄

☁ 3. Upload your invoice and unlock   ⌄

Figure 11.1: Packt unlock landing page on desktop

Step 3

After selecting your book, sign in to your Packt account or create one for free. Then upload your invoice (PDF, PNG, or JPG, up to 10 MB). Follow the on-screen instructions to finish the process.

Need help?

If you get stuck and need help, visit `https://www.packtpub.com/unlock-benefits/help` for a detailed FAQ on how to find your invoices and more. This QR code will take you to the help page.

Note: If you are still facing issues, reach out to `customercare@packt.com`.

‹packt›

packtpub.com

Subscribe to our online digital library for full access to over 7,000 books and videos, as well as industry leading tools to help you plan your personal development and advance your career. For more information, please visit our website.

Why subscribe?

- Spend less time learning and more time coding with practical eBooks and Videos from over 4,000 industry professionals
- Improve your learning with Skill Plans built especially for you
- Get a free eBook or video every month
- Fully searchable for easy access to vital information
- Copy and paste, print, and bookmark content

At www.packtpub.com, you can also read a collection of free technical articles, sign up for a range of free newsletters, and receive exclusive discounts and offers on Packt books and eBooks.

Other Books You May Enjoy

If you enjoyed this book, you may be interested in these other books by Packt:

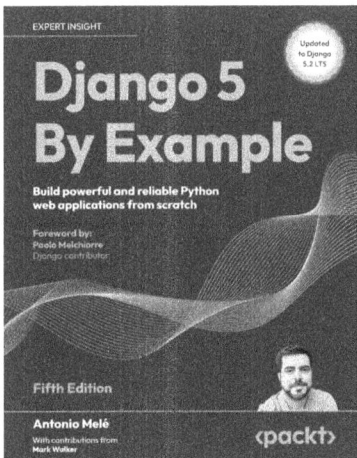

Django 5 By Example

Antonio Melé

ISBN: 978-1-80512-545-7

- Use various Django modules to solve specific problems using the latest features
- Integrate third-party Django applications into your project
- Build complex web applications using Redis, Postgres, Celery/RabbitMQ and Memcached
- Set up a production environment for your project with Docker Compose
- Build a RESTful API with Django Rest Framework (DRF)

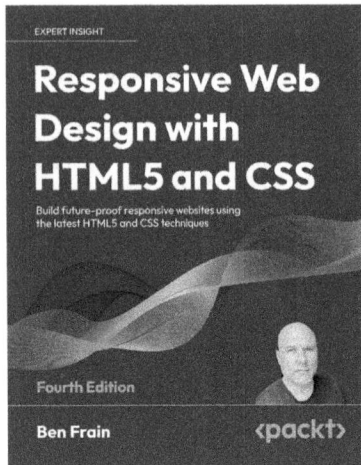

Responsive Web Design with HTML5 and CSS

Ben Frain

ISBN: 978-1-80324-271-2

- Use media queries, including detection for touch/mouse and color preference
- Learn HTML semantics and author accessible markup
- Facilitate different images depending on screen size or resolution
- Write the latest color functions, mix colors, and choose the most accessible ones
- Use SVGs in designs to provide resolution-independent images
- Create and use CSS custom properties, making use of new CSS functions including 'clamp', 'min', and 'max'
- Add validation and interface elements to HTML forms
- Enhance interface elements with filters, shadows, and animations

Packt is searching for authors like you

If you're interested in becoming an author for Packt, please visit authors.packtpub.com and apply today. We have worked with thousands of developers and tech professionals, just like you, to help them share their insight with the global tech community. You can make a general application, apply for a specific hot topic that we are recruiting an author for, or submit your own idea.

Share your thoughts

Now you've finished *The GitHub Copilot Handbook*, we'd love to hear your thoughts! Scan the QR code below to go straight to the Amazon review page for this book and share your feedback or leave a review on the site that you purchased it from.

https://packt.link/r/1806116634

Your review is important to us and the tech community and will help us make sure we're delivering excellent quality content.

Index

www.ingramcontent.com/pod-product-compliance
Lightning Source LLC
Chambersburg PA
CBHW081056220326
41598CB00038B/7119

The GitHub Copilot Handbook

Cross-functional product teams are under constant pressure to build and ship faster, but too much time is lost to manual coding, slow reviews, and fragmented workflows. GitHub Copilot streamlines day-to-day coding so your team can focus on delivering value to users while maintaining high quality on real projects.

Written by industry experts Rob Bos and Randy Pagels, this book shows how GitHub Copilot supports your work from start to finish. You'll learn how to turn ideas into tasks, write code with fewer hiccups, spot problems earlier, and understand errors when things go wrong. You'll also see how Copilot suggests improvements in pull requests and helps fix common build issues, enabling teams to keep moving and ship with confidence.

You'll integrate GitHub Copilot into daily routines, share it across roles, and make it stick with simple checklists and clear examples. You'll also track what works, set guardrails, and build an internal community.

By the end, you'll know when GitHub Copilot helps – and when it doesn't – and you'll be ready to write, review, and ship code with confidence on real projects.

WHAT YOU WILL LEARN

- Apply GitHub Copilot across the full software development life cycle
- Understand how AI powers the suggestions and chat features
- Boost productivity by automating tests, reviews, and pipeline fixes
- Integrate Copilot into IDEs and GitHub.com for maximum value
- Roll out Copilot across teams with proven onboarding strategies
- Build a knowledge-sharing culture with Copilot community champions

Get a free PDF of this book

packtpub.com/unlock/9781806116638

ISBN 978-1-80611-663-8

90000

9 781806 116638

Hands-On
MLOps on Azure

Automate, secure, and scale ML workflows with the
Azure ML CLI, GitHub, and LLMOps

Banibrata De